What if They Gave a Crisis and Nobody Came?

What if They Gave a Crisis and Nobody Came?

Interpreting International Crises

Ron Hirschbein

PRAEGER

Westport, Connecticut
London

Library of Congress Cataloging-in-Publication Data

Hirschbein, Ron, 1943–
    What if they gave a crisis and nobody came? : interpreting
international crises / Ron Hirschbein.
        p. cm.
    Includes bibliographical references and index.
    ISBN 0–275–96043–9 (alk. paper)
    1. International relations. 2. Nuclear crisis control. 3. United
States—Foreign relations—Soviet Union. 4. Soviet Union—Foreign
relations—United States. I. Title.
JX1391.H57   1997
327.1'747—dc21   97–18725

British Library Cataloguing in Publication Data is available.

Library of Congress Catalog Card Number: 97–18725
ISBN: 0–275–96043–9

First published in 1997

Praeger Publishers, 88 Post Road West, Westport, CT 06881
An imprint of Greenwood Publishing Group, Inc.

Printed in the United States of America

The paper used in this book complies with the
Permanent Paper Standard issued by the National
Information Standards Organization (Z39.48–1984).

10 9 8 7 6 5 4 3 2 1

This book is dedicated to Tim Carroll:
Encouragement when necessary;
Criticism when essential

CONTENTS

ACKNOWLEDGMENTS

This study stresses the highly problematic, interpretive nature of international reality. However, the contributions of colleagues, organizations, and family to this project require no interpretation; their role is obvious—they made it possible. Bob Jackson, Director of California State University, Chico's Center for International Studies, encouraged me to investigate international crises during my 1989 sabbatical. Thanks to Alan Greb, I pursued this study at the University of California's Institute for Global Conflict and Cooperation in La Jolla. The research of Fen Osler Hampson and Gloria Duffy prompted me to investigate the crises that inform this study. Jim Skelly's Discourse Group provided an ideal situation to hazard my preliminary thoughts, and Sandy Lakoff offered adroit commentary on the first incarnation of my inquiry.

After the sabbatical I profited from correspondence and interviews with a variety of political actors and analysts. Accordingly, I wish to thank Raymond Garthoff, Ralph Earle and the family of Ray Cline (who sent materials after his untimely death). I also wish to acknowledge my indebtedness to the research and insight of Victor Turner, Clifford Geertz, Bart Bernstein, Steve Nathanson, and Michael Shapiro. Conversations with local scholars such as Larry Bryant, Greg Tropea, Jeff Livingston, and Bob Jackson proved invaluable. (I am particularly indebted to Larry's filigreed theory and practice of interpretive inquiry.)

I also wish to thank Jerry Sanders for the opportunity to offer a seminar on my research in his Peace and Conflict Studies Program at the University of California, Berkeley. (I am particularly grateful for colleague Carolyn Nordstrom's enthusiasm and insight.) And, as fate would have it, Jim Skelly once again fostered my efforts by inviting me to offer a crisis seminar during a recent sabbatical at the United Nations University in Austria.

The inquiry was facilitated by a National Endowment for the Humanities Fellowship; indeed, NEH Program Specialist Robert Bolin showed remarkable insight into what I was trying to accomplish. And stipends from my institution, California State University, Chico, enabled me to visit the John F. Kennedy Presidential Library in Boston, and the Richard M. Nixon Presidential Library in Alexandria. Of course, no research inside the Beltway would be complete without out a visit to the privately funded National Security Archive. Personnel at these institutions were invariably attentive and helpful. And I would be remiss if

I did not mention the unflagging enthusiasm and technical support provided by James Sabin and Jason Azze of Praeger Publishing.

Before I wrote books, I thought that families were merely acknowledged pro forma in venues such as this. This is not the case. My wife, Lee, suggested that my immoderate interest in crises may be a sublimation for my mid-life crisis—a possibility I could not dismiss until she concluded that I was too old for such an episode. Whatever the case, she was wonderfully supportive during the tribulations that produced this book. It understates the case to suggest that my family was involved: at age 11, my son Jonah could differentiate between the excesses of postmodernism and the hermeneutic methods invoked here. And, putting to rest the usual mother-in-law jokes, Mary Walker remained unnaturally cheerful even during the darkest days of research and manuscript preparation.

Finally, I am especially indebted to Tim Carroll's nuanced and ironic critique of my work.

I know not what to say to it; but experience makes it manifest, that so many interpretations dissipate the truth, and break it. Who will not say that glosses augment doubts and ignorance, since there is no book to be found . . . which the world busies itself about, whereof the difficulties are cleared by interpretation. The hundredth commentator passes it on to the next, still more knotty and perplexed than he found it. When were we ever agreed among ourselves: "this book has enough; there is no more to be said about it?" Do we find any end to the need of interpreting? . . . There is more ado to interpret interpretations than to interpret things; and more books upon books than upon any other subjects: we do nothing but comment upon one another. Every place swarms with commentaries. . . . Is it not the common and final end of all studies? Our opinions are grafted upon another; the first serves as a stock to the second, the second to the third, and so forth.

—Montaigne
Essays

INTRODUCTION

THE CURSE OF HERMES

We are all prisoners of a rigid conception of what is important and what is not. We anxiously follow what we suppose to be important while what we suppose to be unimportant wages guerrilla warfare behind our backs, transforming the world without our knowledge and eventually mounting a surprise attack on us.

—Milan Kundera[1]

In the fall of 1962, just before the congressional election, President John F. Kennedy learned that he had been deceived by Soviet diplomats: U-2 reconnaissance revealed that the Soviets were secretly constructing a nuclear missile base in Cuba. Kennedy and his most trusted advisers privately concluded that the base did not bestow any strategic advantage upon the Soviets.[2] Nevertheless, according to their own lights, they hazarded grave risks by promoting the episode as a crisis—the fear of nuclear holocaust was palpable.[3] The president publicly demanded that Chairman Nikita Khrushchev dismantle the installation. At the same time, he relied upon a secret diplomatic channel to facilitate negotiations between his brother, Robert F. Kennedy, and Soviet Ambassador, Anatoly Dobrynin.

In order to compel Soviet compliance, Kennedy escalated the confrontation by blockading their fleet, ordering an unprecedented strategic alert, and conveying a message to Dobrynin through his brother—dismantle the base promptly or the United States will destroy it. (Dobrynin indicates that he construed the demand as a statement, but Khrushchev understood it as an ultimatum.[4] Apparently, it's a matter of interpretation.) These negotiations, however, were not as seamless as they appeared for a generation. Simultaneously, Robert Kennedy proposed a secret deal, a quid pro quo: the United States would secretly remove its missiles from Turkey and promise not to invade Cuba—as Khrushchev insisted—if the Soviets publicly removed their missiles from Cuba, agreed not to deploy offensive weapons, and promised not to reveal this clandestine arrangement. (I shall argue that this desperate attempt to resolve the crisis through an ultimatum and a compromise is the "essence of indecision.") In any case, while the Kennedy brothers hoped the ultimatum and compromise would somehow prompt their adversary to back down, they feared they were on the brink of nuclear war; indeed, Robert Kennedy allowed that he and his brother *expected* to be involved in such a war in a matter of days. He hoped for the best but expected the worst: according to most accounts this was the closest the world has come to nuclear war. Kennedy's joust on the abyss is the most memorable crisis of the nuclear age.

In the fall of 1970, just before the congressional elections, President Richard M. Nixon learned that he had been deceived by Soviet diplomats: U-2 reconnaissance revealed that the Soviets were secretly constructing a nuclear submarine base at Cienfuegos Bay in Cuba. The president and his national security adviser, Henry Kissinger, agreed that this action violated the informal understanding that resolved the 1962 confrontation. More disturbing still, they shared the same dire perception: the submarine base posed a more formidable threat than the land-based missiles the Soviets had attempted to deploy earlier. In Kissinger's words, it was a "quantum leap" in Soviet strategic capability. It was as if the Soviets were inviting Nixon to the gravest crisis of the nuclear age, but he found it inconvenient to attend.[5] The president was distracted by other matters, thought it unwise to have a crisis before the election, and had his heart set on visiting the Mediterranean to watch the Sixth Fleet fire its guns.[6] Accordingly, Nixon instructed his advisers to make sure that no crisis occurred; he vacationed in Europe as planned. Kissinger, however, wanted to make a crisis move—albeit one dramatically different from Kennedy's bravura crisis. Before Nixon departed, Kissinger prevailed upon the president to allow him to meet secretly with Dobrynin to resolve the provocation secretly, quietly, and diplomatically. He succeeded. This prudent resolution of what might have become the gravest crisis of the nuclear age is all but forgotten, even among the participants themselves.

The similarities and differences between these episodes raise challenging issues regarding the theory and practice of international crises. Why did seemingly comparable events—the surreptitious construction of Soviet nuclear bases in Cuba—evoke radically different responses on the part of two administrations? Specifically, why did Kennedy take grave risks while Nixon downplayed the situation? And, turning to the same administration, why did Kissinger define the base as a crisis while Nixon did not; and why was Kissinger's approach to crisis management markedly different from both Kennedy's and Nixon's? (Cognitively oriented analysts such as Robert Jervis argue that discrepancies in decision-making are due to disparities in perception generated by different modes of cognitive processing.[7] However, to reiterate, Nixon and Kissinger shared the same perception of Soviet actions.) Finally, why has Kennedy's daring resolution of the 1962 episode become an unforgettable, exemplary metaphor for future confrontations—the very métier for assessing potential leaders,[8] while Kissinger's prudent and successful management of the 1970 episode quickly faded into obscurity?

These issues raise three fundamental questions regarding crisis construction, management, and remembrance that are the focus of this inquiry, questions that must be resolved if crises are to be prevented or managed prudently. These concerns are the exclusive domain of social scientific approaches to politics. Humanistic inquiry has not realized its potential for illuminating these questions. This is unfortunate, because the interpretive methods (hermeneutics[9]) prominent in the humanities are attuned to the rapidly changing context of international relations: a milieu that is transforming political actors from observers of unmistakable facts to interpreters and authors of cryptic texts and symbolic performances. If wars are too important to be left to the generals, crises are too dangerous to be left exclusively to the social scientists:

Why do American political actors define an event as a crisis in the first place? Due to the symbolic turn in international relations in the overdeveloped world, a crisis is not something "out there," an objective event that can be observed, measured, and classified. Today, actors experience the international world vicariously through the words and images of others. They have become interpreters of cryptic texts and symbolic performances. Given this symbolic context, a crisis is a conceptual strategy—a metaphorical narrative that actors read into their texts and performances to render them intelligible, communicable, and dramatically self-validating. Specifically, I argue that a situation is constructed as a crisis when it is likened to a previous crisis narrative indelibly etched in an actor's memory and inscribed in his[10] texts—a saga remembered as a critical juncture requiring urgent, perilous choices. Crisis managers, of course, are not merely interpreters. They are also authors and actors: once actors interpret a text or performance as a crisis, they struggle to restore the status quo ante by authoring communiqués and improvising scenarios.

Why are some crises managed prudently, while others are not, despite access to comparable knowledge and resources? Crisis management is influenced by a variety of personal and political factors. I direct attention to an overlooked determinant—the genre of the narrative authored and improvised to manage the crisis. Thinkers as diverse as Thucydides and Habermas[11] claim that two archetypal narratives are invoked to manage crises. (Ceremonial Washington is modeled after Greek edifices, and missiles are named after Greek gods. Perhaps it is not too farfetched to suggest that crises are also modeled after resonant Greek scripts that echo through the centuries.) In any case, these contending narratives construct crises in markedly different ways: (1) the existential narrative scripts a daring strategy for accomplishing heroic feats in dramas that reveal the truth about men and events; (2) the clinical narrative prescribes prudent treatment for restoring homeostasis in the international body politic. These arresting metaphors have been used to explicate crises in ancient Greek city-states and crises of advanced capitalism. Yet, strangely, the possibility that the dialectical interplay between these resonant narratives informs recent international crises has not been considered. I correct this omission.

Why are some crises enshrined as templates for future confrontation while others quickly fade into oblivion? To paraphrase Kundera, this study is also about remembering and forgetting. I argue that national memory is determined by two related factors: (1) the image of the actor who constructed and promoted the crisis—Kennedy gets better press than Nixon; (2) the genre of the narrative—heroic narratives with happy endings are much preferred. As Machiavelli counseled, it is preferable to appear to tread the well-worn path of those enshrined as great men.

A PREMATURE POSTSCRIPT

> Rather ironically, while people are more or less continuously engaged in hermeneutic or interpretive activity in their day-to-day routines . . . these "meaning-making" practices have largely been overlooked or dismissed as inconsequential by many students of human behavior.
>
> —Robert Prus[12]

Colleagues who graciously reviewed various incarnations of these opening paragraphs recognized my authorial strategy. Some agreed I cast a tempting hook: given the renewed interest in these figures, a fresh take on Kennedy's joust on the abyss played off against a little-known Nixon/Kissinger episode with the Soviets might captivate the reader. Others considered these episodes ancient history: Why not explicate more recent crises? And, not surprisingly, the comparisons between the Cuban episodes were, to say the least, controversial, as was my stress on the interpretive dimension of crisis construction and inquiry. Sympathetic colleagues found the comparisons apt and fruitful. What better confirmation of my thesis—a paraphrase of the wisdom of Epictetus: It is not the world that is the source of our crises, but our interpretation of the world. Others were less generous. They cautioned that since these episodes are incommensurate, my comparison is cavalier; my problematic, tendentious. Surely, the "Missiles of October" were a momentous challenge to the Kennedy presidency, if not to national security, while the Cienfuegos business was a minor diplomatic skirmish—a brief detour in Kissinger's grand strategy of triangular diplomacy.

To be sure, like other analysts, I chose the Cuban crises to make a point: seemingly comparable events can elicit dramatically different responses among political actors. From the plethora of possible case studies we tend to select those that suit our agendas. We do so for a variety of reasons. Episodes such as the Cuban missile crisis are difficult to overlook—they are dramatic and intriguing. I would be remiss if I did not comment upon the most harrowing crisis of the Cold War—the Cuban missile crisis. Since this is the most thoroughly investigated episode, a wealth of material is available (given the problems with declassification, only limited material is available on recent crises).[13] Our a priori interpretive schemes also influence our selection; indeed, as we shall see, these interpretive strategies determine what counts as data. Realists, for example, are fond of examples of actors responding similarly to comparable international exigencies. And those who rely upon bureaucratic models cite instances of domestic bureaucratic politics determining elite responses to international challenges. Like the proponents of these two competing schools of crisis interpretation, I am not indifferent toward case studies that make my case.

Now I am not urging that two wrongs don't make a right—but three do! I am suggesting that, in general, prevailing interpretations are not sufficiently self-reflective about their inevitable tendentiousness: we cannot avoid such bias; we can only recognize it. I must allow that my case studies were selected, in part, to drive home a point: prevailing approaches do not account for the incommensurate risks Kennedy hazarded, nor do they account for the fact that comparable challenges can elicit dramatically different responses among actors within and between administrations. There are other rationales—or rationalizations—for my choices. Comparing and contrasting the 1962 and the 1970 episodes also illustrates the neglected role of historical memory in the construction and evaluation of crises. Crises resolved through momentous risks leave an indelible impression, while those resolved patiently and quietly are soon forgotten. In effect, this study investigates the hallowed and the forgotten crisis narratives of American culture.

However, to reiterate, critics urged that I had no business comparing episodes they deem incommensurate. Initially, I was tempted to respond by reminding critics that Nixon and his closest advisers, such as Kissinger and Haldeman, saw parallels, as did respected analysts such as Hampson.[14] Heeding Oscar Wilde's advice, I would deal with the temptation by giving in to it. Surely, my sources and argumentative strategies were a match for theirs! Further reflection diminished such bravado—I began to realize what I was doing. For the most part my critics and I agreed upon the facts, but we disagreed about how to make sense of the facts. It was a matter of interpretation.

Of course it would not suffice to respond glibly, "It's a matter of interpretation!" Such an unvarnished pronouncement would likely strike friend and foe alike as a transparent attempt to reduce crisis inquiry to utter subjectivity. (Such argumentative strategy is not unknown to our students. Confronted with argumentation and evidence that undermine their position, they have been known to retort: "Well that's just your opinion, and my opinion is as valid as yours!") Recognizing that—like a crisis itself—crisis inquiry is a matter of interpretation does not relegate us to such whimsical subjectivity. Our choice is not between positivism and fantasy. Several caveats are in order:

I do not deny the existence of empirical political realities: Soviet missiles and submarines were all too real. Rather, I explicate official interpretations of these realities, especially those authored and improvised by the "interpreter in chief," the president of the United States.[15] In the process I also confront the competition: prevailing interpretations of the Cuban crises. Even a cursory glance at the literature reveals that crises are subject to contesting interpretations. Mainstream and revisionist historians marshal evidence for their respective positions. Likewise, the international relations literature chronicles the ongoing disputes of realist, bureaucratic, and cognitive approaches to crises, to name but a few. No wonder anyone trying to make sense of an episode such as the Cuban missile crisis is bedeviled by contesting interpretations. As we shall see, there is no agreement even among Kennedy's Ex Comm advisers: some attribute his resolution of the episode to a brilliant, carefully calibrated strategy; others claim that the nation emerged unscathed due to "plain dumb luck." Scholarship fares no better. The crisis is variously celebrated as Kennedy's finest hour, or the lowest point in human history.

It is, however, possible to evaluate contesting narratives. I am not an unrepentant postmodernist who, enchanted by playful nihilism, is intent on deconstructing crises into fictive language games and entertaining performances. I shall argue that just as it is possible to evaluate contesting interpretations of unfamiliar cultures, so it is possible to evaluate interpretations of a culture far removed from our personal and professional lives—the exotic world inside the Beltway.[16] True, the evaluative criteria I propose will not satisfy positivist standards, but with Aristotle we can only hope for precision appropriate to the inquiry. Anthropologists such as Clifford Geertz are well aware of what is entailed; interpretation involves judiciously reading meaning into a cryptic text: "Doing ethnography [or explicating crises] is like trying to read (in the sense of 'construct a reading of') a manuscript—foreign, faded, full of ellipses, incoherence, suspicious emendations and tendentious commentaries. . . ."[17]

By claiming that crisis construction and analysis are matters of interpretation, I do not commit the cardinal sin of crisis inquiry—reductionism. My account does not dismiss the research and insights of other scholars. On the contrary, it is profoundly indebted to their contributions. And certainly I have not found *the* magic key that unlocks the secrets of the Cuban crises, let alone all crises. Since I recognize that there is indeed no end to interpretation, it would be the height of folly to claim that I have somehow divined *the* definitive account of something as complex and variegated as international crises.

My goal is modest. I simply try to accomplish an intellectual task that should have been completed long ago: contextualizing the notion of "crisis." I recognize that at other times and places a crisis was something "out there": a clear and distinct event that would prompt virtually anyone to hazard urgent, perilous choices. (The British invasion of the United States during the War of 1812, Nazi air attacks on Coventry, and civil wars in places such as Ethiopia are such crises. These events were immediately experienced by many people, and the obvious threats they posed required little interpretation.) In recent times, however, in places like the United States, crises are precipitated by cryptic reconnaissance data, communiqués, military maneuvers, and the like. These texts and performances do not speak for themselves, nor do they lend themselves to unequivocal interpretation. On the contrary, they spark acrimonious disputes among political actors. For example, there was heated speculation within the Ex Comm regarding why the Soviets deployed the missiles, and what words and gestures might compel them to remove the weapons. Curiously, Nixon's response to what he regarded as a more formidable threat—a Soviet nuclear submarine base—was blasé, while Kissinger was more exercised.

Entertaining the possibility that, in the present context, a crisis is an interpretation of the highly symbolic artifacts of international relations, presents formidable challenges for those of us foolhardy enough to analyze these episodes. Despite our social scientific pretensions we are relegated to the role of hermeneuticists—interpreters of interpretations. To be sure, we can devise interpretations that fit the facts—they are on target. But there is no bull's-eye: *the* interpretation that provides an irrefutable, conclusive account of a crisis, let alone crises in general. Because actors have heeded Machiavelli's counsel, interpreting international crises is at best daunting, at worst chimerical: "It is necessary to know well how to disguise . . . and to be a greater pretender and dissembler."[18] Only the most naive would accuse political actors of pathological truth telling, especially in crisis situations. Our efforts to make sense of crises are impeded and enormously complicated by what I call the Curse of Hermes.

Afflicted by the curse *actors have become suspicious interpreters, dissembling authors and impostors, and improvisers of cryptic texts and performances. And analysts—despite our scientific aspirations—are not observers of obdurate facts; we have become interpreters of official interpretations. Our interpretations can be on target, but there is no bull's-eye—no "smoking gun," no conclusive proof. Accordingly, our interpretations are invariably incomplete and contested.*

The legend of Hermes provides the method and metaphors that inform this study. It generates fertile images and techniques that lead to a more nuanced, subtle understanding of crises: Hermes—ever the suspicious but charming courier and trickster—is the archetypal diplomat and crisis manager. The theory and practice of international crises are bedeviled by a hermeneutics of suspicion.

THE CURSE OF HERMES

Hermes was the son of Zeus. He presided over commerce, wrestling . . . even over thieving, and everything, in short, which required skill and dexterity. He was the messenger of Zeus, and wore a winged cap and winged shoes. He bore in his hand a rod entwined with two serpents, called the caduceus.[19]

Today, of course, the culture of the spectacle and commodity reduces Hermes to the icon of FTD Florists. The former deity is relegated to delivering bouquets and—if advertisements are to be believed—forgiveness for contrite husbands. The ancients afforded more majesty and mystery to the son of Zeus. Hermes was charged with interpreting the creeds and passions of the gods to mortals. (Interpreting the creeds and passions of political actors is a more daunting task!) But Hermes, himself a god, was not content to be a mere messenger. He was a discoverer of great secrets—mysteries unknown even to other gods. And his supreme confidence was usually justified—his sword could cut through anything. Unlike Prometheus, the selfless Titan, he was not a trustworthy friend to humanity, a benefactor who would suffer exquisite torture to enable mortals to discover the truth. True, at times, Hermes warned mortals of impending disaster. But he often toyed with hapless mortals sometimes for higher ends, but often for the perverse pleasure of deceiving vainglorious humanity. He was *the* consummate trickster, a supple deceiver who tricked Zeus himself, and the guarantor of hubris to smug mortals. Indeed, Hermes could well be the patron god—or demon—of diplomacy and crisis management: he relied upon charm and guile to convey misleading messages that caught his fancy. The legend reveals a being with powers of enchantment that would awe Kennedy and Kissinger, a supple trickster who outclassed JFK while descending to depths that would have embarrassed even Tricky Dick.

True, like any effective diplomat, Hermes could not be caught in a blatant lie: his power of deception would vanish with such transparent deceit. But neither was it in his nature to reveal the entire truth. Kissinger's tribute to Bismarck's dissembling diplomacy could well be a gloss on Hermes—or Kissinger himself:

> Sincerity has meaning only in reference to a standard of truth of conduct. The root fact of Bismarck's personality, however, was his incapacity to comprehend any such standard outside of his will. For this reason, he could never accept the good faith of any opponent; it accounts, too, for his mastery in adapting to the requirements of the moment. It was not that Bismarck lied—this is much too self-conscious an act—but that he was finely attuned to the subtlest currents of any environment and produced measures precisely adjusted to the need to prevail.[20]

Hermes' missions often reflected the venality of his father. In order to rescue Zeus's mistress from the ultimate intelligence network of his day—Argus, the hundred-eyed Panoptes—Hermes became an impostor, a winsome shepherd boy. Relying upon his allure and ruthlessness, he charmed Argus with fanciful tales, put him to sleep, and slew him.

Like any diplomat worthy of his portfolio, Hermes negotiated with the devil himself. In one of the more harrowing hostage crises, Hermes was sent to the Underworld to persuade Hades to release the fair Persephone. Hermes had good reason to doubt Hades' good faith. Like any worthy adversary, the god of the Underworld was also skilled in the art of trickery: he charmed the maiden into eating the forbidden fruit. Hermes, ever the adroit negotiator, made a virtue of necessity—politics was always the art of compromise. We learn that in what might have been the first joint custody settlement: "a compromise was made, by which she was to pass half the time with her mother, and the rest with her husband, Hades."[21]

Hermes was also involved in shuttle diplomacy with the likes of King Priam and the venturesome Odysseus. Relying upon his legendary charm and wile, he guided the faltering king down the right path. And, unable to dissuade the impetuous Odysseus from his dangerous ventures, Hermes bestowed the latest Olympian technology upon him so that he might survive and prevail.[22]

Whether out of sheer boredom or perversity, the gods relished putting humanity through relentless ordeals. Indeed, ceaselessly testing mortals was an obsession on Olympus. The fortunate mortals who prevailed against all odds lived in glory; others suffered a cruel fate. Hermes was no exception. Ever the impostor, he appeared when least expected to tempt and test mere mortals.

Finally, Hermes bestowed what is at once a blessing and a curse upon his progeny—an indelible memory. It should become clear that Kennedy, Nixon, and Kissinger suffered the hubris of indelible memory. Relying upon the secondary sources of their remembered past, they interpreted the novel challenges of the present in terms of the clichés of yesteryear. It is a commonplace that those who cannot remember the past are condemned to repeat it. This inquiry is informed by a more subtle insight: those who cannot forget the past are condemned to repeat it.

The legend of Hermes spawned a venerable inquiry known as hermeneutics. The inquiry originated with medievalists who combined inspiration and arcane rules to divine the true meaning of ambiguous Scripture. It has gone in and out of vogue during the last millennium. As an eighteenth century scholar, Johann Martin Chladenius, opined:

> Many centuries ago, scholars considered the production of interpretations to be one of the most prestigious endeavors, and because there were no principles which would have enabled these to be done reasonably . . . many interpretations ended unhappily and . . . the disciplines which were built on interpretations were completely devastated. . . . Finally, there was no alternative but to toss out all these interpretations and to start all over again.[23]

In the hands of more recent philosophers and anthropologists hermeneutics evolved into diverse methods designed to interpret the ambiguities of lived, human experience.[24] The literature is vast and complex, especially when authored by Teutonic philosophers. However, in essence, there is nothing complicated about hermeneutic social inquiry. It presupposes that humans inhabit an ambiguous world of texts and performances crying out for interpretation. Hermeneutics interprets the meaning of these artifacts. Most interpreters abide by implicit, general standards—deliberate falsification is eschewed. Nevertheless, meticulous, fair-minded hermeneuticists often interpret the same facts with contesting narratives. Curiously, analysts who claim to rely strictly upon empirical methods cannot avoid the trials and tribulations of hermeneutic inquiry. Indeed, as I shall argue, regardless of their pretensions, crisis analysts are closet hermeneuticists reading favored retrospective interpretations into the hallowed crises of the past.

This, then, is the first curse of Hermes: actors no longer inhabit a world of obdurate, unmistakable threats, a world in which they are mirrors of nature clearly reflecting the contours of international reality—a world grasped through mere perception. The international world, to be entirely unoriginal, is seen through a glass darkly: cryptic texts and evanescent performances are the essence of international life. Current provocations are decidedly ambiguous, and are experienced vicariously through electronically transmitted texts and performances. More daunting still, actors seldom communicate clearly and distinctly. On the contrary, they have become impression managers intent upon concealing their intentions. In Jervis' telling phrase, they "threaten on the cheap" with enigmatic symbols and gestures.[25] And, as Kennedy's secret deal illustrates, actors intrigue against friend and foe alike. No one is to be trusted—ultimately, not even one's self.

Given this symbolic turn in international relations, de rigueur accounts of the role of perception—and misperception—in crisis construction and management are not fully adequate. No doubt actors would much prefer a world of unmistakable, tangible challenges and obvious solutions—a brave old world in which courageous deeds vanquish foes. This is not their fate. In the not-so-brave new world depicted in this study, actors interpret and author texts—briefings, communiqués, and the like; and they improvise literary maneuvers—symbolic performances that "send messages" rather than accomplishing military feats.

Specifically, as we shall see, the Cuban missile crisis was sparked and resolved by texts.[26] Most narrations of the event begin with the U-2 reconnaissance photos that were examined by CIA official Ray Cline.[27] He, in turn, communicated his interpretation of the data to the president's national security adviser, McGeorge Bundy. Bundy communicated with the president, and Kennedy responded by convening an ad hoc advisory group—the Ex Comm. While there are useful game-theoretic and bureaucratic models of such decision-making, these models overlook the defining feature of Ex Comm deliberations—hermeneutics.[28] The lived experience of the Ex Comm reflected more kinship with medieval monks disputing Scripture than with laboratory scientists testing disconfirmable hypotheses. The parallels are striking. Like other recent crisis managers, the Ex Comm spent 13 days disputing contesting interpretations of texts and performances: just as the monks pondered why Paul wrote a second missive to the Corinthians, so the cabal of the "best and the brightest" ruminated about why Khrushchev sent a second guided missive on the last, fateful Saturday of the crisis. Kennedy and the others were self-congratulatory about their clever, if less than virile, response—the "Trollope ploy." Like the ingenue in Trollope's Victorian novel, they ignored the harsh message, and responded to the words they wanted to hear.

Actors, of course, are interpreters *and* authors. Like their counterparts in other recent crises, the Ex Comm members labored under circumstances that even the most draconian editor would not impose: somehow they had to quickly find the right words to prevent the situation from veering out of control and precipitating a war no one wanted. Or, in Tim Carroll's telling metaphor, perhaps Kennedy and his associates can be likened to magicians conjuring up incantations: like the Sorcerer's Apprentice, Kennedy and the others sought the magical words and compelling gestures to avert a disaster that was, in part, their own doing.

Hermes, of course, delighted in vexing mortals with such ordeals. Kennedy, Nixon, and Kissinger were constantly put to the test—or put themselves to the test. "Crisis" was the idée fixe in their thought and deed. They wrote voluminously about these ordeals that they construed as tests of their worth. They were consumed by crises: one would be hard pressed to think of writings of Kennedy, Nixon, and Kissinger that were *not* preoccupied with the trials and tribulations of great men. No wonder Robert McNamara remarked, "There is no more diplomacy, just crisis management."[29] It is only fitting that biographers chronicle the lives of these officials as sagas of relentless crises.[30]

These tests were not always successfully met because of yet another curse: Hermes bestowed these actors with an indelible, albeit selective, memory. Enchanted by received wisdom, they made sense of a disturbing, ambiguous present by likening it to the simple verities of the remembered past. This reliance upon historical analogies exaggerates similarities between past and present while concealing the differences. In so doing, it distracts actors from the novel reality of the present. (As McNamara recently confessed, such misleading historical analogies led to the tragedy of Vietnam.[31]) Einstein was prescient: modern weaponry changed everything but our thinking.

Just as generals are always fighting the last war, so actors are always managing a previous crisis. Kennedy interpreted the world in terms of the fateful "Munich Syndrome" of the 1930s;[32] and Kissinger could not forget the diplomatic legerdemain of nineteenth century figures such as Metternich and Bismarck. What of Nixon? Hermes bestowed a unique hubris upon the thirty-seventh president. Contrary to the "newest" Nixon's representation of himself as a latter-day elder statesman, he was not a captive of the great causes of his day—or of days gone by for that matter; he was imprisoned by his own psychologically impoverished past. Without undue respect for Oliver Stone's cinematic rendition, the saga of Richard Nixon is not the high Shakespearean tragedy of a Richard III. It is the low tragedy of the anti-hero of *Death of a Salesman,* Willy Loman—a man who felt cheated by life. Like the feckless Willy Loman, Nixon was a vulnerable "Everyman" who merely wanted to be well-liked in the here and now. His crises were impurely personal ordeals sparked by humiliation and embarrassment.

Joke books define a diplomat as "someone who lies for his country." However, the suspicion endemic to foreign affairs is no laughing matter for diplomats or crisis managers: trust does not come easily in a cynical world. As every messenger from Hermes to Kissinger has realized, being caught in blatant lies destroys one's credibility. The adroit crisis manager must become a trickster or an impostor—a deceitful purveyor of ambiguous threats and half truths. Through cunning and guile, actors become impostors on the world stage: they convince others—and sometimes themselves—that they are not who they are.[33] This then is the fourth and most ironic curse. The pirouette of deception known as diplomacy and crisis management foments a hermeneutics of suspicion in which, to paraphrase Kissinger, only the naive attribute good faith to friend or foe. Ironically, charm and duplicity fail because no one is trusted.

Examples are plentiful. Kennedy failed to charm Khrushchev; indeed, the Cuban missile crisis may have occurred because the wily Russian peasant didn't take the jaunty youth's oaths about preserving the Monroe Doctrine seriously. And during the crisis, Cline allows that he had difficulty convincing United Nation's Ambassador Adlai Stevenson of the existence of Soviet missiles in Cuba because the Central Intelligence Agency had lied to the ambassador about an incident during the Bay of Pigs fiasco. (Like the American public, the ambassador was falsely told that an aircraft that attacked Cuba was a Cuban plane piloted by a defector. In reality, it was an American plane conducting a CIA operation.) Cline explains:

> I took the photographs [of the Soviet installations in Cuba] up to Adlai Stevenson at the UN. He was very skeptical because he had been burned in the Bay of Pigs operation. I said, "We are absolutely telling you the truth: the CIA may have lied to you in the past, but they are not lying now."[34]

American actors, of course, have no monopoly on dissembling. Soviet adversaries were far from candid. Quite correctly, no one assumed that the Soviets were compulsive truth tellers—or inveterate liars, for that matter. An incident recounted by Dobrynin reveals why Soviet officials confounded American actors—and their own inner circle. Simply put, he was not informed about his own government's deployment of missiles in Cuba: "In seeking to keep the secret, Moscow not only failed to inform me of so dramatic a development as its plans to station nuclear weapons in Cuba but virtually made its ambassador an involuntary tool of deceit."[35]

Of course, given the hermeneutics of suspicion that informs politics, truthfulness is often dismissed or treated with derision, especially in regard to the likes of Richard Nixon. Much to his chagrin, even his Republican allies would not believe "Tricky Dick" when told the truth during the fund crisis (an episode in which Nixon was accused of using a secret fund for personal extravagances). This humiliating episode—the template for subsequent Nixon crises—was resolved through the "Checkers Speech." And, for a time, Kissinger seemed to possess the supreme confidence of Hermes—surely the Harvard don's rapier wit could cut through anything. His charm and duplicity proved remarkably successful—until he acquired the reputation of a duplicitous charmer. No wonder Ole Holsti, an influential analyst, concludes that, "It is almost axiomatic that adversaries in an intense international crisis will not trust each other very much[;] it is hard to be sanguine that much can be done to alter this condition."[36]

The most ironic curse involves self-deception, or what Erving Goffman calls "deep acting."

> One finds that the performer can be fully taken in by his own act; he can be sincerely convinced that the impression of reality he stages is the reality. When his audience is also convinced . . . about the show he puts on—and this seems to be the typical case—then, for the moment at least, only the sociologist or the socially disgruntled will have any doubts about the "realness" of what is presented.[37]

Did Kennedy truly believe that he was a profile in courage because he "went eyeball to eyeball" with Khrushchev, and his adversary blinked first? And could it be that the new Nixon came to believe that he had become a revered elder statesman who surmounted the venality of the old Nixon? Finally, despite the failures at the close of his diplomatic career, did Kissinger believe that he, and he alone, was the Platonic physician/statesman of his generation—the "doctor of diplomacy?" Like the actors themselves, we will probably never know.

Determining whether political action is deep acting is not, to understate the case, the only difficulty facing an interpreter of crises. Analysts invoke congenial social scientific apparatus to get a handle on crises. These episodes are variously represented as the outcome of gambling to attain strategic advantage, bureaucratic maneuvering, or psychological processes. But could it be that these representations are more akin to interpretive strategies read into enigmatic texts and performances than to unvarnished empirical descriptions? Even the most uncompromising positivist is found in the archives—not the laboratory—struggling to make sense of the raw data of international crises—ambiguous texts.

I suspect that this unnerving recognition that we are interpreters of interpretations is largely tacit and inchoate in mainstream discourse; and yet the recognition may be percolating toward the surface. (Indeed, if this inquiry accomplishes nothing else, it should call attention to the unthought, unquestioned presuppositions and limitations of prevailing crisis inquiry.)[38] The literature is gradually allowing that social scientific accounts fall far short of their Promethean dream: a synoptic theory that definitively explains crises while generating predictions that are at once precise, accurate and disconfirmable. Moreover, as Holsti concludes, even more modest goals may be unattainable. In his view, while social scientific approaches have much to offer, "It is unlikely that the behavioral sciences will ever be in a position to offer lawlike prescriptions that will enable those who must make decisions in crises to transcend the awful dilemmas . . . they face."[39]

Finally, like Hermes, we cannot lie, but neither can we tell the whole truth. We cannot emulate the methods of natural science, let alone the results, but we are guided by its ideals: we do not deliberately mislead or falsify. We struggle to fashion fair-minded, coherent interpretations that are on target—they fit the facts. But, despite our virtue, we invariably miss the bull's-eye—a definitive, indisputable interpretation of a crisis. We continually uncover intriguing facts, but—cursed by Hermes—what we truly crave eludes us: a conclusive account of why the crisis occurred, why it was managed as it was, and why it is remembered or forgotten. Like Montaigne, we realize that our interpretations will invariably be incomplete and contested. There are both obvious and more subtle reasons.

Obviously, uncritically and enthusiastically embracing a colleague's interpretation is a bad career move. Analysts do not win friends, but they do influence people, by criticizing colleagues, questioning received wisdom, and devising provocative interpretations that don't venture too far beyond the respectable pale. However, we invariably miss the bull's-eye for a less obvious reason: there is no bull's-eye to be hit. Social scientific inquiry can put crisis inquiry on target by discovering the facts. But making sense of the facts is more of a literary project than a scientific endeavor. As Isaiah Berlin observes, it is often the novelist, not the strategist, who is bestowed with astute political judgment. Dostoevsky may prove more useful than Clausewitz in making sense of crises:

[Political judgment] seems to me to be a gift akin to that of some novelists, that which makes such writers as . . . Tolstoy or Proust convey a sense of direct acquaintance with the texture of life; not just the sense of a chaotic flow of experience, but a highly developed discrimination of what matters from the rest.[40]

To be sure, we are on target when we rely upon prevailing approaches to delineate crisis fundamentals—salient facts needing no interpretation. For example, claiming that the Cuban missile crisis occurred in October 1962 during the Kennedy presidency, when the Soviets deployed strategic nuclear weapons in Cuba evokes no controversy. (However, to invoke an extreme example used by philosophers to make a point, asserting that Barry Goldwater was Khrushchev's adviser during the crisis misses the target.) We seem to get closer to the bull's-eye when we discover that widely accepted claims are misleading. For example, prior to recent revelations of the secret deal it was a commonplace that Khrushchev backed down because of Kennedy's cool courage. As Robert Smith Thompson explains: "For three decades . . . the 'lesson' of the Cuban missile crisis has persisted in the textbooks of our minds: when confronted by aggression, you hang tough, stay cool, show flexibility over minor points, but never yield on major ones; plan to operate with surgical precision, but keep the bludgeon conveniently nearby."[41] Thompson wrote his book to demonstrate that this was not the case: the secret deal acceded to Khrushchev's demand for a quid pro quo—American missiles were quietly removed from Turkey five months after the crisis. (Nevertheless, the Kennedy legend persists despite the fact that it misses the target.)

In any case, few analysts are content merely to chronicle the facts or even to demythologize by uncovering closely guarded secrets. We do not merely want to know what occurred; we want to understand *why* it occurred—what was the point? We yearn for the ever-elusive Holy Grail, *the* conclusive interpretation: a definitive grasp of a crisis that evokes an epiphanic "Aha!" response from esteemed colleagues, if not from the actors themselves. Or, to squeeze more life out of the previous metaphor, we seek a "smoking gun" that will enable us to hit the bull's-eye.

For example, there is virtual consensus among scholars that Kennedy escalated the crisis to dangerous levels while simultaneously orchestrating a secret deal that acceded to Soviet demands. Some analysts claim that JFK learned from past mistakes and crafted a carefully calibrated, two-track strategy—the traditional carrot-and-stick approach. I suggest that Kennedy was confused and desperate—grasping at straws. Just as JFK was indecisive during the Bay of Pigs and the Berlin confrontations, he remained indecisive during the Cuban missile crisis. Naturally, I marshal facts and inferences to support this account. The competition does the same. Unfortunately, there is no "smoking gun"—no authoritative reference point—to demonstrate conclusively the plausibility of my interpretation. No august tribunal exists to bestow its imprimatur upon our cherished interpretations. As Tim Carroll explains:

The "Smoking Gun" is the new root metaphor for the transcendence of the vagaries of interpretive interpretations. There are times, admittedly rare, when a fact
emerges that is so conclusive it overrides the tendency and ability to cling to
"cherished interpretation."[42]

While it is logically possible that I will uncover a "smoking gun" to valorize
my interpretation, I doubt that it is *historically* possible. What sort of revelation
would irrefutably valorize my take on the risks and compromises that Kennedy
orchestrated simultaneously? A deluge of newly declassified documents in which
Kennedy and his associates unequivocally endorse my interpretation would be
helpful. Unfortunately, real possibilities are more limited than such fantasies.
Responding to the concerns that inform this study, I offer *an* interpretation of
crisis construction, management, and remembrance that is on target, but surely
this is not *the* interpretation—not *the* bull's eye. Historian Michael Hunt explains
the predicament of crisis interpretation with painful clarity:

There is not one but several good stories to tell in each dangerous international
confrontation, and depending upon whose perspective the story reflects, the
identity of the aggressor and victim will change. Those who write and read these
stories . . . must do so from a complex body of evidence, in the face of openly
competing claims, and with the specter of relativism fluttering quietly over-
head.[43]

I strive to tell a good story about these dangerous confrontations, an account
that is at once ironic and iconoclastic. I offer a novel, and perhaps fruitful
account of vintage Kennedy, Nixon, and Kissinger crises.

INTERPRETING INTERNATIONAL CRISES: A FIRST TAKE

There is scarcely a society without its major narratives which are recounted, re-
peated and . . . recited in well-defined circumstances: things said once and pre-
served because it is suspected that behind them there is a secret or treasure.
—Michel Foucault[44]

Crisis Construction

A crisis occurs when an actor interprets a text or performance by likening it
to a crisis narrative of the remembered past—a critical juncture requiring urgent,
hazardous choices. In the words of political theorist Murray Edelman, "A crisis,
like all other news developments, is a creation of the language used to depict it;
the appearance of a crisis is a political act, not a recognition of a fact or a rare
situation."[45] I presuppose that the remembered past is inscribed in an actor's
texts; therefore, I turn to these texts to decipher an actor's concept of "crisis."
This perspective generates specific hypotheses about the case studies explicated
in this study: I argue that Kennedy defined the nuclear missile base in Cuba as a
crisis because he likened it to the crises depicted in *Why England Slept* and *Profiles in Courage*. Nixon did not define what he deemed a more threatening situation as a crisis because the surreptitious construction of a nuclear submarine

base did not resemble the personal embarrassments recounted in *Six Crises*. Kis-singer, however, defined the base as a crisis because he likened the threat to the nineteenth century crises narrated in his texts.

These hypotheses are based upon further presuppositions about the origin and nature of international crises that should be made explicit. Confronting a text or performance that captures his interest, an actor invokes what Ernest May and Richard Neustadt call the "Goldberg Rule." These Harvard scholars attribute the rule to the folk wisdom of one far removed from academe. Responding to the their account of their method of inquiry, critical oral history:

> Avram Goldberg, a scholar and gentleman who happens also to be the chief ex-ecutive officer of Stop and Shop, a New England chain of . . . stores . . . ex-claimed, "Exactly right! When a manager comes to me, I don't ask him, 'What's the problem?' I say, 'Tell me the story.' That way I find out what the problem really is."[46]

May and Neustadt were rightly impressed by Goldberg's insight: in order to understand an issue, we read a story into the experience. But due, perhaps, to disciplinary biases and constraints, they construe such stories as mere cognitive maps: schemes that attempt to describe reality. With apologies to Bach, I offer a "Goldberg Variation," a brief philosophic critique. May and Neustadt are correct as far as they go: political actors have cognitive needs—they want to know what's happening. But, like the rest of us, actors do not live by cognition alone: they also have hopes and values. Put more technically, like many other analysts, May and Neustadt fail to distinguish between perceptions and conceptions. Per-ceptions construct what is occurring; conceptions impose meaning, determine what counts as data, and select the data for interpretations. Further, unlike per-ceptions, conceptions are performative—they prescribe action.

This distinction between perception and conception has profound implica-tions for theories of crisis definition. Actors have teleological and normative needs neglected by prevailing cognitive approaches to international relations. Captivated by a daunting text or performance, an actor is not content merely to perceive what is happening; he must understand *why* it is happening, and *what is expected* of him. Determining why an unexpected, puzzling situation has arisen precipitates a crisis of meaning: somehow an adversary's motives and character must be discovered and evaluated. Determining how one should respond fo-ments an even more formidable challenge, a crisis of identity: the self-discovery of one's conflicting motives and flawed character; a moment of truth, an epiph-any, that reveals the inner chasm between what one is and what one should be.

Cast in the perspective that informs this study, an international crisis begins as a crisis of meaning. Crises are meaning-making projects. Simply put, the facts don't speak for themselves—a text or performance does not somehow announce its meaning and prescribe appropriate actions. The meaning of a communiqué or troop mobilization is not "discovered" (uncovered through observation). It is constructed, and read into a situation by an actor's conceptual imagination. As the philosopher Roy Schafer explains, "Historical situations do not have built into them intrinsic meaning. . . . Historical situations are not inherently tragic, comic or romantic."[47] (He reminds us that a love affair that seemed tragic at sixteen may appear comic at age fifty.)

An unexpected turn of events often provokes puzzlement and vexation. No wonder Kennedy's first response to the discovery of the Soviet base was "How could he [Khrushchev] do this to me?"[48] Perception of events such as clandestine missile deployments presents the problem; interpretation constructs an answer. The facts of the situation were clear; the meaning was not. In the post-Freudian world it is reasonable to suspect that those who orchestrate military deployments may not fully understand their motives. And, as Richard Betts' research suggests, while an actor may be bluffing initially, he may have no idea of how to respond if the bluff is called.[49] Indeed, in a world cursed by Hermes, actors often conceal the meaning of their acts from their adversaries and from themselves. Equivocal texts and performances are fashioned to keep an adversary guessing. Or a forthright actor may be unable to communicate his meaning because he lacks communicative skills—texts and performances lose something in the translation. And given the "Munich Syndrome," actors like Kennedy are reluctant to meet personally with adversaries in order to decipher their intentions.

However, crises are not simply meaning-making projects. Certain situations are construed as crises because they confront an actor with a challenge even more formidable than the problem of meaning. Actors often endure crises because they are captivated by texts and performances that call their very identity into question. Ordinarily actors take their identity for granted. The smooth, habituated patterns of routine existence present no occasion to question one's identity—it is tacit, unquestioned, and uncontested. However, during troubled times of crisis, these tacit self-representations are made explicit and challenged. In other words, confronted with an enigmatic text or performance, an actor is not content to understand "What's the story?"; it does not suffice merely to construct and express an interpretation of a text. A more menacing, unsettling question is broached: "Who am I?" Certain crises throw actors into situations in which they feel compelled somehow to live up to mythic, larger-than-life narratives militated by the remembered past. As we shall see, during the Cuban missile crisis there was, among other things, an identity crisis. When Kennedy went "eyeball to eyeball" with Khrushchev, would he be a Chamberlain or a Churchill? (A daunting dilemma in an age of assured destruction.) Likewise, during the Cienfuegos episode Kissinger wanted once again to demonstrate that he was not an irrelevant academic; he expected himself to live up to the ideal of the Platonic physician/statesman—the doctor of diplomacy. Nixon's quest for authenticity was less grandiose. Like Willy Loman, he merely wanted to escape derision and ridicule. Put more positively, he wanted to be taken seriously and to be respected. Nixon crises are about managing Nixon, not about managing foreign affairs.

Metaphorical crisis narratives are frequently invoked to resolve these issues of meaning and identity. These metaphors are not merely rhetorical embellishments or cognitive maps. They are, in effect, containers for resonant narratives. For example, the popular discourse move of likening a proposal to Chamberlain's policy of appeasement does not merely describe reality; it reiterates an entire morality play: a prefigured script in which negotiation and compromise invariably produce humiliation and defeat. In other words, the policies of the present are sanctified by likening them to an uncontested, remembered past. An inquiry into social memory and narrativity suggests:

> Stories do more than represent particular events: they connect, clarify, and interpret in a general fashion. Stories provide us with a set of stock explanations which underlie our predisposition to interpret reality in the ways that we do.[50]

It is, of course, logically possible for an actor to interpret a text or performance in diverse ways: "crisis" is not the only possible interpretation. In his oft-quoted Farewell Address, Eisenhower admonished his successors to resist the temptation to construe any international challenge as an acute crisis demanding risk-taking and hasty judgment. Likewise, noted experts warn of the perils inherent in nuclear age crises. Conceivably a provocation can be disregarded or interpreted as a problem—a chronic affliction to be resolved quietly and patiently in due course. It can be lamented as an irredeemable tragedy, or promoted as an acute crisis demanding urgent, perilous choices. However, crisis narratives are more attractive than contending interpretive schemes for a variety of reasons. Interpreting a challenge as a chronic problem suggests that an actor can live with the challenge, and that others—perhaps a committee, a bureau, or even a rival—can resolve the situation through routine problem-solving skills. But mere problem-solving does not valorize an actor's preconceived destiny. And interpreting an event as a disaster suggests that the terrible has already happened—there's nothing to be done. For example, President Reagan did not gain in stature by interpreting the 1983 Soviet destruction of a Korean airliner as a disaster. However, as we shall see throughout the study, crisis narratives provide a formulaic interpretation that fulfills an ensemble of needs. Unlike problems or disasters, crises prescribe what an actor must do to be immortalized as a statesman/hero. No wonder crises are expected and welcomed among elites—unfortunately, they seldom get the ones they want.

Of course, like other cherished, interpretive strategies, the concept of "crisis" is naturalized. Actors and analysts alike presuppose that a crisis is something "out there," something akin to a natural disaster that occurs behind the backs and against the will of political actors. Somehow, it is "necessary" (to use one of the most overworked terms in international relations discourse) to interpret certain texts and performances as crises. As Peter Berger remarks: "The statement 'I must' is a deceptive one in almost every social situation. It is to pretend something is necessary that in fact is voluntary."[51] A crisis, then, is not brought to life by events beyond human control—crises are made, not born. True, an actor may not be self-reflective and aware of the process and dangers of reification. It may not occur to him that interpreting a text or performance as a crisis is a decidedly human act.

In sum, prevailing analysis recognizes the essential international, domestic, and subjective ingredients that set the stage for a crisis. Subsequent chapters illustrate that these episodes can occur through sudden changes in the balance of power, domestic bureaucratic machinations, or misinterpretations of adversarial intentions. However, the *sufficient* condition for a crisis is obvious, but over-looked. No crisis is enacted unless an actor conceptualizes a text or a perfor-mance as a crisis. In the final analysis, this book is about the role of human activ-ity, particularly elite values and aspirations, in the construction, management, and remembrance of crises.

Crisis Management

Certain crises are managed prudently, while others are not, for a variety of reasons. Commenting upon crisis construction and management, historian Ran-dolph Starn observes that the "Father of Scientific History [Thucydides] left more room for the tragedian than some of his interpreters, for such a framework could lend itself to drama as well as science."[52] The literature persuasively dis-cusses diverse structural and subjective impediments to prudent crisis man-agement.[53] This study considers a factor that has long been overlooked: the genres of the narratives invoked to manage crises. The Cuban episodes offer a telling clue. I suspect that the 1970 episode was managed adroitly, while the 1962 episode was not, because—for a variety of personal and political reasons—these episodes were constructed and managed in accord with different crisis narratives. These narratives are scripted into what Victor Turner calls a "social drama": ceremonial theatrics in which a decision-maker improvises resonant nar-ratives to understand why he is experiencing a threat, and what must be done to attain his preconceived destiny. The cultural stock of crisis narratives is limited. Therefore, in general, crises are derivative and formulaic. They are based upon narratives authored by the ancient Greeks that persist because they provide a classical account of an unnerving crisis experience—a story with a happy end-ing.

To reiterate, this study explicates two genres of crisis narrative—the exis-tential and the clinical. Literary critic Northrop Frye calls the former "romantic narratives": sagas that transform supernatural myths into idealized human dramas. Human heroes replace gods as the protagonists aspiring to a glorious end. Romantic narratives occur on a vertical plane: the would-be hero embarks on a quest and ascends to a prefigured destiny. According to Frye, these grand narratives are the favorite mode of national storytelling. In contrast, clinical (or what Frye calls "realistic" grand narratives) occur on a horizontal plane: eschew-ing heroic encounters, suspicious of faith in progress, let alone human perfect-ibility, these narratives—a favored genre of the political realist—are civics les-sons in preserving the status quo and preventing disaster.[54]

Jürgen Habermas' nuanced account of these genres is exceedingly useful for interpreting the vintage Kennedy, Nixon and Kissinger crises explicated in this inquiry. He suggests that romantic grand narratives (what I call existential crises) signify "the turning point in a fateful process that, despite all objectivity, does not simply impose itself from outside and does not remain external to the identity of the persons caught up in it."[55]

He explains that these fateful life crises are, in the final analysis, crises of identity precipitated by contradictions within the person:

> The contradiction . . . is inherent in the personality systems of the principal characters. Fate is fulfilled in the revelation of conflicting norms against which the identities of the participants shatter, unless they are able to summon up the strength to win back their freedom by shattering the mythical power of fate through the formation of new identities.[56]

Habermas contrasts these internal crises with realistic grand narratives (what I refer to as medical crisis models):

> The concept of crisis . . . [is] familiar to us from its medical usage. . . . The critical process, the illness, appears as something objective. A contagious disease, for example is contracted through external influences on the organism; . . . it can be observed and measured with the aid of empirical parameters. The patient's consciousness plays no role. . . .[57]

This clinical representation of "crisis" connotes a predicament in which political actors—or patients—are deprived of their sovereignty by forces acting behind their backs and against their wills. My account of the management of the Cuban episodes explicates the dialectic interplay of the two narratives.

The Existential Crisis: A Strategic Drama in which a Would-Be Hero Reveals his True Character.

In the words of Nietzsche: "[Existential] crises show that there are still things that men prize more than life and property."[58] In this familiar, formulaic narrative the protagonist no longer enjoys the charmed life of his youth. Fate casts him in the final crisis of his life: a dark night of the soul in which he is scourged by relentless self-doubt and humiliation. Existential crises vex the self at its very core by threatening the beliefs, values, and aspirations that infuse life with meaning and direction. There are no experts adept at resolving threats to the integrity of the self with tried-and-true methods. Everyone is a rank amateur when it comes to the dark night of the soul.

Such crises afflict a wide variety of individuals for countless reasons. Leaders such as Kennedy seem exquisitely vulnerable to such episodes when unexpected circumstances call their preconceived identity and destiny into question. I am not the first to note Kennedy's affinity for ancient Greek narratives. As Arthur Schlesinger remarked: "The President's ethos was more Greek than Catholic. He took his definition of happiness from Aristotle—the full use of your powers along lines of excellence."[59]

Kennedy took certain adversarial challenges personally: they were interpreted as the climax of a drama that reveals the truth about men and events—the ultimate test of courage and cunning that reveals what a leader is made of. Like other would-be heroes, he confronted what Turner calls "liminality" during his defining crisis. Disoriented by an unexpected, ambiguous event, and uncertain of what was required, he abandoned his familiar life script—it offered no answers, let alone solace. In Turner's telling phrase, he was "betwixt and between metaphors"; the uncanny episode could not be likened to anything in experience—there were no comforting metaphors, just cruel confusion. Kennedy was lost; he was in the dark about how to respond to the unanticipated Soviet challenge.

Periods of liminality can lead to inconsolable despair, but they can also produce periods of remarkable fecundity. The would-be hero sometimes devises a novel variation on familiar heroic themes. Improvising this new metaphor, he embarks upon an uncharted and perilous journey, tempts the Fates by risking everything, confronts a riddle posed by a dilemma, and triumphs if worthy (or perishes, at least politically, if not). Such theatrics are staged with great alarm and fanfare while the world watches. Kennedy improvised a new metaphor on the world stage—the gradual escalation doctrine. But this novel metaphor failed—or so it seemed to Kennedy. The missiles remained in Cuba and became operational; and a series of unexpected developments and alarming mishaps revealed that events were careening out of control.

The guardians of the Kennedy memory invoke a favorite presidential aphorism—"To govern is to decide." They laud his decisiveness. According to legend, Kennedy made courageous, yet carefully calibrated, decisions that consummated his heroic quest. Personifying "grace under pressure," he became a profile in courage.[60] Critics indict what they regard as Kennedy's reckless decisions: supposedly he eschewed diplomacy in favor of confrontation. Both accounts miss the point. Offering a take on the crisis that has something to offend everyone, I argue that Kennedy was imprudent and reckless precisely because he was indecisive. Unable to extricate himself from liminality, fearing the ship of state was capsizing, he grasped at straws and simultaneously tried to be a heroic Churchill on the world stage while acting out a conciliatory Chamberlain script in camera.

Ironically, however, Kennedy's indecisiveness may have inadvertently saved the day. Just as Khrushchev's mixed messages disturbed the Ex Comm by suggesting that the Soviet leader was no longer in control, perhaps Khrushchev became fearful and willing to settle due to Kennedy's mixed messages. Likewise, Nixon's profound indifference to the Cienfuegos episode was a blessing in disguise. His blasé attitude allowed Kissinger to intervene at a decisive moment.

The Medical (Hippocratic) Crisis: A Tactic for Averting Disaster.

Actors such as Dr. Kissinger look upon themselves as specialists well versed in diagnosing and treating afflictions of the international body politic by restoring homeostasis. There is, of course, nothing new about this conception of "crisis"; it can be traced to the Platonic conception of the physician/statesman, a conception succinctly framed by Goethe when he wrote: "All transitions are crises; and is a crisis not a sickness?"[61] This conceptualization arises from an interrelated series of clinical imagery.

Adversaries such as communists are likened to a disease. In his "long telegram," for example (one of the first articulations of what would become containment policy) George Kennan relied upon various physiological and psychiatric metaphors to diagnose the Soviet affliction and to prescribe the proper treatment.[62] Unlike those enduring their ultimate test during an existential crisis, the physician/statesman is responsible for treating others' afflictions, not his own. It is presupposed that those charged with caring for the body—or the international body politic—are not the best judges in their own case. Given their ideological passions and lack of expertise, politicians may overreact to a situation or fail to respond to a serious affliction. The physician/statesman remains cool, collected, and professional. Crises constructed and managed in accord with this medical model are not taken personally; they are viewed with clinical detachment. A crisis is likened to a routine—albeit serious—medical affliction.

This medical genre is vintage Kissinger. Conceiving himself as the Platonic physician/statesman, both knowledgeable and wise, the "doctor of diplomacy" took charge, excluded amateurs, diagnosed the malady, prescribed the tried-and-true treatment—dissembling diplomacy—and intervened at the decisive moment to restore the balance of power in the international body politic. Kissinger was self-reflective. He cautioned that international relations involve selecting the right metaphor. He chose well in managing the Cienfuegos crisis. The clinical metaphor resulted in a peaceful resolution of what could have been the most harrowing episode of the Cold War. Even the best metaphors, however, are plagued by what can be a fatal liability—they are misleading. Despite Kissinger's wishful thinking, the international world is not a patient to be medicated, and he was not in possession of some uncanny synoptic wisdom. To be sure, Kissinger's erudition and supple diplomacy should be lauded. However, the appropriate place must be given to what his predecessor, Dean Acheson, called "plain dumb luck": Kissinger happened to be in the right place at the right time.[63] For a time his skillful application of realpolitik successfully resolved a series of confrontations. But, as he would discover, there would come a time when neither friend nor foe would support his tropes. Everyone from North Vietnamese officials to Republican critics rejected his self-serving metaphors.

REMEMBERING AND FORGETTING

As Richard Reeves reminds us, it wasn't Schlesinger or Sorensen who cast the image of Kennedy that still thrills the world. It was Jacqueline Kennedy telling Theodore H. White: "At night before we'd go to sleep, Jack liked to play some records. The lines he loved to hear were: 'Don't let it be forgot, that there once was a spot, for one brief shining moment that was known as Camelot.' There will be great Presidents again, but there'll never be another Camelot."[64]

This study, it will be recalled, is also about remembering and forgetting. I suspect that our national memory of a crisis is determined by two not unrelated factors: the image of the actor who constructed and promoted the crisis, and the genre of the crisis narrative. First, however, national memory must be defined. Sociologists James Fentress and Chris Wickham begin their perceptive study of collective memory by drawing a salient distinction between knowledge and memory. Knowledge claims are factual assertions about the external world. Such impersonal descriptions can be likened to a message passed from one person to another: the message conveys information, but it is not the hallowed property of one individual. Memory, on the other hand, is a cherished interpretation of the past—a heritage. To be sure, national memory is a social product, but it is intro-jected as a sacred part of the self. The authors conclude: "Thus, unlike objective knowledge which belongs to us only in a contingent and temporary way, person-al memories are indissolubly ours; they are part of us."[65]

Looking at the remembrance of crises specifically, I sense little reluctance to accept new knowledge about the Cuban missile crisis. There is no hesitation, for example, on the part of analysts to incorporate recent revelations regarding the number of Soviet troops and weapons deployed in Cuba in 1962; evidently, such matters are not taken personally. Interpretive memories, however, are taken per-sonally. Indeed, it sometimes appears that our cherished interpretations are immune to the facts. It is unlikely, for example, that McNamara's recent reve-lation that the Cuban missile crisis was more dangerous than he initially sus-pected will alter the views of Kennedy champions. Likewise, the revelation of the secret deal does not mollify his critics. By the same token, it seems unlikely that Nixon's insistence on avoiding another Cuban crisis will change his image held by friend or foe. As Thomas Kuhn argues, we must be besieged by anom-alies before we consider abandoning cherished paradigms. Applying this insight to international relations, Tim Carroll suggests that new-found revelations such as McNamara's simply prompt some quick reshuffling of our cherished a priori interpretations.

As Fentress and Wickham demonstrate, nations as a whole embrace certain memories—cherished interpretations of the national past; indeed, it is these shared memories that cement national identity. In the United States, for example, virtually every schoolchild learns that Washington chopped down the cherry tree, Lincoln freed the slaves, and Kennedy was a profile in courage. The con-struction and popularization of these memories is rarely a spontaneous act gener-ated by firsthand experience—or sustained inquiry and reflection, for that matter. Even the recent past is experienced vicariously through the media, and political elites are not averse to manipulating the media to construct and manage national memories. As Edelman stresses, even relatively recent episodes such as the Cuban missile crisis are elite constructions popularized by the media and legit-imized in mainstream textbooks: "The mass public does not study and analyze detailed data about missile installations in Cuba. It ignores these things until political action and speeches make them symbolically threatening . . . and it then responds to the cues furnished by the actions and the speeches, not to direct knowledge of the facts."[66]

There is nothing conspiratorial in all this. Just as we cannot, apparently, live without enemies, life seems unbearable without heroes. The powers that be oblige. In the words of Ernest Becker:

> Heroism is first and foremost a reflex of the terror of death. We admire most the courage to face death; we give such valor our highest and most constant adoration; it moves us deeply in our hearts because we have doubts about how brave we ourselves would be.[67]

Just as shamans promote the collective myths of tribal cultures, the elites of advanced industrial society promote their own congenial myths—it is simply the way things work. Fentress and Wickham explain:

> National memories are imposed on other classes from above, by public and private means: schooling, newspapers, books, and radio and TV programmes. They are linear in their conception of time and indeed teleological: very explicitly, all of them lead up to and legitimize their present situations. . . . They are thus hegemonic, and totalizing: alternative memories are regarded as irrelevant, inaccurate, and even illegitimate.[68]

My first visits to the official presidential libraries convinced me of the plausibility of this analysis. The memory of President Kennedy is celebrated in an impressive structure designed by I. M. Pei (in consultation with Jacqueline Kennedy) and situated on a promontory in Boston Harbor. The Nixon Library was just another converted warehouse in a rundown district of Alexandria, Virginia. (The library was subsequently moved to the new National Archives facility in College Park, Maryland. The privately funded Nixon Library is in Yorba Linda, California.) It was as if the Kennedy Library extols our ideals, while the Nixon Library presents us the way we are. This sentiment is poignantly expressed in Oliver Stone's *Nixon*:

> Near the end of the movie . . . Nixon stands before a looming oil portrait of John F. Kennedy. It's the JFK of Camelot: at ease, upper-class handsome. Looking up at his old foe, Stone's defeated Nixon has his epiphany about the American people. . . . "When they look at you, they see what they want to be. When they look at me, they see what they are."[69]

To indulge in further "anecdotage," initially I had hoped that the documents within these presidential libraries would somehow confirm or disconfirm my memories of Kennedy, Nixon, and Kissinger—and their crises. But there were no great secrets or treasures, no startling revelations. I found that, like the medieval hermeneuticists, I could gerrymander the documents to support my cherished interpretations. I tried to resist the temptation, but I realize that I was cursed by Hermes. As social theorist R. I. Moore admonishes: "It would be comforting to think of memory as a simple record. . . . Of course, it is nothing of the kind: it is an artefact [*sic*] and a trickster, and an active trickster at that, not merely a relic of the past, but the past shaped and adapted to the uses of the present. . . ."[70]

I did sense, however, considerable pressure to embrace the national memory of recent presidents, and their characters and crises. As the controversy about the American decision to use atomic weapons in World War II suggests, those who question cherished national memories are indicted as "revisionists" or worse. Biographers such as Richard Reeves seem increasingly sensitive to the ideological role of national memory. He argues that the guardians of the Kennedy legend have managed to represent him as a robust and daring young adventurer who matched heroic vows with courageous deeds:

> After the assassination of President John F. Kennedy . . . Richard Goodwin tried to console Robert Kennedy by saying: "Julius Caesar is an immortal, and he was only emperor of Rome for a little more than three years." "Yes," Bobby said, "but it helps if you have Shakespeare to write about you." That's certainly true, but taking no chances . . . Caesar wrote about himself first. John Kennedy intended to do the same . . . emulating his hero, Winston Churchill. The 35th president never got the chance, but his memory . . . [was] well served by two talented assistants: Arthur M. Schlesinger, Jr. and Theodore Sorensen did their best to immortalize their fallen leader.[71]

However, it appears that Kennedy is remembered as a martyred hero, not a fallen leader. His leadership in promoting his domestic agenda was unremarkable, and both of his champions agree that he didn't take a leadership role with the Ex Comm by building consensus. He is lionized as the hero who took charge, acted alone, and miraculously emerged alive, only to be martyred in a bizarre assassination. Kennedy fiascoes such as the abortive Bay of Pigs invasion are recounted as "learning experiences" that enabled the young president to grow in courage and wisdom. That he accepted personal responsibility for the fiasco is yet another sign of virtue. Likewise, his frequent peccadilloes—affairs that would scandalize if not destroy other administrations—not only are overlooked, they are seen as further proof of Kennedy's virility and daring. Not surprisingly, Kennedy's defining crisis—the Cuban missile crisis—is treated as *the* brief shining moment of Camelot. Popular commemorations such as the televised *The Missiles of October* depict brilliant, good-natured men in Washington carefully calibrating a highly creative strategy while apparatchiks in the dimly lit Kremlin hatch nefarious plots. And it should become clear that mainstream academic literature is equally enthusiastic about Kennedy and his crises. No wonder historian Garry Wills quips, "Kennedy has become the opiate of the intellectuals."[72]

Nixon is treated less generously. Arguably, he was no worse than other recent presidents. He was neither the first nor the last to conduct clandestine operations against opponents. As *The Haldeman Diaries*[73] intimate, he probably prolonged the Indochina war for domestic political reasons. But surely there is nothing commendable about Kennedy's involvement, to say nothing of the unprecedented risks he hazarded to remove missiles that, in his view, did not alter the strategic balance. As various biographers suggest, we love to hate Nixon because he reminds us of our own shadow side; he was indeed in Tom Wicker's words, "one of us." Reeves laments: "Perhaps we should get used to this new posthumous Nixon because it seems to be the one that works best on film and television. . . . It may be that no Presidents are heroes to their . . . valets, but the stumblebum Nixon seems ludicrous to me. No one in his right mind ever took him to be the demented clown being portrayed now."[74]

What some call Nixon paranoia may simply have been social awareness: He realized that he was disliked, even ridiculed, just for being Nixon. His campaign managers astutely avoided using the "N word" during the 1972 campaign when they urged the public to "Reelect the President" rather than to "reelect Nixon." In any case, I sense reluctance to credit Nixon for his accomplishments, and surely no one is tempted to romanticize him. According to the Nixonian apocrypha, Hannah Nixon told her son, "You've got to get out and scratch; you won't get anywhere on your good looks."

Looking at crises narratives per se, it appears that existential narratives are more memorable than clinical narratives for a variety of reasons. Existential narratives, in which an actor risks everything and miraculously emerges alive, offer a perverse, breathless excitement that punctuates the monotony of everyday experience for both actors and their audiences. They are also seductive because they embody wishful thinking: the complexities of international politics are reduced to a Manichaean drama in which the forces of light—led by a daring hero—vanquish evil.

Realistic narratives, on the other hand, involve bargaining and compromise. Even though the actors in these narratives accomplish heady feats in the real world, they are given little credit. A specialist intervening with routine treatment to save a life does not receive the acclaim afforded to existential heroes in sports, entertainment, or politics. In the real world, politics may be the art of compromise, but living in reality isn't necessarily the most attractive option.

AUTHORIAL STRATEGY

Catchwords are hard to resist; one wonders how often "crisis" has flowed off historian's pens . . . with little more than the force of fad. If politicians and pundits could counterfeit crises, why not historians?

—Randolph Starn[75]

Chapter 1: The Present as a Foreign Country

In order to understand the process of crisis construction, management, and remembrance, Chapter 1 contextualizes a notion that has long been stripped out of context and naturalized—the concept of crisis. I argue that, in the overdeveloped world, crises occur in a domain foreign to prevailing social scientific approaches to international relations. Due to the symbolic turn in international relations, actors are no longer observers of unmistakable threats perpetrated by adversaries with transparent motives. Responding to advances in communication and weaponry, actors rely upon impression management rather than military strategy to reestablish the status quo ante in crisis situations. Actors have become interpreters of artifices, and authors and improvisers of crisis scripts appropriated from their life and culture.

Given this transformation in international affairs, there is a marked difference between crisis interpretation in theory and in practice. In theory, analysts seem reluctant to acknowledge the interpretive nature of their inquiry. While theoretic professions of the positivist credo are no longer penned de rigueur, analysts do not proudly proclaim that they are interpreters of those official interpretations of texts and performances known as crises. In practice, however, analysts are closet hermeneuticists who blur genres in order to explicate the meaning of particular crises.

Chapter 1 critiques the interpretive practices of the competition—three influential interpretive strategies. These strategies render crises intelligible by reading favored interpretations into these episodes. These interpretive strategies are invariably tendentious. They determine what counts as data and how the data will be explicated. Specifically, realists interpret crises as unexpected exigencies precipitated by international events that upset the precarious balance of power. Bureaucratic models adduce an additional dimension to crisis construction and management: the machinations of domestic bureaucratic competition and bargaining. Unlike the realists, this model is attentive to organizational politics. Finally, individuated approaches emphasize the role of cognitive and affective processes on crisis construction and management. Accordingly, they are attentive to the predicament of individual actors amid dangerous uncertainty.

As Robert Keohane (a former president of the International Studies Association) suggests, these approaches offer retrospective interpretations of particular crises rather than predictions regarding future crises, let alone crises in general. In any case, while these competing accounts offer insight into aspects of the crises explicated in this study, given their interpretive bias, they are not on target in accounting for the most problematic aspects of these crises: (1) the mystery of the Cuban missile crisis: why did Kennedy take incommensurate risks in order to compel his adversary to withdraw the missiles? (2) why—despite decades of excoriating Kennedy's appeasement of Cuba—did Nixon fail to make a crisis move in response to the surreptitious construction of a Soviet nuclear submarine base in Cuba?

Chapter 2: A Hermeneutic Primer

Chapter 2 has the unenviable task of defining hermeneutic inquiry. Even though actors and analysts alike are de facto hermeneuticists reading interpretations into the artifacts of international life, the term is not in wide usage—to say the least. Indeed, given the association of "hermeneutics" with a world in which truth was found in sacred texts rather than the mathematical book of nature, the term understandably gets bad press among those wedded to social scientific inquiry. The term seems arcane and elusive, especially to those with traditional social scientific backgrounds.

Indebted to the "indoor" hermeneutics of philosophers such as Dilthey and Gadamer, and the "outdoor" hermeneutics practiced by anthropologists such as Turner and Geertz, to explicate crises at other times and places, I discuss the presuppositions, methods, and problematics associated with this self-reflective, avowedly interpretive approach to crisis explication. Turner's concept of "liminality" merits special emphasis because it illuminates the critical juncture in existential crises experienced by Kennedy and Nixon. "Liminality" refers to that phase of a crisis in which familiar metaphors become irrelevant and dangerous, and no new metaphors are on the horizon to take their place. The would-be statesman/hero is thrown into an existential darkness "betwixt and between metaphors"—neither here nor there. During this terrifying phase of the heroic journey, the actor either improvises new metaphors to redeem himself or suffers abysmal failure or worse.

The chapter relies upon Turner's account of Becket's life crisis to illustrate the approach. I conclude by reflecting upon the seemingly intractable problems endemic to avowedly interpretive approaches such as mine, or implicitly interpretive approaches such as those of the competition.

Chapter 3: The Essence Of Indecision

Detecting a remarkable match between Kennedy's words and deeds, Chapter 3 examines his texts in order to explicate his concept of crisis. *Why England Slept* and *Profiles in Courage* reveal that Kennedy's defining life crisis was ultimately a crisis of identity presaged by his texts. To be sure, the Cuban missile crisis cannot be reduced to a single factor; but it cannot be understood without reference to Kennedy's existential predicament: Would he be a Chamberlain or a Churchill?

My reading of Kennedy is iconoclastic and ironic. The Kennedy credo was "to govern is to decide." However, his defining crisis was marked by indecision. Initially, he could not decide whether to be a Churchill or a Chamberlain. While he recklessly acted as if he were Churchill in public, in private he improvised a new metaphor—gradual escalation strategy. This strategy offered hope—for a brief and shining moment. However, since this strategy failed to remove the missiles, as his domestic adversaries had warned, he lapsed into liminality. He was trapped between strategic metaphors. Emulating Churchill might spark a nuclear holocaust, and mimicking Chamberlain would certainly be political suicide. But these were indelible metaphors. Out of desperation he decided to be both Churchill and Chamberlain. In haste, his brother presented the Soviets with a strident message (remove the missiles quickly or look out!) and simultaneously acceded to Khrushchev's demands by secretly trading the Cuban missiles for American Jupiter missiles based in Turkey.

Ironically, Kennedy's indecisiveness may have been a blessing in disguise. His inconsistent messages may have frightened Khrushchev by suggesting that Kennedy was losing control over events. (This is precisely how the Ex Comm responded to Khrushchev's inconsistencies.) It is not unreasonable to assume that Khrushchev's own indecisiveness about how to deal with Kennedy and the Cuban situation—which was rapidly veering out of control—may have prompted him to end the confrontation.

Nevertheless, due to effective posthumous impression management—along with a popular will to believe—Kennedy is lionized as a profile in courage, a gallant young president who had the guts to stand up to Khrushchev. More disturbing still, the putatively triumphant gradual escalation strategy became the template for the fiasco in Vietnam and for imprudent nuclear war-fighting doctrines.

Chapter 4: What if They Gave a Crisis and Nobody Came

The Cienfuegos incident presented an ideal opportunity for Nixon to prove that he—not his nemesis, John F. Kennedy—was a profile in courage. It provided a pretext from him to come to the aid of his party by playing the communist card for political advantage and, in the process, resolving what he and his closest advisers regarded as a serious threat to national security.

Again, I find remarkable correspondence between the crisis narratives inscribed in a president's texts and his deeds. Specifically, I argue that Nixon passed up the opportunity because Cienfuegos was not the sort of incident that fomented Nixon-style crises. He was surprised when Chou En-lai told him that "he felt he knew me through my book, *Six Crises*, which had been translated into Chinese."[76] In this chapter, I, like Chou, read between the lines to determine what Nixon conceptualized as a crisis, and what he downplayed or ignored. *Six Crises* (for the most part, an account of Nixon's tenure as vice president) should disabuse the reader of the increasingly influential myth that foreign relations was Nixon's abiding concern. His words and deeds suggest that Nixon was preoccupied with managing Nixon, not foreign affairs. Given the myth, or even more mundane expectations, one would think the vice president of the United States would have been exercised by episodes such as the Korean War, the Soviet detonation of the H-bomb, events in Indochina, the Suez crisis, the Soviet invasion of Hungary, Sputnik, and the Soviet downing of a U-2 reconnaissance plane, to list but a few instances. Not so. The latter-day Nixon represented himself as a statesman who profoundly altered history—a Wilson or a Churchill. But his deeds, especially his crisis improvisations, suggest that he was more like Willy Loman—a tragic figure who wanted to be respected and well-liked in the here and now. *Six Crises* and *Death of a Salesman* are of the same genre: both portray the low tragedy of men haunted by misfortune and humiliation, insecure men who felt cheated by life, yet nevertheless embraced the American dream.

True, Nixon would later write of the "lonely decisions" he made in foreign affairs, but his fire-in-the-belly crises were invariably venal and personal. Vintage Nixon crises—resolved by gambits such as the Checkers speech, the Kitchen Debate, and the "I Am Not a Crook" Watergate apologia—were venal and personal. They were sparked by rejection and humiliation—situations that would not let Nixon forget that he was not well-liked.

But ironically, Nixon's indifference to international challenges served the rest of us well, at least in 1970. Given his preoccupation with other matters, such as domestic enemies and his pending vacation, he declined to attend a potential Götterdämmerung. Lacking the glamour and the impression management skills bestowed upon Kennedy, Nixon, of course, still gets bad press. In any case, leaders are seldom remembered, let alone lionized, for what they didn't do.

Finally, I argue that Kissinger construed the Cienfuegos incident as a crisis because he determined that Soviet actions upset the balance of power. As we shall see, he resolved the confrontation through virtuoso dissembling—even Hermes would have been impressed. If Nixon was a victim of his failures, Kissinger was a victim of his success. Due to early successes such as Cienfuegos, he acquired the reputation of a charming but duplicitous diplomat. Unfortunately, his clever, tenacious diplomacy in response to the challenge at Cienfuegos Bay was soon forgotten, even by Kissinger himself.

Chapter 5: The Past as Prologue

Despite (or due to) the widely acknowledged unpredictability of international affairs, one prediction—a veritable truism—inspires confidence: crises will remain a prominent and dangerous feature of international life. I suspect that future leaders will continue to construe these episodes as heroic tests of their preconceived destiny. Eisenhower's admonition to construe unexpected challenges as problems one can live with, to be resolved quietly and patiently in due course, will be disregarded. Like the poor, crises will always be with us for two reasons:

1. Like poverty, crises have become an accepted (and from an elite viewpoint, useful) institution, an unquestioned social practice. Since crisis discourse has become the lingua franca inside the Beltway, a wide array of disparate events are conceptualized as crises—critical junctures that test a leader's mettle.

2. There are strong personal and political incentives for sustaining this practice. Leaders seldom view themselves as lackluster caretakers managing chronic problems. Perhaps every age is deemed a time of crisis—an epochal turning point—because leaders want to make an indelible and dramatic impression on history. Crises are initiation rites that mark the passage from politician to revered statesman.

Interpreting the texts and performances of international life as crises also fulfills a host of less grandiose political needs. The high drama of crises punctuates the monotony of everyday experience, distracts attention from more pressing personal and social matters, galvanizes support for policies that demand risk and sacrifice, and boosts an incumbent's popularity. I conclude that the nature of the crises awaiting us depends upon our future leaders' conceptual universe. Given the lethality of modern weapons and the uninhibited nature of military strategy, heroic narratives may end in tragedy. Unlike the triumphant Greek dramas, no deus ex machina awaits in the wings to save us from ourselves.

NOTES

1. Milan Kundera, *The Book of Laughter and Forgetting* (New York: Penguin), 106.

2. The Cuban missile crisis has generated a voluminous literature. This study is particularly indebted to archival material provided by the John F. Kennedy Presidential Library in Boston, and the National Security Archive (NSA) in Washington, D.C. Many pertinent NSA documents are contained in Laurence Chang and Peter Kornbluhs' *The Cuban Missile Crisis, 1962* (New York: New Press, 1991). Works by participants include: Robert F. Kennedy, *Thirteen Days: A Memoir on the Cuban Missile Crisis* (New York: W.W. Norton, 1969); Arthur M. Schlesinger, Jr., *A Thousand Days: JFK in the White House* (Boston: Houghton Mifflin, 1965); Theodore Sorensen, *Kennedy* (New York: Harper & Row, 1965); George Ball, "JFK's Big Moment," *The New York Review* (February 13, 1992); McGeorge Bundy, *Danger and Survival* (New York: Random House, 1988); Raymond L. Garthoff *Reflections On The Cuban Missile Crisis* (Washington: The Brookings Institution, 1987); Nikita Khrushchev, *Khrushchev Remembers* (Strobe Talbot trans. and ed.), (Boston: Little Brown, 1970); Anatoly Dobrynin, *In Confidence* (New York: Times Books, 1995). Secondary sources include Robert Divine, *The Cuban Missile Crisis* (Chicago: Quadrangle Books, 1971); Graham Allison, *The Essence of Decision: Explaining the Cuban Missile Crisis* (Boston: Little Brown, 1971); Robert Jervis, *The Logic of Images in International Relations* (Princeton: Princeton University Press, 1970); and *Perception and Misperception in International Politics* (Princeton: Princeton University Press, 1976); Richard Ned Lebow, *Between Peace and War: The Nature of International Crises* (Baltimore: Johns Hopkins University Press, 1981); Richard Ned Lebow and Janice Gross Stein, *We All Lost the Cold War* (Princeton: Princeton University Press, 1994); Barton J. Bernstein, "The Week We Almost Went to War," *Bulletin of the Atomic Scientists* (February 1986); James A. Nathan, *The Cuban Missile Crisis Revisited* (New York: St. Martin's Press, 1992) the essays by Nathan, Bernstein, Lebow and Chang are of particular interest; James G. Blight and David A. Welch, *On The Brink: Soviets and Americans Reexamine the Cuban Missile Crisis* (New York: Hill and Wang, 1989); James G. Blight, *The Shattered Crystal Ball: Fear and Learning in the Cuban Missile Crisis* (Lanham: Rowman & Littlefield, 1992); Richard Reeves, *President Kennedy: Profiles of Power* (New York: Simon and Schuster, 1993); Michael Beschloss, *The Crisis Years* (New York: HarperCollins, 1991); Gerald S. Strober and Deborah H. Strober, *"Let Us Begin Anew": An Oral History of the Kennedy Presidency* (New York: HarperCollins, 1993); Robert Smith Thompson, *The Missiles of October* (New York: Simon and Schuster, 1992); Bruce J. Allyn, James G. Blight, and David A. Welch, "Essence of Revision," *International Security*, (Winter 1989/90); Tim Carroll, "The Cuban Missile Crisis: Representations and Misrepresentations," paper presented to the American Popular Culture Conference, Las Vegas, March 26, 1996.

3. Based upon his interviews with the participants, Blight discusses the fear of nuclear war in his *The Shattered Crystal Ball*; the fear precipitated by the crisis is discussed in primary sources such as the works of Robert Kennedy and Nikita Khrushchev.

4. Dobrynin, 86.

5. As McGeorge Bundy (Kennedy's national security adviser) notes, like Nixon, President Ronald Reagan did not lose sleep over Soviet nuclear submarines. "He had no interest in constructing a comparable strategic provocation as a crisis: . . . in 1984 the capabilities of Soviet submarines in the Western Atlantic—essentially parallel to those of the missiles . . . in Cuba—were sensibly pronounced untroubling by Ronald Reagan: 'If I thought there were some reason to be concerned about them, I wouldn't be sleeping in this house tonight.'" *Danger and Survival*, 450.

6. Perhaps because the crisis was not constructed and managed in accord with the hallowed crisis narratives of our culture, the material on the 1970 episode is scant. Participants discuss the episode in: Richard M. Nixon, *The Memoirs of Richard Nixon* (New York: Grosset & Dunlap, 1978); Henry Kissinger, *The White House Years* (Boston: Little Brown, 1979); H. R. Haldeman, *The Haldeman Diaries* (New York: Putnam, 1994); H. R. Haldeman, with Joseph DiMona, *The Ends of Power* (New York: Times Books, 1978); Raymond L. Garthoff, "Handling the Cienfuegos Crisis" in *International Security* 8, no. 1 (1983); Dobrynin, *In Confidence*. Secondary sources include Steven E. Ambrose, *Nixon,* vol. 2, (New York: Simon and Schuster, 1989); Seymour Hersh, *The Price of Power* (New York: Summit Books, 1983); Tom Wicker, *One of Us: Richard Nixon and the American Dream* (New York: Random House, 1992). The 1962 and 1970 incidents are compared and contrasted in Garthoff, and in Fen Hampson, "The Divided Decision-Maker: American Domestic Politics and the Cuban Crises" in Charles Kegley and Eugene Witkopf, eds., *The Domestic Sources of Foreign Policy* (New York: St. Martin's Press, 1988); and in Gloria Duffy, "Crisis Prevention in Cuba" in Alexander George, ed., *Managing U.S.-Soviet Rivalry* (Boulder: Westview Press, 1979).

7. See Jervis's *Perception and Misperception*; cognitive approaches to crises will be discussed in more depth in Chapter 1.

8. In what was, perhaps, the only memorable moment of the 1988 vice presidential campaign, Lloyd Bentsen taunted his opponent, Dan Quayle, "You're no John F. Kennedy." Bentsen was alluding to what he construed as Kennedy's adroit resolution of the Cuban missile crisis. And as Christopher Matthews remarks in "Ready for Prime Time" *San Francisco Examiner Magazine* (April 28, 1996), 8: "To the delight of . . . the 1992 Democratic convention, organizers showed a grainy film clip of 16-year-old Clinton being greeted by the hero-president [JFK] himself. The few frames . . . provided a moment of magic: it was as if young Arthur himself had just pulled the sword from the stone."

9. Chapter 2 explains the nature of the hermeneutic inquiry that informs this inquiry. A working definition should suffice here. Hermeneutics presupposes that cultural artifacts—such as crises—are ambiguous; that is, they can be plausibly subject to two or more interpretations. Accordingly, hermeneutics devises insights and methods for interpreting such ambiguity.

10. In general, gender-specific terms are used because the crises explicated in this study were male endeavors.

11. Randolph Starn discusses the conceptualization of "crisis" from Thucydides forward in "Historians and Crisis," in *Past and Present*, (Fall 1971); also see Jürgen Habermas, "What Does a Crisis Mean Today?" in Steven Seidman, ed., *Jürgen Habermas on Society and Politics* (Boston: Beacon Press, 1989).

12. Robert Prus, *Symbolic Interaction and Ethnographic Research* (Albany: State University of New York Press, 1996), 34.

13. Impediments remain: many documents are still classified, and certain key documents—such as RFK's calendar and drafts of his memoir on the crisis—are either missing or unavailable to independent investigators.

14. See, for example, Kissinger, Haldeman, Hampson, and Duffy, cited above.

15. See Denise Bottsdorff's discussion of crisis promotion in her *Presidents and the Rhetoric of Foreign Crises* (Columbia: University of South Carolina Press, 1993).

16. Chapter 1 discusses four evaluative criteria. I argue that for a narrative to be on target, it should be internally coherent; correspond to the facts known and discovered, contextualize the actors and events, and attend to the dialectic aspect—the contradictory features—of human reality. Of course, analysts who share these criteria may agree that

their interpretation fulfills these criteria, yet their respective interpretations may be diametrically opposed. In this not uncommon situation, I can think of no authoritative tribunal for judging contesting interpretations that would satisfy the disputants and other analysts.

17. Clifford Geertz, *The Interpretation of Cultures* (New York: Basic Books, 1973), 10.

18. Niccolo Machiavelli, *The Prince* (Ware: Wordsworth Editions, 1993), 138.

19. The legend of Hermes recounted in Thomas Bulfinch's *The Golden Age of Myth and Legend* (Ware: Wordsworth Editions, 1993), 9.

20. Quoted by Bruce Mazlish in *Kissinger: The European Mind in American Policy* (New York: Basic Books, 1976), 91.

21. Bulfinch, 69.

22. Bulfinch recounts this saga on 297.

23. Quoted by Kurt Mueller-Vollmer in Kurt Mueller-Vollmer, ed., *The Hermeneutics Reader* (New York: Continuum, 1989), 5.

24. Joseph Bliecher offers a succinct but penetrating account of hermeneutic social inquiry in "On Hermeneutics" in *The Blackwell Dictionary of Twentieth Century Social Thought* (London: Blackwell, 1989).

25. See Jervis's discussion in *The Logic of Images in International Relations.*

26. Due to the advent of postmodernism, there is controversy as to whether texts describe, create, or—indeed—*are* reality. I argue that texts, broadly construed, are the substance of international relations. As such, they both describe and interpret reality. However, since description and interpretation are inextricably linked, a congenial interpretation of a text is often naturalized and taken to be an account of an objective phenomena rather than a way of merely rendering such phenomena intelligible.

27. Due to his illness, and subsequent death, I was unable to continue my correspondence with Mr. Cline. I am grateful to his family for sending pertinent documents.

28. Allison (cited above) offers an influential bureaucratic model; K. A. Oye relates game-theoretic models to international conflict in *Cooperation Under Anarchy* (Princeton: Princeton University Press, 1986).

29. Quoted by Alexander George in "A Provisional Theory of Crisis Management" in Alexander George, ed., *Avoiding War: Problems of Crisis Management* (Boulder: Westview Press, 1991), 58.

30. See the works of Ambrose, Beschloss, Reeve, and Wicker cited above.

31. Robert S. McNamara, *In Retrospect,* Chapter 11.

32. The Munich Syndrome refers to a lesson of history: like Chamberlain—the British prime minister who traveled to Munich to court a rapprochement with Hitler—those who appease enemies encourage further aggression and invite humiliation and defeat.

33. See, for example, Jervis, *The Logic of Images in International Relations.*

34. Strober and Strober, 390.

35. Dobrynin, 74.

36. Ole Holsti, "Crisis Decision Making," in Philip Tetlock, Jo Husbands et al., *Behavior, Society and Nuclear War, vol. 1* (Oxford: Oxford University Press, 1989), 49.

37. Erving Goffman, *The Presentation of Self in Everyday Life* (Garden City: Doubleday, 1959), 17.

38. See Bliecher's discussion of this self-reflective, critical contribution to hermeneutics, 259.

39. Holsti, *"Crisis Decision Making,"* 56.

40. Isaiah Berlin, "On Political Judgment" in *The New York Review*, October 3, 1996.

41. Thompson, 356.

42. Tim Carroll, personal communications, July 5, 1996.

43. Michael Hunt, *Crises and U. S. Foreign Policy* (New Haven: Yale University Press, 1996, 425.

44. Michel Foucault, "The Order of Discourse" in Michael Shapiro, ed., *Language and Politics* (New York: New York University Press, 1989).

45. Murray Edelman, *Constructing the Political Spectacle* (Chicago: University of Chicago Press, 1988), 31.

46. Richard Neustadt and Ernest May, *Thinking in Time* (New York: The Free Press, 1986), 106.

47. Roy Schafer, "The Appreciative Analytic Attitude and the Construction of Multiple Histories," in *Psychoanalysis and Contemporary Thought* (1979), 3:24, 23.

48. See McGeorge Bundy's discussion of the incident in *Danger and Survival,* 414.

49. See Richard Betts, *Nuclear Blackmail & Nuclear Balance* (Washington: Brookings Institution, 1987).

50. James Fentress and Chris Wickham, *Social Memory* (Oxford: Blackwell 1988), 51.

51. Peter Berger, "Society as Drama," in Dennis Brisset and Charles Edgley, eds., *Life as Theatre* (Chicago: Aldine, 1975), 16.

52. Starn, 4.

53. The literature is voluminous. In addition to the work of George cited above, see Holsti's also cited above.

54. See Dorothy Ross' account of Frye in her "Grand Narrative in American Historical Writing: From Romance to Uncertainty," *American Historical Review* (June 1995).

55. Jürgen Habermas, *Legitimation Crisis* (Boston: Beacon Press, 1973), 2.

56. Ibid.

57. Ibid. 1.

58. Quoted in Starn, 8.

59. Arthur M. Schlesinger, Jr., *Robert Kennedy and His Times* (Boston: Houghton Mifflin, 1978), 601.

60. Theodore Sorensen, "Kennedy Vindicated," in Robert Divine, ed., *The Cuban Missile Crisis* (Chicago: Quadrangle Books, 1971).

61. Quoted in Starn, 7.

62. "Mr. X" essay in *Foreign Affairs* attributed to George Kennan; see Kennan's discussion of the article in his *The Cloud of Danger* (Boston: Little Brown, 1978).

63. See Acheson's essay, "Plain Dumb Luck," in Robert Divine, ed., *The Cuban Missile Crisis* (Chicago: Quadrangle Books, 1971).

64. Richard Reeves, "Nixon Revisited by Way of the Creative Camera," in *New York Times*, December 17, 1995, sect. 2, 1.

65. Fentress and Wickham, 5.

66. Murray Edelman, *The Symbolic Uses of Politics* (Urbana: University of Illinois Press, 1988), 172.

67. Ernest Becker, *The Denial of Death* (New York: The Free Press, 1973), 11-12.

68. Fentress and Wickham, 134.

69. Stryker McGuire and David Ansen, "Stone Takes on Nixon," *Newsweek,* (December 11, 1995): 67.

70. R. I. Moore's editorial comment in Fentress and Wickham, viii.

71. Reeves, "Nixon Revisited," 1.

72. Garry Wills, *The Kennedy Imprisonment* (Boston: Little, Brown, 1981), 49.

73. See Ambrose's "Introduction" to the *Diaries.*

74. Reeves, 41.

75. Starn, 5.

76. Richard Nixon, *In the Arena,* (New York: Simon and Schuster, 1990), 12.

CHAPTER 1

THE PRESENT AS A FOREIGN COUNTRY

We are all natives now, and everybody else not immediately one of us is an exotic. What looked once to be a matter of finding out whether savages could distinguish fact from fancy now looks to be a matter of finding out how others across the sea or down the corridor organize their significative world.

—Clifford Geertz[1]

It is widely presupposed that crisis inquiry is the exclusive domain of prevailing approaches to politics. Accordingly, avowedly interpretive inquiry has not realized its potential for illuminating the social dramas we call international crises. This is unfortunate because crises occur in a realm foreign to prevailing approaches, a realm more familiar to interpretive approaches to social action. Actors, as I have suggested, are no longer observers of unmistakable events; they are interpreters of cryptic texts and symbolic performances. And, given this situation, analysts are not detached observers, mirrors of nature accurately reflecting machinations inside the Beltway. It is tempting to suggest that we have gone through the looking glass to become interpreters of official interpretations. But such an Alice in Wonderland allusion is not entirely apt. Our interpretations are not impure fantasy: they take the facts into account—indeed, they try to account for the facts. But our interpretive strategies are not *determined* by the facts. They are congenial, a priori schemes devised to gain entrance to an alien world far removed from our personal and professional lives—the elite subculture that controls the fate of the earth.

The possibility that crises occur in a world alien to ostensibly social scientific approaches that dominate the literature prompts the questions explored in this chapter:

Why is the present a foreign country? If the past is a foreign country—a realm crying out for interpretation—so, a fortiori, is the present. As Edward Bruner observes: "We talk of our special anthropological methodology for reconstructing the past, as if the present were not equally constructed."[2] And, throughout his career, political theorist Murray Edelman has stressed the increasingly symbolic nature of domestic American politics.[3] Indeed, I argue that given the symbolic turn in international relations, it is reasonable to conclude that the present is more of a construction than the past. Accordingly, this chapter examines the radical transformation in communication and weaponry that precipitated this symbolic turn in international relations, ushering in a world foreign to prevailing perspectives.

Have analysts recognized this symbolic turn in international relations? A philosophic answer is in order—yes and no. In theory, analysts profess their devotion to empirical methods that observe, classify, and generalize data in accord with social scientific paradigms. In practice, however, they tacitly respond to the symbolic turn in international relations by (in Geertz's telling phrase) blurring genres in order to interpret ambiguous words and deeds. Despite their theoretic inhibitions, analysts have become closet hermeneuticists unable to resist the temptation to attribute motives to political actors. However, for the most part, they are unwilling to openly discuss their interpretive practices and the problems they entail. The time has come to acknowledge this variance between theory and practice.

How adequate are prevailing interpretations of crises? While my critique is hardly exhaustive, I examine the competition: three influential interpretations of crisis construction and management. These perspectives, in effect, move from world politics, to domestic politics, to the politics of particular personalities. The first, political realism, attends to the power politics of nation states amid a world of international anarchy. The second, bureaucratic politics, concerns itself with the machinations of elite bureaucratic competition and bargaining. Finally, individuated approaches focus upon the cognitive and affective dispositions of particular actors. To be sure, the competition illumines many crises of the past, and offers insight into aspects of the episodes considered in this study. However, they do not adequately explain two pressing concerns of this study: (1) Why did Kennedy take incommensurate risks in order to resolve the Cuban missile crisis? (2) Why did Nixon fail to make a crisis move in response to the surreptitious construction of a Soviet nuclear submarine base in Cuba?

THE SYMBOLIC TURN IN INTERNATIONAL RELATIONS

> Our age is even more hermeneutic than it is postmodern, and the only meaningful question to be raised at this stage is whether there is ever a time when we refrain from interpreting.
>
> —Richard Shusterman[4]

Political actors seldom refrain from interpreting, for good reason. They are cast into a world in which unequivocal communication between adversaries with transparent motives about unmistakable events has been supplanted by contesting interpretations of cryptic texts and symbolic performances. And, as we shall see, in this post-Freudian world, actors themselves allow that they are not always conversant with their motives, let alone those of their adversaries. As Ernest Cassirer observed:

> Physical reality seems to recede in proportion as man's symbolic activity advances. Instead of dealing with the things themselves man is in a sense constantly conversing with himself. He has so enveloped himself in linguistic forms . . . in mythical symbols or religious rites that he cannot see or know anything except by the interposition of [an] artificial medium.[5]

The transition from a world of obdurate threats to national survival to a realm of evanescent challenges to symbolic values did not occur ex nihilo, nor did it occur solely in some ethereal realm of ideas. The transition is due, in large measure, to dramatic changes in communication and weapons technology. As communication theorist Mark Poster explains:

> Every age employs symbolic exchange which contain internal and external stuctures, means and relations of signification. Stages in the mode of information may be . . . designated as follows: face-to-face; orally mediated exchange; written exchanges mediated by print; and electronically mediated exchange. . . . In each stage the relation of language and society, idea and action, self and other is different.[6]

Poster is not merely observing that face-to-face communication is being supplanted by electronically transmitted messages; he is calling attention to a more disturbing development—increasingly, words no longer refer to things. This is evident in the construction and management of crises. At one time "crisis" referred to an objective event that virtually anyone would call a crisis, an unmistakable threat. For example, when the Madisons saw the White House burn, and when Lincoln heard secessionist gunfire across the Potomac, they observed situations that most everyone would deem a crisis. Today, crises are seldom sparked by direct observation of objective events; they are precipitated by interpretations of texts and performances. Kennedy and his advisers were interpreters, not observers. They were puzzled by a situation that was unanticipated and ambiguous, if not inchoate—the discovery of Soviet missiles in Cuba. The Ex Comm deliberations involved interpreting Soviet actions and sending the right message to Khrushchev. (As we have seen, the best and the brightest sought salvation in Trollope's literary ploy rather than the strategies of Clausewitz.) In any event, they spent relatively little time discussing the objective features of the weapons. As Richard Betts explains, "The Ex Comm paid scant attention to calculations [regarding the mechanics of Soviet weapons]; emphasis was placed upon the political and symbolic import of the deployment in Cuba."[7]

Kennedy and his closest advisers were not exercised by Khrushchev's actions because the missiles posed a tangible, unmistakable threat to American survival. However, the New Frontier impression managers were not indifferent toward appearances: as Sorensen urges, a crisis occurred because it might *appear* to friend and foe alike that the Soviets gained some strategic advantage.[8] Their concerns were more symbolic than strategic: they were preoccupied with interpreting Soviet motives, and with authoring texts and performances that would express their own preconceived destiny and somehow persuade Khrushchev to remove the weapons. Kennedy and the others fervently hoped that their words would have the magical power attributed to such symbols by Northrop Frye: "The written word has far more power than a reminder: it recreates the past in the present, and gives us, not the familiar remembered thing, but the glittering intensity of the summoned-up hallucination."[9]

The words authored by the Ex Comm were designed to conjure up visions of American power and resolve in the minds of Khrushchev and his apparatchiks. Indeed, a crisis has become a war of words in which words, not weapons, are used to reestablish the status quo ante. Even a traditional realist such as Schelling concludes that the Cuban missile crisis wasn't governed by calculations of strategic gains and losses; it was a "competition in risk taking." Therefore, the coercive strategy devised was symbolic and psychological, not tactical and military.[10] Indeed, given the symbolic turn in international relations, the explications of Turner and Geertz may be more illuminating than the strategizing of Clausewitz and Schelling.

Nuclear weapons technology also precipitated the symbolic turn in international relations. These apocalyptic weapons render traditional notions of "national security" and "strategic superiority" obsolete. As McNamara warns, it is absurd to presuppose that a more formidable nuclear arsenal bestows any advantage: "I doubt that a survivor—if there was [*sic*] one—could perceive much difference between a world in which 12,000 nuclear warheads had been exploded and one subject to attack by 40,000."[11]

Ever since he left office, McNamara has argued that there is no defense against these weapons. According to the former secretary, had the 1962 crisis escalated into nuclear war, the Soviets—despite their strategic inferiority—very likely would have devastated the United States with dozens of thermonuclear weapons. He urges that the thought of even one such weapon striking an American city evokes images of unparalleled disaster:

> If you go to nuclear war . . . and only a few—maybe even only *one*—bomb gets through to destroy an American city, you—the one who initiated the nuclear war—will have . . . to shoulder the responsibility for the worst catastrophe in the history of this country.[12]

For McNamara, since nuclear weapons have no military use, their role must be symbolic: "The sole purpose of strategic nuclear force is to deter the other side's first use of strategic forces."[13] (As I have argued in previous works, "deterrence" is a symbolic system, a millenarian faith that nuclear weapons have ushered in peace on earth without goodwill toward men. In any case, "deterrence" provides an ideological justification for the development and deployment of weapons whose use would be irrational.[14]) However, even if we grant that deterrence is both a very good reason—and the real reason—for American nuclear endeavors, it is not some objective, measurable phenomenon: at best "deterrence" is speculation regarding elite psychology; at worst, it is an ideology that justifies the development, deployment, and possible detonation of apocalyptic weapons. McNamara seems to share this view when he argues that the acquisition of nuclear weapons is not a military strategy; it is a symbolic performance, an improvisation, designed to convince adversaries of the credibility —and the extremes—of one's resolve.

Just as guns exerted a leveling influence on the Western frontier—an armed weakling was as formidable as anyone else—nuclear weapons exerted a leveling influence on the New Frontier. Diminishing utility—and increasing futility— rapidly approach once an adversary enjoys the capability of delivering a few nuclear weapons. Citing the Cuban missile crisis as a prime example, historian Marc Trachtenberg argues that calculations of superiority or inferiority are virtually meaningless in crises between nuclear powers:

> Would it . . . have made a difference in 1962 if "the relative strategic positions of the Soviet Union and the United States had been reversed?" In 1969 McGeorge Bundy said no: "A stalemate is a stalemate either way around."[15]

In sum, since political actors inhabit a world of cryptic texts and symbolic performances—and all-too-real nuclear weapons—they have a powerful incentive to rely upon words, rather than weapons, to resolve crises. Despite our predilections to the contrary, those of us who try to get a handle on crises find ourselves interpreting a peculiar universe of words and performances. At the moment, this predicament is seldom proclaimed in theory, but it is tacitly acknowledged de facto in practice.

CLOSET HERMENEUTICS

> We might answer Montaigne's question "Do we find any end to the need of interpreting?" . . . How could we find an end . . . when interpretation disguises itself in so many ways, when interpretation masks itself and its desire for absolute knowledge in the drive toward satiety?"
> —Gayle Ormiston and Alan Schrift[16]

Referring to the competition as interpretation disguised as empirical social science may seem tendentious, even narcissistic. (While these prevailing analysts may, on occasion, loosely refer to their inquiries as "interpretations," they generally claim that their conclusions are based upon the usual social scientific procedures, not interpretations read into a situation.) It is, perhaps, forgivable to write a book to persuade colleagues to be more like me by embracing interpretive inquiry. However, it may well be unforgivable to suggest that, whether they realize it or not, colleagues *are* indeed like me. Nevertheless, well aware of my seeming presumption, I claim that the competition is empirical in theory but interpretive in practice. With Paul, I hope to be forgiven, although such presumption is unforgivable. Such presumption is based upon the realization that crisis inquiry has undergone profound changes during the last three decades. This chapter offers an account of the largely unrecognized impact of these changes on the competition.

At the risk of sounding overly magisterial, it is tempting to liken these changes to the transformation undergone by the natural sciences during the last three centuries. Classical physicists saw themselves as passive observers of nature; their efforts were dominated by what Foucault calls "the will to know":

> At the turn of the sixteenth century . . . there appeared a will to know . . . [that limited intelligible inquiry] to observable, measurable, classified objects; a will to know which imposed on the knowing subject . . . a certain position, a certain gaze and a certain function (*to see rather than to read, to verify rather than to make commentaries on*). [italics mine][17]

But could it be that, as Thomas Kuhn argues, even natural scientists are interpreters of natural phenomena, not mere observers?

> Hermeneutic interpretation . . . is how such [scientific] discovering is done. No more in the natural than in the human sciences is there some neutral, culture-independent, set of categories within which the population—whether of objects or of actions—can be described.[18]

Despite Kuhn's insight, early crisis investigators interpreted the natural sciences as purely empirical, non-interpretive endeavors. Suffering from physics envy, emulating what they took to be scientific methods, they naturalized crises by assuming they were part and parcel of this familiar realm of classical physics—an objective thing "out there" that could be observed, measured, and classified. In this world, blessed by Prometheus, it was expected these empirical procedures would generate testable hypotheses that would, one day, usher in scientific explanations. Many were convinced that such explanations would subsume particular events under general mechanical-causal laws; and eventually, these explanations would generate a comprehensive theory of phenomena such as crises. What was sought was an elusive treasure wonderfully described by historian David Samuels as "facts . . . of the stern Germanic variety envisioned by von Ranke, fixed, immutable facts that sat like Roman coins in the palm of your hand, waiting to be brushed clean of the dirt of accumulated centuries by the wire-hairbrush of historical truth. . . . "[19]

Alas, cursed by Hermes, we dig through the archives only to uncover dog-eared texts, not glistening treasures. Our oral histories produce contradictory glosses on performances that we rightly regard with suspicion, not hallowed revelations. Once, however, analysts were strong in the faith that such facts could be uncovered, and that they would yield scientific explanations of phenomena such as crises. During my graduate school days, influential analysts such as J. David Singer evangelized on behalf of empirical methods. In 1966 he predicted:

Within a decade, almost every graduate school in the country will have some faculty who have been trained in scientific method, and assertions to the effect that "you can't quantify diplomatic variables," or "international politics are too complicated to be treated scientifically" will sound as absurd as they do now when said of biology, psychology or economics.[20]

Ironically, Singer's prediction did not come true. Indeed, since we cannot predict trends within our own disciplines, it seems unlikely that we will be able to predict the vicissitudes of international relations in the foreseeable future. True, some schools (such as practitioners of game theoretic research) still keep the faith. However, despite their theoretic professions, the practice of influential analysts has become eclectic and interpretive; perhaps the time will come when international relations theory will reflect these changes more accurately.

Consider the apparent evolution of Richard Ned Lebow's methodological perspective. In 1981 he invoked the conceptual apparatus of empirical social science in his perceptive study of twenty-six crises: "The sample is sufficiently comprehensive to permit generalization to be made with a reasonable degree of confidence."[21] And his discourse referred to variables (both dependent and in-dependent), sampling, hypotheses, and such. Yet, his actual inquiry blurred genres. (He recalls his graduate school days with dismay. According to Lebow, the political science program derided his interests as too historical. Returning the favor, the historians did not take well to his political interests.) Undaunted, he advanced adroit explications that incorporated studies in history, political science, and social psychology. Most significantly, he went beyond—or behind—observations of publicly observable behavior, and offered accounts of actors' inner experiences—namely, their styles of cognitive processing. In 1990 he published a piece that interpreted traditional and revisionist accounts of the Cuban missile crisis.[22] And it is noteworthy that his 1994 account of two Cold War crises (authored with Janice Stein) dispenses with professions of scientific procedures, and begins with a decidedly hermeneutic problem: embedding texts in their political context in order to judge their reliability and meaning. Moreover, he fashions narratives to explicate the motives of the actors in the Cuban missile crisis.[23]

By the late 1980s Robert Keohane used his Presidential Address to the International Studies Association to express doubts about the possibility of a science of international relations:

Deterministic laws elude us, since we are studying the purposive behavior of relatively small numbers of actors engaged in strategic bargaining. In situations involving strategic bargaining, even formal theories with highly restrictive assumptions fail to specify which . . . outcomes will occur.[24]

He stressed that the best that could be hoped for is what Geertz calls "local knowledge": "We must understand that we can aspire only to formulate conditional, context-specific generalization rather than to discover universal laws, and our understanding of world politics will always be incomplete."[25]

Keohane noted a profound difference between theory and practice. In theory, many prevailing accounts of international relations are empirical projects putatively guided by the methodology of the physical sciences. In practice, however, analysts interpret the crisis literature and struggle to pen insightful interpretations of political thought and action. These interpretations rely upon what Geertz calls "thick descriptions": teleological accounts of *why* actors think and act as they do. Indeed, it appears that regardless of an analyst's intentions, it is difficult to practice social inquiry without attributing motives to others. Typically, our congenial a priori interpretations are inextricably mixed with our observations. As Geertz concludes, "What we call our data are really our own constructions of other people's constructions of what they and their compatriots are up to."[26]

Keohane, indebted to Geertz, recognized what his colleagues are up to: in theory, analysts claim to explain crises in the manner of natural scientists. In practice, they interpret these episodes in the manner of humanistic inquiry: they devise thick descriptions and weave them into narratives:

> How much insight does Realism [or other prevailing approaches] provide into contemporary world politics? . . . We can draw inspiration from Clifford Geertz' discussion of the role of theory in anthropology. Geertz argues that culture "is not a power, something in which social . . . events can be causally attributed; it is a context—something within which they can be intelligibly—that is, thickly—described." The role of theory, he claims, is "not to codify abstract regularities but to make thick description possible. . . ."[27]

And like Geertz, Keohane suggests that in theory, prevailing social scientific approaches represent themselves as forward-looking. There is much discussion of hypotheses and prediction. Analysts seem to celebrate their empirical pedigrees with apparent indifference, if not obliviousness, to the symbolic turn in international relations. In practice, however, as I've suggested, analysts pen commentaries on the crises of yesteryear. (As Kierkegaard realized in his ruminations, life is lived forward but thought backwards.) It is hardly surprising that, in the final analysis, prevailing accounts offer retrospective interpretations of crises rather than explicit predictions, let alone laws of crisis construction, management, and remembrance.

It appears that in practice, if not in theory, analysts have come to recognize that the international realm is not governed by deterministic laws or even "constitutive rules" that seem commonsensical to those of us in the academy. In other words, political actors are not considerate enough to think and act just like academics. Adding proverbial insult to injury, not only are analysts relegated to the role of interpreting official interpretations of reality, we are destined to have our interpretations discarded or—at best—endlessly contested. The competition readily admits that it does not offer a synoptic account of international crises: the episodes cannot be explained definitively in the manner Newton explained mechanics. Unfortunately, less grandiose objectives also remain elusive: despite their intriguing, often heuristic accounts of previous crises, the predictive value of prevailing approaches is, admittedly, limited.[28] Nevertheless, as I shall argue, these approaches play a crucial role in explicating various crises: the crises that fomented World War II cannot be understood apart from realpolitik; clearly, bureaucratic maneuvering played a role in certain decisions made by the Ex Comm; and how can any critical juncture be understood without reference to the disposition of the actors involved?

Since, as Keohane suggests, prevailing inquiry struggles to understand purposive activity, it is understandable that—despite its scientific pretensions—it is actually informed by a decisive, albeit unrecognized, interpretive dimension. By making this tacit dimension explicit, I hope to reveal that crisis explication is invariably uncertain, incomplete, and contested. For example, the competition often interprets the meaning of a crisis by describing the deeds of an actor and drawing inferences regarding intentionality from these deeds. Such inferences are generally based upon unexamined assumptions about psychological processes. At best, such assumptions are educated guesses, not invariable laws of nature. Indeed, these inferences often seem self-confessional. Could it be that these psychological assumptions reveal what analysts believe their motives might be for such actions in such situations?[29] In any case, given the symbolic turn in international relations, deeds seldom speak for themselves; inferences regarding intentionality are invariably contested.

These tremulous inferences about intentionality are fashioned into retrospective interpretations consonant with a particular perspective. Not surprisingly, realists interpret crises as a struggle for power amid the anarchy of nation states. This perspective, for example, illuminates the crisis precipitated by the terribly tangible threat of Nazism; however, it is less useful in explaining the symbolic social dramas of the nuclear age. Bureaucratic approaches stress the role of organizational competition and bargaining in crisis construction and management. This perspective aptly directs inquiry to the bureaucratic machinations that shape routine foreign policy, but it is of limited value in interpreting the crises explicated in this study: crucial decisions were made by the Kennedy brothers and their closest confidants, not representatives of competing bureaus; and the 1970 episode was managed exclusively by Kissinger, an actor who excluded competing bureaucracies from routine policy-making, and certainly, from crisis management. Finally, individuated approaches attend to the role of cognitive and affective processes in crisis construction and management. These approaches go beyond old paradigms in favor of explicating the inner lives and lived experiences of political actors. At first, as we shall see, such explications were restricted to accounts of cognitive processing. Recently, however, analysts have ventured further by exploring the role of adaptive anxiety in managing the Cuban missile crisis. These new paradigms are heady contributions. Unfortunately, to reiterate, cognitive approaches do not explain why Nixon and Kissinger responded in dramatically different ways to their shared cognition regarding the threat posed by the Soviet submarine base. And, as I shall argue, adaptive anxiety was a dimension of the Cuban missile crisis, but not the only dimension. A dialectical, two-dimensional reading of Kennedy and his associates better accounts for the more puzzling aspects of this joust on the abyss.

The competition labors under a common liability: lack of conceptual clarity as to what it is about. Wedded to old paradigms, terms such as "explanation" and "interpretation" are used interchangeably, if not promiscuously. (Allison, for example, subtitles his influential study *Explaining the Cuban Missile Crisis*.) Unfortunately, this casual usage blurs crucial distinctions that reveal the qualitative differences between these terms, a difference that is not merely semantic—I am not being precious with words. The purposive interpretations of crises found in virtually every school of analysis are far different from the long-sought natural science style of explanation. For example, the Newtonian framework readily explains the trajectory of a guided missile. However, interpreting Khrushchev's purposes in deploying these missiles in Cuba is, to say the least, problematic; and understanding the risks Kennedy took to compel the removal of these weapons is more puzzling still.

In sum, political action is interpreted, not explained. We do not explain crises by subsuming them under invariable laws. We interpret them by attributing conscious, preconscious, or unconscious motives to actors. In so doing, we satisfy cognitive, teleological, and normative needs. And of course, coming out of the closet and admitting that we seek interpretation, not explanation, confronts us with an unavoidable problem: ascribing motives to social action.

Edward Bruner is well aware of the need for such interpretive efforts: "Narrative structures serve as interpretive guides, they tell us what constitutes data, defines topics for study, and . . . transforms . . . the alien to the familiar."[30] Just as actors invoke crisis narratives to render certain texts and performances intelligible, analysts superimpose their own narratives upon these sagas to render them intelligible. To be sure, these favored narratives serve a cognitive function by representing the facts. But they are not merely cognitive devices, as is widely supposed. As Keohane suggests, an analyst's a priori interpretive strategies determine the facts selected for scrutiny and the techniques employed to make sense of these facts. (Indeed, our initial conceptualization determines what counts as data. As Allison quips, what he regards as data—competition among bureaucrats—is dismissed as gossip by realists.)[31]

Interpretations, then, are not merely cognitive maps. To press the analogy, interpretive schemes determine what territory will be mapped, the destination sought, the strategy for reaching the goal, and the meaning of the journey. As Kuhn stresses, these strategies are the templates (paradigms) that guide mapmaking in the natural sciences and in social inquiry:

> Paradigms prove to be constitutive of . . . research activity. . . . Paradigms provide scientists not only with a map but also with some of the directions essential for map-making. In learning a paradigm the scientist acquires theory, methods and standards together, usually in an inextricable mixture. Therefore, when paradigms change, there are usually significant shifts in the criteria determining the legitimacy both of problems and of proposed solutions.[32]

Given the myriad facts of international life, such selectivity is unavoidable. Even rigorous positivists arbitrarily determine when a crisis begins and ends, and the facts to be emphasized or ignored. Most important, unlike explanations, interpretations are teleological: they account for facts by assigning meaning to these events. As McGeorge Bundy, a principal actor in the Cuban missile crisis, reminds us, actors and analysts alike are concerned with the meaning of the facts. As an actor and analyst, Bundy stresses that he was concerned with *the* salient issue of the crisis: What did Kennedy and Khrushchev think they were doing?"[33] In other words, what was the point: *Why* did these men think and act as they did? These actors, of course, are not depicted as billiard balls moved by forces beyond their control. They are represented as autonomous agents caught in dilemmas, trying to make the best of a bad situation.

Of course, as we shall see throughout this study, interpreters who agree on the facts often superimpose contesting interpretations. As Kenneth Burke, the grammarian of motives, reminds us:

> It is good . . . to remember that there are various theories of psychoanalytic interpretation in violent disagreement with one another. Further, the scorn of the Marxians with their brand of economic psychoanalysis, is that . . . the Freudians can be in turn interpreted as a retreat from the economic facts and the class struggle which are "really" at the heart of our motives.[34]

As Burke suggests, not only do interpreters disagree, they seldom take an actor's account of his/her purposes at face value. Generally, these accounts are viewed with suspicion or are dismissed in favor of explications of preconscious or unconscious motives. (Imagine a Freudian blithely accepting an obsessive-compulsive's account of his excessive hand-washing, or a Marxist accepting the National Association of Manufacturers' account of itself at face value. Behaviorists are no different. Imagine Skinner's response to an actor certain that she is an autonomous agent unmoved by thoughts of external rewards.)

While Hannah Arendt may attribute excessive acumen to historians, she rightly emphasizes that actors caught in the fray are seldom the best judges of their motives:

> Action reveals itself fully only to the storyteller . . . to the backward glance of the historian, who indeed always knows better what it was all about than the participants. All accounts told by the actors themselves, though they may in rare cases give an entirely trustworthy statement of intentions . . . become mere useful source material in the historian's hands and can never match his story in significance and truthfulness. What the storyteller narrates must necessarily be hidden from the actor himself. . . . Even though stories are the inevitable results of action, it is not the actor but the storyteller who perceives and "makes" the story.[35]

I suspect that our efforts to render crises intelligible will improve when we acknowledge the interpretive dimension of our inquiry and the problematic that it entails. Well aware of the hazards of attributing motives to myself, let alone to others, I suggest that colleagues are reluctant to confront the problematic of purposive action because it presents a classic, philosophic puzzle: it confronts inquiry with issues that are crucial, difficult, and likely irresolvable. Sociologists James Fentress and Chris Wickham are well aware of our predicament:

> When it is a question of ascertaining whether or not some human act has really taken place . . . [historians] cannot be too painstaking. If they proceed to the reasons for that act, they are content with the merest appearance, ordinarily founded upon one of those maxims of common-place psychology which are neither more nor less true than their opposites. When historians peep across the fence they see their neighbors in . . . sociology, just as complacent in relying on . . . platitudes which are naive, simplistic, or obsolete.[36]

They may not be exaggerating. Noted historian Natalie Davis allows that she interprets events by superimposing her psychological assumptions upon the data.[37] Other justly influential historians follow suit. True, they vow merely to describe the facts, but they quickly succumb to the temptation to interpret the facts by ascribing motives to actors. Consider the case of Stephen Ambrose. He begins a definitive Nixon biography by declaring: "As a biographer, I am concerned with what Nixon said and did, planned and hoped, attempted and achieved. I confess that I do not understand this complex man." However, he proceeds to articulate his understanding of Nixon and his devious motives. Ambrose's volley of attributions is thickly descriptive: "He was devious, manipulative, driven by unseen and unknowable forces, quick . . . to blame and slow . . . to forgive, passionate in his hatred, self-centered, untruthful, untrusting and at times . . . despicable."[38]

Throughout the work, Ambrose offers thick descriptions of the life and times of Richard Nixon. We learn, for example, that Nixon couldn't imagine living without campaigning, and accordingly, he moved to New York to have instant access to the international media. He could, however "pretend he was moving there for his family's sake, not his own."[39] Indeed, virtually every page of the volume expresses the author's attempt to understand Nixon.

While Nixon does not mention Ambrose by name, he is bemused—or so he claims—by the motives critical biographers ascribe to him. He aptly recognizes the self-confessional element in interpretive efforts:

> I always find it amusing when psycho-historians I have never met conclude that I have what they consider to be a warped personality. Usually they trace it to my poor, lower-middle-class family. In fact, these pseudo-biographers are telling you more about themselves than about me. . . .[40]

Surely Ambrose would not be surprised by Nixon's response. Yet, he fails to confront this difficulty. How should the reader respond? Is Nixon's account of himself more believable than Ambrose's representation? Or is Ambrose's representation more credible? Do you have to be a chicken to judge an omelet?

Likewise, Dobrynin claims that his account of the Cuban missile crisis is authoritative. He urges that no one questions his recall of events, and that his interpretation is based upon his meticulous notes.[41] However, the ambassador's declaration did not deter American analysts (and their Russian and Cuban counterparts) from penning contesting accounts of the crisis.

Somehow, Kissinger biographer Bruce Mazlish's supreme confidence surpasses Dobrynin's:

> In sum, I would go so far as to say that I "know" Kissinger better now than does any single friend of his or person whom I interviewed, and perhaps better than Kissinger knows himself; I hope the reader will be in the same position at the end of the book.[42]

While I profited from Mazlish's inquiry, I do not regard the biography as definitive. Mazlish did not have the last word: a number of Kissinger biographies appeared after his work was published. There is no need to compound examples. Analysts interpret crises by freely attributing motives to the actors. Most of these interpretations lack self-reflection: little is said about the problematic aspects of assigning motives to others; indeed—as we've seen—some interpreters are supremely confident despite the difficulties inherent in such an enterprise. Not only are certain salient questions unresolved, they are seldom asked. I do not broach these questions because I am foolhardy enough to believe that I can solve these conundrums that have plagued philosophers for millennia; rather, I want to stress the host of difficulties that bedevil those of us who labor to understand what makes political actors tick. A mercifully brief sampling of the problematic would include the following:

1. Is elite motivation as transparent as many analysts seem to imply? As we shall see, Kennedy allowed that he was not always conversant with the essence of his decisions.

2. With Burke, should we consider the possibility that our assumptions about motivation—assumptions regarded as perfectly natural, if not inevitable—are actually social constructions? That is, our cherished notions of motivation reflect peculiar circumstances, rather than invariable laws of human motivation. (Understandably, sectarian societies attribute religious motives to action, while those in commercial societies interpret action in terms of pecuniary motives.)

3. In any case, how do we gain access to motivation? We are not mind readers, and given our hermeneutics of suspicion—a proper response to the political spectacle—we seldom take actors' accounts of themselves at face value.

4. Our interpretations are invariably contested, often by the actors themselves. Which—if any—of the public and private versions of Kennedy, Nixon, and Kissinger should we believe?

By tradition, or perhaps by default, such questions are relegated to philosophers. If analysts are rather facile in attributing motives to actors, certain postmodern philosophers go to the other extreme by denying the possibility of explicating motivation. As Michael Shapiro suggests, Geertz reflects the philosophic inheritance of Dilthey and Gadamer (the philosophic foundation of this study) as he strives to render the exotic more familiar. In other words, for Geertz, while the present will remain a foreign country, it can become a less puzzling place in which we can converse with the natives. However, philosophers such as

Foucault and Derrida are intent upon deconstructing such attempts to fix meaning, even temporarily. The more these philosophers think about it, the more alien the present becomes. As Shapiro explains:

> Whereas hermeneutically oriented investigators . . . try to disclose more abiding and stable modes of subjectivity by confronting one manifestation that is familiar with one that is exotic, the genealogist [in the manner of Foucault] takes a familiar interpretation and confronts it with another interpretation from a different historical period. This has the effect of rereading the present forms of subjectivity in a way that denaturalizes them . . . and produces, thereby, a distancing or, in Foucault's terms, a "dissociating view . . . capable of shattering the unity of man's being."[43]

I don't wish to succumb to the joys of postmodern sects by abandoning the search for meaning. In my view, some motives are transparent and others are opaque. The motive forces in crisis situations lie betwixt and between: they are neither obvious nor wholly unintelligible. There are obvious cases of political motivation. There is, for example, little difficulty in understanding what makes Capitol Hill lobbyists tick. (The motives of tobacco industry lobbyists, for example, seem transparent. However, the motivations for constructing and promoting a crisis are less obvious, even to the actors themselves.)

I propose that it is possible to better understand an actor by penetrating his conceptual horizon and imaginative universe. Actors depict their ideals, if not their intentions, in their texts; and the historical record reveals whether their decisions were governed by these ideals at critical junctures. Our interpretive strategies, of course, will be disputed. The next chapter discusses four criteria for determining whether an interpretation is on target. (Suffice it to assert at this point that claims about intentions can be judged against deeds. For example, the Watergate tapes belie Nixon's account of himself, and lend credence to Ambrose's rendition. Likewise, the risks that Kennedy hazarded suggest that avoiding nuclear war was not his overarching motivation.) However, while we can demonstrate that an interpretation is on target, it is unlikely that we can hit the bull's-eye. Usually, we look in vain for a smoking gun. Put less metaphorically, the quest for a conclusive piece of evidence that definitively valorizes our favored interpretation is elusive, if not chimerical.

In any case, explicating crises in terms of elite motivation is problematic—yet necessary. We cannot make sense of a crisis without understanding the meaning an actor knowingly and unknowingly assigns to the drama. Our best interpretive efforts are bound to be contested or dismissed; and—unlike our colleagues in the natural sciences—we cannot definitively prove the truth of our claims to the inevitable doubters. The recognition of this predicament ought to make us humble and tolerant. We can, perhaps, make a virtue of necessity. It might be helpful to begin with the admission that, like our colleagues in the humanities—indeed, like the actors we study—we are interpreters of texts and performances, not laboratory scientists titrating solutions. As Turner urges, "I would plead with my colleagues to acquire the humanistic skill that would enable them to live more comfortably in those territories where the masters of human thought and art have long been dwelling."[44]

The dubious nature of interpretation calls for self-reflection and caution: being certain of our facts does not imply that we should be supremely confident of our interpretations. At the same time we must resist the facile relativism that makes no distinctions between contending interpretations: all interpretations are not created equal. Recognizing the inevitability of multiple interpretations of the same event need not produce quiet despair; it can prompt us to enter into robust conversations with those who offer contesting interpretations. The next section makes such an effort.

THE COMPETITION

> One human being can be a complete enigma to another [or to himself or herself]. We learn this when we come into a strange country with entirely strange traditions; and what is more, even given a mastery of the country's language. We do not *understand* the people. (And not because of not knowing what they are saying to themselves.)
>
> —Ludwig Wittgenstein[45]

While my critique is hardly exhaustive, I examine the theory and practice of three influential interpretations of crisis construction and management. Despite their obvious differences, they have much in common. Like all interpretive practice, the competition struggles to render the enigmatic world more familiar. It does so by reading favored narratives into crisis texts and performances. These narratives, as we have seen, determine a priori what counts as data and how the data will be interpreted. There are, of course, significant variations on this theme. To reiterate, political realism attends to the power politics of nation states in a world of international anarchy. Bureaucratic politics concerns itself with domestic politics—the machinations of elite bureaucratic competition and bargaining. Finally, individuated interpretations focus upon an actor's cognitive and affective dispositions.

As Montaigne recognized long ago, there is nothing new about my authorial strategy in this chapter. I begin by interpreting the competition's interpretations. With some notable exceptions, perhaps the greatest liability of the analysts who advocate realist, bureaucratic, and individuated approaches is that they are unaware of the interpretive dimension of their inquiry. Accordingly, they are not fully cognizant of the strengths and weaknesses of their hermeneutic attempts to render crises intelligible. I intend to develop a general evaluation of the competition and judge its utility for explicating the crises that inform this study. I entertain an ironic possibility: fully conscious interpretive perspectives might offer more compelling retrospectives *and* more useful predictions regarding the construction, management, and remembrance of future crises.

Realism

> Realism is a necessary component in a coherent analysis of world politics be-
> cause its focus on power, interests, and rationality is crucial to any understand-
> ing of the subject.
>
> —Robert Keohane[46]

Political realism can be defined simply; that's much of its appeal. Realists believe that it's a jungle out there, and only the strong and the clever survive and prosper. More precisely, realists presuppose that:

1. The international world is composed of sovereign states that are not beholden to any supernational authority—the international realm is anarchistic.

2. States are rational actors that set realistic—albeit selfish—goals and act accordingly.

3. States seek to survive and to expand their power. (Power is generally understood as the capability of invoking military might to maintain and expand hegemony.) Further, this pursuit of power is seldom tempered by moral scruples.[47]

Henry Kissinger, both a theorist and a practitioner of realpolitik, puts this interpretive framework to good use in his latest tome, *Diplomacy*.[48] He interprets a series of conflicts—beginning with Richelieu and ending with Gorbachev—as the outcome of a ceaseless struggle for power among sovereign entities. Many of his explications are persuasive, especially his account of the rise of Nazism. He rightly concludes that Hitler's threat should have been judged in terms of the Nazi military capability rather than Hitler's cynical profession of peaceful intentions.

Whether we read a realist such as Niebuhr[49] (the theologian of realism) or Kissinger, a plausible generalization emerges. Much to the regret of those who long for a world order, the first presupposition of realism is accurate: we are thrown into a world of sovereign nation states. To be sure, there are international organizations, and various international regimes and protocols—tacit mores and etiquette that ordinarily temper foreign relations. Moreover, various non-governmental organizations (NGOs) often play an unsung role in international conflict resolution. Nevertheless, it would be difficult to think of a crisis in which a great power agreed to international mediation. In any case, the Cuban episodes explicated in this study were resolved by representatives of sovereign nation states, not international organizations or NGOs.

The second presupposition, however, is problematic for several reasons. The notion of "state" is obviously reified: political actors, not states, make decisions. This objection is, of course, something of a straw man; few realists literally embrace Louis XIV's proclamation, *"L'etat, c'est moi!"* The salient issue is this: Are political actors rational actors that set realistic goals and act accordingly? They are in realist theory; but are they in practice? According to Schelling, the key premise of realism is "not just intelligent behavior, but . . . behavior motivated by a conscious calculation of advantage."[50] Since, in the world according to political realism, this instrumental rationality is durable, we can rely upon actors behaving like CPAs at critical junctures. They may err and miscalculate, but their intentions are transparent and unswerving: they want to know what must be done to maximize their advantage, and they act appropriately.

As the foregoing analysis suggests, realists find actors inhabiting a familiar landscape, the realm of noonday commerce—the everyday world of cost/risk/ benefit analysis. As Allison argues, this presupposition is just that, a presupposition. Such premises are not derived empirically; they are more closely akin to philosophic rationalism: realists assume they can understand foreign policy by reasoning about how they would act, were they political actors.

Consider Schelling's invocation of the rational actor model: the Hobbesian notion that political actors invariably seek to maximize personal advantage while avoiding pain. Given the folly and mayhem that mark our century, celebrations of the triumph of reason in collective life are premature. Lasswell seemed to speak to our hapless century when he characterized politics as "the process by which the irrational bases of society are brought out into the open."[51] Cast in this perspective, a crisis is a pretext for attaining what Freud deemed the ultimate pleasure: the expression of long-repressed, forbidden impulses.

The reduction of politics to psychopathology is overstated, but is it more hyperbolic than the realist faith in durable instrumental rationality? To be sure, ordinarily actors reality-test and act accordingly. They are rational enough to get elected and to accomplish a variety of goals. However, a mounting body of evidence suggests that rationality is not durable, especially in the midst of a crisis. As Holsti, an analyst not unsympathetic to prevailing interpretations, concludes in his study of stress during crisis decision-making:

> The evidence suggests that policy making under circumstances of crisis-induced stress is likely to differ in a number of respects from decision-making processes in other situations. More important, to the extent that such differences exist they are likely to inhibit rather than facilitate the effectiveness of those engaged in the complex task of making foreign policy choices.[52]

Looking at the Cuban episodes explicitly, to what extent were Soviet and American actors rational? While this question will be discussed in depth in Chapter 3, this first take responds directly to the second presupposition of political realism. Referring to this presupposition as a "rational actor model" is something of a misnomer: realists insist that rational action—stipulating achievable, self-aggrandizing goals and acting accordingly—is not simply a heuristic construction or a working hypothesis, it is a law of nature, an uninterpreted fact of international life. The rationality that realists attribute to actors is transparent, uniform, and predictable: any reasonably intelligent, alert actor should respond in the same way to the same situation. The situation, in effect, compels the action. Indebted to Hobbesian mechanistic metaphors, realists seem to liken actors to iron filings invariably attracted to one behavioral pole—maximizing power.[53] Consider the teaching of an influential realist, Hans Morgenthau: "The struggle for power is universal in time and space and is an undeniable fact of experience. . . . Regardless of social, economic, and political conditions, states have met each other in contests for power."[54]

However, as political theorist Jim George stresses, despite their pretensions of practicing a discipline akin to classical textbook physics, realists are "silent hermeneuticists." He cites Morgenthau's classic *Power Among Nations,* which insists that in order to understand an actor, "We [must] look over his shoulder when he writes his dispatches: we must listen in on his conversations with other statesmen; we [must] read and anticipate his very thoughts."[55] As he concludes:

> Realist scholarship, following these broad hermeneutic principles, must do more than simply reaffirm the anarchy of the system. . . . It is interested, rather, in a more profound kind of historical and cultural understanding of the relationship between states. [56]

The realists believe they understand actors: indeed, they can read their minds—actors are (to update Hobbesian figures) "hard-wired" to maximize state power. However, as critics have long stressed, statecraft is not as clear and distinct as the realists would have us believe. There was, for example, protracted controversy within the Ex Comm—and within Kennedy himself—about the proper response to the Soviet missiles. Stevenson argued for negotiation and compromise while General Curtis LeMay (the top Air Force officer) urged an immediate attack. Nixon, of course, remained indifferent to the Soviet submarine base, while Kissinger construed Soviet actions as a crisis. Jervis' criticism of realism is apt:

> If a situation were so compelling [as the realists presuppose] then all people would act alike, decision-makers would not hesitate nor feel torn among several alternative policies, nor would there be significant debates within the decision-making elite. In fact, key decisions that are so easily reached . . . stand out because they are so rare.[57]

Further, in the world according to political realism, the Cuban missile crisis should never have occurred. With the exception of CIA Director John McCone, Kennedy and his advisers were astonished by Khrushchev's move. Their astonishment was due, in large measure, to their faith in the quintessence of realism—deterrence doctrine. According to this doctrine, the credible threat of nuclear and conventional reprisals made it unthinkable for Khrushchev to challenge American interests. He was well aware of American nuclear and conventional superiority, particularly in the Caribbean. Moreover, on two occasions in September 1962, Kennedy vowed that offensive Soviet weapons would not be tolerated in Cuba. However, as Allison argues, deterrence doctrine is not based on an inductive canvass of a large number of cases, but upon a priori assumptions about rational action.[58] Such assumptions proved wrong: Khrushchev was not deterred from installing nuclear missiles in Cuba. As Raymond Garthoff (a State Department adviser to the Ex Comm) remarks, "The United States, for its part, did not deter the Soviet Union from making its decision to deploy its missiles in Cuba and embarking on deployment."[59] Realists conclude that deterrence failed because Khrushchev's decision to deploy the weapons was not guided by cost/risk/benefit analysis. But to what extent were Kennedy and his confidants rational actors? Many Ex Comm members concede that the Soviet move did not change the strategic balance. As Bundy notes, "most agreed that the Cuban missiles did not change the strategic balance, not at all."[60]

Nevertheless, by promoting the episode as a crisis, "the best and the brightest" hazarded risks incommensurate with any possible gain—thermonuclear war. In his latest book, McNamara reveals that the danger was much greater than he originally estimated: the Soviets had 162 nuclear warheads in Cuba and approximately 40,000 troops; the local Soviet commander was, evidently, authorized to use tactical nuclear weapons against American invaders:

> Clearly, there was a high risk that, in the face of a U.S. attack—which, as I have said, many in the U.S. government, military and civilian alike, were prepared to recommend to President Kennedy—the Soviet forces in Cuba would have decided to use their nuclear weapons rather than lose them.[61]

And, as McNamara has continually stressed in his writing and public appearances, he would have ordered a nuclear response that would have precipitated World War III.[62] This willingness to risk everything belies Morgenthau's minimalist notion of rationality—assuring the survival of the nation state as a physical, political, and cultural entity. Nevertheless, Morgenthau characterized Kennedy's crisis management as "the distillation of a collective intellectual effort of a high order, the like of which must be rare in history."[63] Lebow suggests that such uncritical praise may reveal more about Morgenthau than about Kennedy: perhaps it reveals the Dean of Political Realism's need for cognitive consistency—knowingly risking self-destruction is not consonant with his system. Or could it be that Morgenthau embraced the image of the president promulgated by the guardians of Kennedy memory?

In any case, throughout his discussion of the 1962 episode, Bundy represents himself and Kennedy's other trusted advisers as consummate realists. However, he concludes that Kennedy's hazardous stand against the Soviet base—a posture that fomented unprecedented peril—was not based upon some realist calculation about the balance of power (or the appearance of such a balance). Kennedy simply had a gut feeling that the Soviet missiles had to go despite the risks:

> Just what was it that made it so clear to Kennedy . . . that [he] should take a firm and flat stand against Soviet nuclear weapons in Cuba? *It was not a calculation of strategic balance.* . . . It was not that these weapons made Castro more secure. . . . It was not the fear of nuclear weapons landing on American soil. . . . It was not even all these points together. *It was something different: a visceral feeling that it was intolerable for the United States to accept on nearby land of the Western Hemisphere Soviet weapons that could wreak instant havoc on the American homeland.*[64] [italics mine]

Victor Turner's observation about crises at other times and places comes to mind: "People will die for values that oppose their interest and promote interests that oppose their values."[65]

Finally, what are we to say about the third canon of realism, the claim that states invariably seek power, and that such pursuits are seldom inhibited by moral qualms? Abandoning his youthful idealism, the mature Niebuhr argued that it is naive, even dangerous, to presuppose that states are capable of moral sensitivity. According to Niebuhr, nation states commit Original Sin every generation in their idolatrous pursuit of God-like power.[66] Surely Niebuhr and the others are right about morality among nations: sterling examples of selflessness in international relations are rare. It is the realist notion of power that is decidedly problematic. According to this notion, states cherish their survival above all else. To illustrate the plausibility of this claim, realists depict crises that occurred when national survival was threatened. But when, to be rhetorical, was the last time the survival of the United States was seriously threatened? The War of 1812 and the Civil War posed such a threat, and the triumph of the Axis Powers during World War II may have threatened national survival. However, looking at recent history, political theorist Arnold Wolfers concludes: "A glance at history will suffice to show that survival has only exceptionally been at stake, particularly for the major powers."[67]

Cold War crises between the superpowers were not about national survival, nor were they about the expansion of geopolitical power as understood by the realists. (No crises occurred when the Soviets invaded Hungary or when the United States invaded Indochina.) The Cuban missile crisis was about appearances and symbols: the Ex Comm was concerned with issues such as the *appearance* of Soviet advantage; and with presidential image and bargaining reputation. Likewise, the Ex Comm initially refused to trade the Turkish missiles because it would give the *appearance* of weakness. Since it had long been determined that these weapons posed more of a political liability than a strategic advantage, Kennedy had previously ordered policy studies about how to remove the missiles without offending the Turks. (Such studies present further interpretive issues: was JFK merely requesting an inventory of options? Was he seriously considering removing the missiles? Did he construe the study as an order? Did he anticipate needing the missiles later as bargaining chips, in any case?) Jervis captures the essence of the crisis when he argues that an immediate, public withdrawal of the Turkish missiles might have ended the crisis, but Kennedy refused because he was preoccupied with appearances. Specifically, it might appear that Kennedy, like Chamberlain, was an appeaser:

> What mattered was that others would interpret such a move as . . . the willingness of the United States to retreat under pressure. . . . If the Russians had asked the United States to change the color of its postage stamps the problem would have been essentially the same.[68]

The trade occurred sub rosa, again, because of *appearances*. Given its emphasis on tangible military power and traditional strategic thinking, realism is not well-equipped to understand a world in which actors rely upon words, images, and appearances to attain their ends.

As a realist, it is not surprising that Kissinger interpreted the Cienfuegos episode as a crisis because the Soviet submarine base bestowed military advantages upon the USSR. Strangely, other "realists" disagreed. Many of Kissinger's colleagues disagreed because they held that such enhancements of Soviet advantage were meaningless in an age of assured destruction. Surprisingly, as we shall see, the "hawks" in the Nixon administration construed Soviet actions as purely symbolic acts designed to show that the Soviets were on a par with the United States. Even Kissinger's narration about the power politics inherent in this episode departs from classical realism. He did not believe that the Soviet move threatened national survival; that is, that the Soviets were about to launch. His concern was more symbolic: acquiescing to the submarine base would impair U.S. prestige and bargaining reputation.

In sum, realism seems to account for certain crises of the past: challenges that occurred in a world of obdurate facts and unmistakable threats. And surely today's leaders are not indifferent toward calculations of strategic advantage. However, realist interpretations seem rigidly reductive and inattentive to the symbolic turn in international relations.

Bureaucratic Politics

Treating national governments as if they were . . . individuals . . . obscures as well as reveals. In particular, it obscures the . . . fact of bureaucracy: the "maker" of government policy is not one calculating decisionmaker but is rather a conglomerate of large organizations and political actors.

—Graham Allison[69]

Unlike the realists, Graham Allison recognizes that he and his colleagues seek thick descriptions that—to paraphrase Geertz—explicate the underlying narrative themes that contextualize events and infuse them with meaning. Consider the overarching questions that inform his *The Essence of Decision,* and the research of most other analysts: Why did the Soviets place the missiles in Cuba? Why did the United States respond with a blockade? Why were the missiles withdrawn? As he recognizes, such questions cannot be resolved with "thin descriptions"—accounts of publicly verifiable facts; somehow motives must be interpreted; somehow the actions of the principal players must be rendered intelligible. Like Geertz, Allison stresses that facts and interpretations are inextricably mixed, and are colored by a priori interpretive strategies:

Most of the . . . facts are not simple facts. Rather, they are points that emerge when one mixes traces of evidence with judgments; one is inclined to accept or reject the judgments depending upon the logic of the model within which he is working.[70]

While Allison does not invoke the vocabulary of hermeneutic social inquiry, he is obviously aware of many of the salient distinctions. Clearly, he recognizes that diverse interpretations—including his—are conceptual lenses, not empirical generalizations. Pressing the metaphor, he urges that these lenses magnify facts congenial to the conceptual model, and throw other salient facts out of focus. For Allison, learning how to focus is more of an art than a science: "The use of public documents . . . is an art. Transfer of these skills from the fingertips of artists to a form that can guide other students of foreign policy is [Allison's bureaucratic] model's most pressing need."[71]

Unlike much of the realist discourse, Allison entertains contesting interpretations in his "three takes" on the Cuban missile crisis; and he also critiques his competition's strengths and weaknesses. And, like the rest of us, he is well-disposed to his own interpretive strategy. But due, perhaps, to disciplinary biases and constraints, even the most perceptive analysts such as Allison seem unaware of the discipline that spent millennia both refining and problematizing this art—hermeneutics. With the exception of Keohane and several others, they are not conversant with of some of the more fruitful "outdoor" approaches to interpreting social action developed by Geertz and Turner, approaches I call cultural hermeneutics.

Therefore, it is not surprising that, despite his incisive criticisms of realism, Allison shares a cherished realist assumption: political actors inhabit a familiar world. Indeed, for those of us in the academy, his world is probably more familiar (indeed, painfully familiar) than the realist realm of rational action: it is a realm of bureaucratic politics in which contending bureaus vie for power and advantage. Cast in this perspective, the world inside the Beltway resembles Clark Kerr's "multiversity": an almost ungovernable institution in which rival bureaucracies compete for everything from parking spaces to lucrative grants. Beleaguered presidents—whether they preside over a university or a nation—have the unenviable task of exacting compromises pleasing to no one. Allison delineates the bureaucratic paradigm with more precision when he explains that: "National behavior in international affairs can be conceived of as something that emerges from intricate and subtle, simultaneous, overlapping games among players located . . . in a government."[72]

Unlike the realists, Allison is attentive to the role of domestic politics in the formulation and execution of foreign policy. He does not claim that bureaucratic elites are indifferent to the needs of the nation, but neither are they oblivious to their careers and to the needs of their organizations.[73] He makes his case by scanning the literature on the role of bureaucratic competition and bargaining in decision-making. The literature review is compelling. For example, he cites Samuel Harrington's *Common Defense,* an account of the role of the Department of Defense, the military, weapons contractors, and other bureaucratic elites in shaping weapons acquisition policy.[74]

Allison's paradigm, of course, does not apply to the Cienfuegos episode: by all accounts it was managed by one man—Henry Kissinger. However, turning to the episode he does consider, his paradigm illuminates various facets of the

Cuban missile crisis, but it fails to account for crucial aspects of the episode. Not surprisingly, he does not dwell upon what he cannot interpret: the mystery at the heart of the crisis—the incommensurate risks hazarded by Kennedy and the others.

Let us begin, however, by turning to Allison's contributions. He argues persuasively that certain key decisions were shaped by bureaucratic politicking.

1. In August 1962, CIA Director McCone determined that Soviet missiles were being installed in Cuba. The CIA, however, was reluctant to embarrass the Kennedy Administration, especially in an election year. Indeed, Kennedy and his associates had long proclaimed (and evidently believed) that no offensive weapons were being deployed in Cuba. (Just two days before the discovery of the weapons, Bundy publicly denied Republican charges that such weapons existed in Cuba.) As Allison quips, "What the President least wanted to hear, the CIA found it difficult to say plainly."[75]

2. Allison argues that the decision to blockade Cuba in order to compel the Soviets to remove the missiles resulted from a bureaucratic compromise. The "hawks" urged an immediate attack on Cuba, while the "doves" urged restraint and diplomacy. By trying to please everyone, the compromise pleased no one. The doves feared the outcome of what could be construed as an act of war, while the hawks urged that the blockade would not, in and of itself, remove the missiles.[76]

Allison is admirably self-reflective regarding the imposition of his model. He realizes that, invariably, he is putting bureaucratic machinations in sharp focus while throwing other dimensions of the crisis out of focus. Curiously, at the onset of his study, he focuses on the mystery of the crisis with terrifying acuity. Unfortunately, the issue blurs quickly and fades from view. To be specific, early on, he recognizes that Kennedy and the others took grave risks to reestablish the status quo ante. He dramatically evokes the unprecedented peril in the first words of his Introduction: "History offers no parallel to those thirteen days of October 1962, when the United States and the Soviet Union paused at the nuclear precipice. Never before had there been such a high probability that so many lives would end suddenly. . . . "[77]

Allison is well aware that, in the view of Kennedy and his confidants, the missiles did not bestow any strategic advantage upon the Soviets. He shares this view, and suggests that Kennedy and the others took grave risks because Soviet actions:

1. Undermined the growing trust between the superpowers.

2. Provoked terrible embarrassment and domestic political problems. He cites the conclusion of Roger Hilsman, a Kennedy adviser: "The United States might not be in mortal danger, but the administration most certainly was."

3. Finally, Allison offers a thick description that has little connection with bureaucratic machinations:

> Khrushchev's action challenged the President personally. Did he, John F. Kennedy, have the courage in the crunch to start down a path that had a real chance of leading to nuclear war? . . . Kennedy had worried, both after the Bay of Pigs

and after the Vienna meeting with Khrushchev, that the Chairman might have misjudged his mettle.[78]

Allison is suggesting that the most harrowing crisis of the Cold War occurred for political and personal, if not venal, reasons: Kennedy knowingly engaged in unprecedented risk-taking due to his political vulnerability; and he willingly risked everything to test his mettle, to show that he, too, was a profile in courage. Somehow, Allison finds such behavior worthy of celebration. Perhaps he expresses his infatuation with existential crisis narratives when he writes: "The Soviet Union looked hard, blinked twice, and then withdrew without humiliation. Here is one of the finest examples of diplomatic prudence, and perhaps the finest hour of the John F. Kennedy Presidency."[79] This claim is dubious. Due to the public performance, Khrushchev was berated by the Chinese and by domestic hawks. Various commentators claim that he was deposed eighteen months later because he appeared to have appeased American leaders.

In any event, as we've seen, Allison focuses on several of the bureaucratic compromises designed to compel Khrushchev to remove the weapons, but he has little to say about the reasons Kennedy made a crisis move in the first place. This is not surprising. These personal and political reasons have little connection with bureaucratic politics as represented by Allison. Indeed, they violate a cherished maxim of bureaucratic politics: bureaucrats are, above all else, survivors.

Recent information, unavailable to Allison when he authored *Essence of Decision*, presents a further difficulty for the bureaucratic model: many of the momentous decisions of the crisis were made by a clique of like-minded individuals, or perhaps by a single individual, not the heads of competing bureaucracies who comprised the Ex Comm. In other words, the essence of decision had little to do with ordinary bargaining and compromise between vested interests. Ultimately, perhaps the essence of decision is to be found in the bargains and compromises Kennedy struck with himself. In any event, Allison and most Ex Comm members were unaware that:

1. After the first Ex Comm meeting, Robert Kennedy met secretly with members of Operation Mongoose (a covert operation designed to overthrow Castro) and stressed that the president was displeased with their lack of progress. He urged them to redouble their efforts.[80]

2. He conducted nightly negotiations with Soviet Ambassador Anatoly Dobrynin.[81] Unknown to his Ex Comm colleagues, Robert Kennedy suggested a quid pro quo to Dobrynin on Friday, October 26.

3. Most significant, after the final Ex Comm meeting on October 27, President Kennedy excluded competing bureaucracies by secretly assembling a coterie of trusted advisers to formulate the strategy that would resolve the crisis. Bundy recounts the secret arrangements unknown to the Ex Comm, let alone the various bureaus and the Congress, arrangements that were a closely guarded secret for a generation:

> The afternoon meeting of ExCom adjourned . . . and a smaller group moved into the Cabinet Room in the Oval Office to talk over the second means of communi-

cation—an oral message conveyed to Ambassador Dobrynin. . . . Those present
. . . with the president were Dean Rusk, Robert McNamara, Robert Kennedy,
George Ball, Roswell Gilpatric, Llewellyn Thompson, Theodore Sorensen, and
I.[82]

Bundy reveals that this clique—which excluded both hawks and doves—
determined that Robert Kennedy would meet secretly with Dobrynin, and confront him with an ultimatum and a secret deal.[83] The ultimatum demanded that
the Soviets dismantle their missiles within twenty-four hours or face American
military action. Allison credits this ultimatum, which he erroneously concludes
was fashioned by the entire Ex Comm, with resolving the crisis. Today, it is (to
say the least) difficult to overlook the secret deal.

The deal acceded to Khrushchev's demands: if the Soviets publicly backed
down, the United States would quietly dismantle the Jupiter installation in Turkey at a later date. (Had they known, Kennedy's detractors might have indicted
the deal as a "profile in appeasement.") Not surprisingly, Bundy discloses that:
"knowledge of this assurance would be held among those present and no one
else."[84] It is difficult not to suspect that the deal—fashioned by a like-minded
group of individuals with little debate—contributed to the resolution of the crisis. (While Robert Kennedy obliquely hinted of this arrangement in his *Memoir*,
apparently, Schlesinger first explained the circumstances and nature of the secret
deal in his *Robert Kennedy and His Times* in 1978.)

Individuated Interpretations

The problem . . . is one of telling current policymakers things they are not at all
prepared to hear about issues they think they already understand.
                                                    —John Steinbruner[85]

Individuated interpretations offer a dramatic and significant departure from
realist and bureaucratic interpretations of international relations. The comparison with natural science is worth reiterating. Just as physics reintroduced the
human subject into the process of doing science, individuated interpretations re-
introduce an actor's inner experience, and cognitive and affective faculties, into
the process of decision-making. As Heisenberg explained, "The science of nature
does not deal with nature itself but in fact with the science of nature as man
thinks and describes it."[86]

To be sure, those who develop individuated interpretations are not oblivious
to the realities depicted by the perspective just discussed. Though Marxist
aphorisms seem passé, perhaps his epigram in *The German Ideology* remains
apt: "Men make history, but not under conditions they choose." Actors cannot
change the fact that they are thrown into a world of sovereign nation states and
contending domestic bureaucracies; these givens are among the parameters within which they must function. However, how they experience and interpret events
within these boundaries, and how they improvise these interpretations, are determined by their cognitive and affective disposition.

Cognitivist Interpretation

I see no reason to believe that political decision-makers are less rational, sophisticated and motivated to understand their environment than are scientists.

—Robert Jervis[87]

Robert Jervis and Richard Ned Lebow are often credited with authoring the cognitive revolution in international relations theory. They redirect our gaze from the world of objective events to the political actor's inner world—the milieu in which events are processed. This venue is not the realm of realism in which reified states make seemingly inevitable decisions. And it is not the realm of bureaucratic politics in which "where you sit determines where you stand." Jervis claims that while bureaucratic interests often shape routine decisions, bureaucrats abandon their parochial interests when they play for high stakes during an international crisis. As I argue in the next chapter, this claim does not seem to apply to Kennedy's military advisers, especially Curtis LeMay.

In any case, cognitivism represents a paradigm shift. Actors are no longer pawns of strategic exigencies and bureaucratic imperatives beyond their control; in a phrase, they are no longer passive subjects whose actions are determined by events. Actors are empowered: their cognition of events informs their actions. Unlike the Newtonian realists, Jervis and Lebow contend that actors *do* make hypotheses, and these hypotheses can and do lead to dangerous misperceptions. They indict realism for its naive empiricism: the view that actors are passive spectators perceiving the unvarnished truths of the objective world. Actors are, as the nomenclature implies, active agents in comprehending the world. Thanks to the authors' considerable efforts, we no longer merely consider events; we analyze an actor's *perception* of events. (Unfortunately, "perception" has become one of the most overused, ill-defined terms in international relations discourse.)

In theory, cognitivists presuppose that comprehension determines action; in practice, they attend to a variety of other factors. For example, in explicating the Cuban missile crisis, ideally a cognitivist should merely articulate Kennedy's belief system—his comprehension of what was occurring—and all else should fall into place. In theory, if we comprehend what the president believed about salient factors such as his adversary's intentions and the strategic threat posed by missiles, his actions will become transparent. But evidently an actor's deeds are not transparent. In practice, cognitivists invoke thick descriptions: accounts of an actor's cognition are invariably fused with explications of his values and hopes.

This critique begins by evaluating cognitivism in theory. It is found wanting. As I have suggested, actors do not live by cognition alone; they have a more fundamental quest for meaning: to reiterate, an actor is seldom content to know merely what is happening; an actor wants to know *why* it is happening *and what is expected* of him—in other words, what's the story? As we've seen, it does not suffice to examine an actor's cognitive map; somehow—to press the metaphor—we must come to understand the story an actor brings into the map reading. In order to do so, our questions cannot be limited to the issue of cognition. To paraphrase T. S. Eliot, if we merely attend to the experience of a crisis, we miss the meaning.

Fortunately, as I argue shortly, cognitivists—like other analysts—seldom slumber in the procrustean bed fashioned by their theory. True, given the deter-minative role they attribute to cognitive processing, some of these writers may appear to suffer from "cognitive insolence." But fortunately, their retrospectives are not limited to accounts of cognition. In practice they invoke thick descrip-tions to impart meaning to events. Jervis and Lebow go beyond their theoretical inhibitions to offer insightful accounts of episodes such as the Cuban missile crisis. In order to demonstrate the role of cognitive processing in determining action, theoretical accounts of cognitivists cite case studies from experimental and social psychology, and, of course, from international relations. These studies demonstrate that faulty cognition often results in erroneous conclusions, poor judgments, and imprudent actions. Jervis, for example, dwells upon imped-iments such as preexisting biases, cognitive dissonance, and the misuse of his-torical analogies.[88]

The authors, however, do not free themselves from what poet William Blake might call the mind shackles of modernity. Like the realists, they presuppose that a crisis is an objective event—something "out there." But unlike the realists, they invoke a more sophisticated epistemology that recognizes that the world is not always perceived accurately. Our perceptions are often clouded by a host of cognitive impediments. Cognitivist scholarship is informed by an overarching in-tention: increasing awareness regarding the impediments to rational decision-making. This task will be accomplished when actors refine their cognitive pro-cessing. In the cognitivists' view, this is no chimerical quest, because there is nothing foreign about the culture inside the Beltway: as Jervis stresses, actors are just like you and I; that is, just like social scientists, they have a will to know—they want to discover the truth and act accordingly.

Perhaps Jervis overestimates the rationality of political actors, or of scien-tists, for that matter. In my view, the incommensurate risks Kennedy hazarded to compel Khrushchev to remove the missiles is not a shining moment in the chronicles of rationality. This claim is, to say the least, controversial. There is, however, considerable consensus that American intervention in Indochina was precipitated by folly and self-deception rather than scientific rationality. Of course, the scientific community itself is not always governed by the unbridled pursuit of truth. Kuhn's influential study (applauded by Jervis) concludes that scientists are often more devoted to cherished paradigms than to the pursuit of truth—they are as irrational and dogmatic as you and I.[89] Worse yet, unlike scientific paradigms, the metaphors that inform political action are seldom sub-ject to rigorous articulation and testing. In any case, perhaps Jervis' comparison of actors and social scientists is too facile. Actors perhaps have more grandiose designs than those of us content to practice the humble craft of social inquiry. We are usually sated by an occasional grant, publication, or promotion; and our pleasures are simple—we delight when others cite our work by interpreting our interpretations. Actors have loftier ambitions, not the least of which is making history.

The cognitivists fail to acknowledge the seductive power of such demons. In my view, decision-making is better understood as a dialectic between rational prudence and irrational bravado.[90] Because cognitivist explications bestow privileged status on cognitive processing and marginalize other dimensions of inner life, they embrace an assumption that simply does not fit the facts. To reiterate their credo: comprehension determines action. Supposedly, rational agents act predictably once they know the truth.[91]

Curiously, Jervis argues that realism does not adequately explain why actors sometimes respond differently to the same event. He concludes that such differences are due to different perceptions. Could it be that actors also respond differently to the same perceptions, and therefore cognitivism is not fully adequate? He dismisses this possibility. In a book that is otherwise meticulously researched, and generally cautious and well argued, Jervis merely asserts the canon of cognitivism:

> That two actors may have the same perception does not guarantee that they will have the same response. But their responses will often be the same, and when they are not, it is usually relatively easy to find the causes of the difference.[92]

As we have seen, Nixon and Kissinger shared the same perception of the threat posed by the construction of a Soviet nuclear submarine base in Cuba. However, Nixon insisted that no crisis should occur. Kissinger, nevertheless, attempted to promote the episode as a crisis. Cognitivists can explain their perceptions, but not their actions. As I shall argue in Chapter 4, in order to understand these dramatically different responses to the Cienfuegos incident, we must invoke the Goldberg Variation: What stories were these actors unwittingly telling themselves about their shared perceptions?

Because it neglects the role of narrativity, the cognitive approach does not adequately explain the mystery of the Cuban missile crisis. As I have argued, the incommensurate risks Kennedy hazarded during the crisis suggest that the will to know, in and of itself, may not determine action. Indeed, Kennedy and the others knew that their gamble entailed horrific risks, yet they persisted. True, he listened to reason, but he was also distracted by a different drummer. Apparently, such elite folly is nothing new. Historian Barbara Tuchman chronicles irrationality in high places in her *March of Folly*. Spanning events from Old Testament sagas to the Indochina War, she concludes that despite tragic failures, leaders who should have know better often persisted in self-defeating actions: they often redoubled their efforts when they forgot their goals.[93]

Cognitivism also invites more formidable theoretic objections. First, it gives insufficient weight to the symbolic turn in international relations. Specifically, it presupposes that, by and large, actors are observers of objective events, rather than interpreters of texts and performances. Second, it presupposes that the will to know is fundamental. I contend that the quest for meaning is primordial; it is this quest that profoundly shapes and colors cognition.

Since the cognitivists rely upon analogies from studies of cognition, it is fitting to begin with a rather standard textbook example of the role of cognition in determining affect and behavior. Consider the following mental experiment. During an uneventful trip to the zoo, you notice that the lion is securely caged. However, the trip would be, to say the least, more eventful if you perceived broken bars on the cage. In this situation, perception determines action. Of course, as the cognitivists stress, international relations are often characterized by ambiguous events. Imagine that you can't tell whether the bars are intact or broken. Assuming that perception determines action, what occurs in such ambiguous situations? (The cognitivists acknowledge that we inhabit such a world.)

However, given the symbolic turn in international relations, the situation is more complicated than they realize. Imagine that you are charged with managing the zoo and that you receive contesting communiqués from experts on the status of the cages. Both experts agree that there is no immediate threat; however they disagree on the long-term viability of the cage. One authority concludes it's a problem you can live with; but the other urges that it's a crisis demanding urgent action at considerable risk to your career.

Unlike their predecessors, recent actors are thrown into such situations. It is difficult to think of any recent situation in which an American actor on the scene directly observed an event, engaged in cognitive processing, and perceived—or misperceived—the event as a crisis. A more accurate "flowchart" would depict intelligence agents authoring interpretations of photographic reconnaissance and the like. These texts are passed on to superiors who, in turn, superimpose their interpretations. (As Montaigne averred, "The hundredth commentator passes it on to the next, still more knotty and perplexed than he found it.") By the time texts reach the highest circles they are often over-interpreted, infused with surplus meaning, and contested.

The documents that reached the Ex Comm did not speak for themselves—they were ambiguous. Kennedy and his associates were thrown into a situation in which they were interpreters, not observers. They did not merely engage in exegesis in which they read meaning out of Khrushchev's communiqués; they also read meaning *into* the communiqués. They were bound by the Fensterheim Rule: "The less well defined the stimulus situation, or the more emotionally laden, the greater will be the contribution of the perceiver"[94]—or interpreter.

Many of the examples cited by Jervis and Lebow concern misperceptions of fairly well-defined events, such as air attacks and troop movements. Jervis discusses Churchill's perception of the dreadfully tangible Nazi threat: the blitzkrieg was immediately experienced; its meaning, obvious.[95] According to Lebow, due to his preexisting beliefs about himself and the military threat posed by the Chinese, General MacArthur dismissed the threat posed by Chinese military intervention during the Korean War.[96]

However, in the present context, crises are not precipitated by air raids and invasions. True, actors may be exercised by an adversary's aircraft deployment and troop movements, but such actions are regarded as means of sending messages, not overt, unmistakable threats. Such symbolic performances present few epistemological problems; concern with cognition is minimal—an actor can readily determine what happened. These symbolic performances present a semiotic problem—transmitting meaning. As McNamara explained to Admiral George Anderson during the blockade of Cuba: "We're trying to send a message, not start a war."[97]

Most significantly, cognitivists are out of touch with the symbolic turn in international relations; texts have literally become the substance of the international world. *It would seem odd and inappropriate to inquire about an actor's perception of a text!* The salient issue is interpretive: What narrative does an actor read into a text to make it intelligible and communicable? Perhaps the cognitivists fail to take cognizance of the symbolic turn in international relations because they privilege cognitive processing at the expense of the more primary processes of inner life. As Geertz urges, "It is not ignorance of how cognition works that stops us from understanding others, it is lack of understanding of their imaginative universe."[98]

According to Geertz, cognition—the will to know—is secondary to a primordial need: the imposition of meaning, drama, and direction upon experience. Jervis and Lebow overlook the possibility that humans are first and foremost symbolizing animals possessed by a compulsion to interpret their experience to themselves and others. He argues that shared cognition does not necessarily lead to comparable actions because individuals are governed by a more fundamental need—the pursuit of meaning. Indeed, cognition itself is not possible apart from an a priori matrix of meaning. Taking a phenomenological stance, he observes that individuals experience meaning, not perception. Perception is an ad hoc reconstruction of lived experience; to paraphrase Dilthey, cognitivists drain pulsating, lived experience of its vitality by reducing it to bloodless perception. For Geertz, and others in the neo-Kantian tradition, we experience gestalts of meaning, not discrete, atomistic perceptions. For example, when we read a text, we are not attentive to individual letters; we attend to words and their referents, and in the process, we read an overall meaning into the text.

This is not to devalue the role of perception in reality testing. But cast in the perspective developed by Geertz and various Continental philosophers, perceptions are like building blocks: what they become depends upon the culturally imposed structure of meaning. But what are these structures? They are the narratives an individual appropriates from his culture that give discrete perceptions form, shape, and meaning.

Going beyond the confines of cognitivist theory, Jervis and Lebow thickly describe aspects of the Cuban missile crisis. Lebow, for example, reads certain motives into Kennedy's actions. According to Lebow, when the president first learned of the missiles: "A furious Kennedy exclaimed, 'he can't do that to me!' The President's 'gut' reaction was to treat the missiles as a personal challenge by Khrushchev involving personal costs to himself."[99]

This gloss on Kennedy is thick description. True, perception is involved. We could conceivably verify the claim that Kennedy made such a statement in response to Bundy's initial briefing about the situation. However, Lebow reads an interpretation into his vicarious perception of Kennedy. I am not criticizing Lebow for offering this interpretation; indeed, I share his perspective. What I am urging is that interpretation is not perception. Unlike perceptions, interpretations cannot be empirically confirmed and—more important—disconfirmed. To be sure, we can conceivably know the words Kennedy used, but how can we verify diverse interpretations of their meaning? Kennedy himself may not have understood his meaning: perhaps his exclamation was a purely emotive expression of surprise and frustration. Or could it be that the expression was merely a favorite figure of speech? There is no need to speculate further. The point of this brief interpretive exercise is that we labor under the Curse of Hermes: since the inevitable interpretations we read into elite actions are not verifiable empirical claims, they are invariably uncertain and contested.

Not surprisingly, Jervis argues that Kennedy's beliefs played a determinative role in his crisis management; he contends that the president would have responded differently if he "had believed that the Russians had placed missiles in Cuba because they felt emotionally or politically committed to protect Castro."[100] Jervis concludes that Kennedy took unprecedented risks because he believed the Soviets were trying to expand their hegemony. This argument is persuasive, but Jervis overlooks a more fundamental concern: what gave rise to Kennedy's belief?

Surely his deeply held convictions did not occur ex nihilo. These convictions must be understood as part and parcel of a resonant narrative—the Cold War cosmology. Jervis contributes to this project de facto in a subsequent chapter when he recounts the mentality that informed Cold War doctrines such as deterrence.[101] However, he does not refer to his account as a narrative.

Likewise, Jervis refers to his interpretive narratives as accounts of perception. Curiously, he uses "perception" and "interpretation" interchangeably. His insightful and justly influential chapter "How Decision-Makers Learn from History" is, perhaps, the most telling instance of his interpretive practices. He states the chapter's problematic as follows: "Where can the statesman find the concepts he needs to *interpret* [italics mine] others' behavior and guide his own actions?"[102] Jervis argues that actors often construct such interpretations by invoking historical analogies: "Learning from history is revealed dramatically when decision-makers use a past event as an analogy for a contemporary one."[103] Such analogies, of course, are tendentious. These persuasive comparisons exaggerate similarities between events while concealing the differences.

Given his theoretical allegiance, Jervis presupposes that these analogies are matters of perception. (However, as I have stressed, it is essential to distinguish "perception" from "conception." The former constructs what is occurring; the latter superimposes meaning upon events.) Specifically, he argues that historical analogies create a "perceptual predisposition." But this "predisposition" is conceptual, not perceptual. Our a priori concepts are more fundamental than cognition; our preconceived narratives govern cognition.

Consider Jervis' account of Truman's decision to intervene in the Korean War. He convincingly demonstrates that Truman likened North Korean aggression in 1950 to Axis Power aggression of the 1930s. According to Jervis, the president was simply drawing a cognitive map—a frame that described what was occurring. In my view, by invoking the analogy, Truman was doing much more. He was not merely describing the North Koreans; he was assigning surplus meaning to the events in Korea. Specifically, he reiterated the remembered past to explain why the North Koreans invaded South Korea, and to prescribe what was expected of the American people and their military. Recasting Jervis' analysis in terms of my perspective, Truman was not merely perceiving; he was conceptualizing a metaphorical narrative.

Perhaps Lebow and Jervis share a common liability: they strip cognitive processing from its context. To be sure, in certain innocuous contexts, historical analogies are simply about perception. For example, if I liken a recent airline schedule to one I saw last month, a typical response might be "So what?" In this context, perceptions carry little meaning. Since there is no agenda, the comparison is not a rhetorical device: no meaning is ascribed to the perception and no action is prescribed. However, the passionate and acrimonious context of international relations is far different. When President Bush likened Saddam Hussein to Hitler, the expected response was not an indifferent "So what?" Bush invoked an impassioned narrative that indicated why Hussein invaded Kuwait and what was expected of the American people.[104]

It is also noteworthy that, despite their theoretical affinity, Jervis and Lebow offer divergent conclusions regarding crucial aspects of the Cuban missile crisis. I sense that Jervis is sympathetic to Kennedy's crisis move while Lebow is not. I do not attribute their differences to impairments or discrepancies in cognitive processing. Both authors display formidable analytic skills and an impressive command of the literature. Rather, I suspect there is a neglected, self-confessional dimension in crisis interpretation. In penning their insightful accounts of the crisis, they reveal a great deal about themselves, and the narratives they read into texts.

Lebow seems aware of this dimension. He does not merely perceive the interpretations of competing analysts; he interprets their interpretations. Once again, I share Lebow's interpretation as to why many mainstream analysts avoid dealing with the most puzzling and disturbing aspect of the crisis: the incommensurate risks Kennedy and the others hazarded.

> The possibility that irrational decision-making could result in nuclear war is frightening. Policy-makers and social scientists have erected defenses to protect themselves from the anxiety that the recognition of this prospect would almost certainly generate.[105]

In sum, Jervis and Lebow privilege the cognitive dimension of individual decision-making, at least in theory. They presuppose that comprehension determines action, and indeed, it sometimes does. However, they do not adequately explain why shared perceptions do not necessarily result in comparable actions, nor do they acknowledge the quest for meaning in generating and shaping perception. And yet, despite these theoretical liabilities, their practice is interpretive. Like the rest of us, they read meanings into crisis texts, and offer thick descriptions of these critical junctures.

Finally, it is noteworthy that Jerome Bruner (a psychologist credited with being an architect, if not *the* architect, of the cognitive revolution) abandoned his strict allegiance to cognitivism in favor of interpretive approaches to inquiry. He explains that reducing individuals to cognitive processors is dehumanizing. What is needed, according to Bruner, is a "hermeneutics of everyday life." He criticizes prevailing schools of thought for treating narrativity as mere decoration. In so doing, these schools ignore the realization that, "We frame the accounts of our cultural origins, and our most cherished beliefs in story form, and it is not the 'content' . . . that grips us, but their narrative artifice."[106]

Commenting upon this interpretive turn, Geertz concludes, "What now comes to the center of attention is the individual engaged with established systems of shared meaning, with the beliefs, the values, and the understandings of those already in place in society as he or she is thrown among them."[107]

Nuclear Angst

We should develop ways to revisit the Cuban missile crisis, phenomenologically, as it appeared and felt at the time . . . we will eventually find ways to move us closer to, [the] shattering fearfulness as we step backward into the forward-moving events of October 1962.

—James Blight[108]

Blight wrote *The Shattered Crystal Ball* in order to resolve a neglected but significant problem: Why did the Cuban missile crisis end more quickly and peaceably than the actors anticipated? He argues that in order to resolve this question, and other significant issues regarding policy-making, an analyst must come to understand an actor's lived experience. By attempting to reconstruct the inner experience of crisis managers, Blight moves inquiry in a fruitful direction. Political actors have not adopted our views on crisis construction and management; perhaps the time has come to understand theirs. Somehow the analyst must recapture the look and feel of a crisis—it's more art than science: "We can study the moon and the stars and the atoms. This is how we have come to understand them. But if we are to understand politics and the people who make policy, we must come to know them."[109]

Blight's approach is simple, even commonsensical: if you want to understand an actor's deeds ask him, and subject his response to critical oral history. Rather than drawing inferences from a priori, retrospective theories of crisis behavior, Blight tries to understand a particular episode—the Cuban missile crisis—in terms I refer to as "subjectivity" (an actor's inner life and lived experience). He refers to this avowedly interpretive approach as phenomenological psychology.[110] Blight does not seek empirical laws of crisis behavior; rather he tries to grasp the emotional life of actors bedeviled by harrowing situations: simply put, What was it like during those final days of the Cuban missile crisis?

It appears, however, that Blight's inquiry is more hermeneutical than phenomenological. As a volume he co-authored, *On the Brink*, indicates, he does not restrict his inquiry to merely explicating an actor's version of his or her intentions and actions.[111] With May and Neustadt, he engages in a "critical oral history":

> Critical oral history requires those former policymakers who participate to do two things: first, to familiarize themselves with . . . documents that, in the event in question, would likely have provided them with the particular information on which their decisions were based. . . . They must also agree to . . . cross-examination by scholars . . . players, and the issues of the time.[112]

According to Blight, the oral history in *On the Brink* provides the data for the interpretation he develops in *The Shattered Crystal Ball*. As he allows, his interpretive strategy is indebted to humanistic thinkers such as Kierkegaard, James, Husserl, and Geertz. Indeed, there are allusions to Plato's *Meno* and to the verses of T. S. Eliot. Finally, he shows sensitivity to certain limitations of the art of interpretation; he suspects that the present is a foreign country:

> One can enter, or reenter, this psychological terrain [the lived experience of those who managed the Cuban missile crisis] only as an alien, but how much better it is to do so in imagination rather than in the full fury of another nuclear crisis.[113]

What interpretation emerges? According to Blight, the crisis ended quickly and peaceably due to the sickening fear that it was veering out of control, careening toward a holocaust no one wanted. True, it may not appear this way in retrospect, but Blight claims that this is how it appeared to the actors at the time. To illustrate his contention, he proposes a mental experiment. Imagine driving down a fog-shrouded road. Suddenly, a dreadful apparition appears, you slam on the brakes and turn back. In retrospect it was only a fallen tree. However, looking at the lived experience, the apparition caused the fear and trembling that made you reverse your course. Likewise, the apparition of nuclear war fomented the angst captured by Kierkegaard—a "fear and trembling," a "sickness unto death"—that made the Ex Comm slam on the brakes.

Blight cites "McNamara's fear" throughout the volume. On that last, fateful Saturday of the crisis not only did McNamara fear that he would not see another sunset, he experienced nuclear angst because the "crystal ball" had begun to shatter. (This metaphor, contrived by the Harvard Nuclear Study group, suggests that actors are ordinarily prudent because they can foresee the horrific consequences of reckless deeds—nuclear war. However, the crystal ball began to crack because actors could not foresee the consequences of their actions clearly and distinctly.) Blight argues that McNamara feared he could not discover a peaceful solution to the American predicament: if Khrushchev refused to remove the missiles promptly, he would be "required" to take actions that would likely precipitate a nuclear war. In other words, the secretary of defense believed he was locked into a dreadful situation.[114] Contrary to the conventional wisdom,

Blight concludes that this palpable apprehension was not an impediment to clear and prudent thinking. On the contrary, it was appropriate and adaptive: it prompted the Americans, and the Soviets, to seek an immediate—if less than ideal—settlement.

Blight's approach is a step in the right direction. Unlike most analysts, he attends to a sorely neglected area: the inner lives and lived experience of political actors. He argues persuasively that an actor's vulnerabilities—indeed, an actor's essential humanity—can prevent harrowing situations from careening out of control. But how adequate is his interpretation of subjectivity? As I've stressed, there is no bull's-eye: it is doubtful that any method can be devised to faithfully capture this dimension of existence; and it is likely that even the most resonant and subtle accounts will be contested or discarded. This is not to say that all interpretations of subjectivity are created equal—they must be on target. Among other factors, the more viable interpretations have a better fit with the facts than the competition. Blight's interpretation of subjectivity is not fully adequate for the following reasons:

1. He targets the angst that vexed Kennedy and the others during the last days of the crisis, but—given his interpretive slant—he does not target the mystery of the crisis: Why did Kennedy and the others get themselves into such a fearful predicament in the first place? Pressing Blight's analogy, why did the best and the brightest knowingly and willfully embark upon a road that led to a fearful precipice? Further, even during the period Blight discusses—the fearful climax of the crisis—principal actors were, apparently, seized by prudent apprehension *and* by reckless bravado. Specifically, the Kennedy brothers prudently offered the Soviets a secret deal while simultaneously issuing an ultimatum. Likewise, McNamara understandably feared the possible consequences of attacking Cuba after the missiles were operational; and yet he endorsed—and by his account almost executed—an attack on Cuba despite the fact that the missiles were known to be operational.

2. He cannot explain such puzzling behavior because he offers a one-dimensional interpretation that neglects the dialectical subtlety of subjectivity. Blight privileges the transparent dimension of subjectivity, a realm that is conscious, static, and consistent. Since he overlooks the preconscious, processual, and contradictory dimension of subjectivity; he cannot explain the peculiar mixture of sobering prudence and intoxicating bravado that bedeviled the Ex Comm.

3. Finally, I do not share one of Blight's determinative criterion for evaluating interpretations of an actor's subjective experience. He argues that a plausible interpretation must have an actor's imprimatur. I find this requirement problematic for a variety of reasons.

Each of these three criticisms warrants elaboration.

Blight offers a perceptive and sympathetic account of the uncanny fear that possessed these actors as events seemingly veered out of control. Unfortunately, he fails to consider the mystery of the Cuban missile crisis: Why did an ordinarily pragmatic politician like Kennedy start down the perilous, fog-shrouded road in the first place? What would prompt an intelligent, reasonable man who loved life to venture onto an unknown byway haunted by the specter of nuclear war? And given a comparable, if not more formidable, Soviet challenge, why did Nixon take a trip to Europe rather than venturing down the road toward nuclear war; and why did Kissinger choose a different path to resolve the confrontation?

Blight is not unaware of the unprecedented risks hazarded by Kennedy and the others. He cites the lamentation of the wife of a member of the Ex Comm: "When I discovered the situation we were in, I couldn't help wondering whether those few missiles in Cuba were really worth risking the destruction of our civilization."[115] Chapter 3 responds to this mystery. Suffice it to say at this point that Blight's explication of nuclear angst is not applicable here. If Kennedy and the others were as fearful of a nuclear holocaust as Blight suggests, they never would have embarked upon "competition in risk-taking," a gamble that involved a public confrontation, a blockade, an unprecedented nuclear alert, and an ultimatum. Worse yet, they knew full well that events might not unfold as planned: in Blight's rather awkward metaphor, the crystal ball may shatter. Nevertheless, they redoubled their efforts to compel Khrushchev to remove the missiles.

Kennedy made a crisis move for a variety of reasons. Sufficient weight, however, must be given to a reason inimical to Blight's exegesis: ever concerned with impression management, Kennedy was driven to overcome his image as an appeaser. His failure at the Bay of Pigs; humiliation at the Vienna Conference; and concessions to Khrushchev during the Berlin crisis confirmed Kennedy's worst fears about himself—it was difficult to build a New Frontier with the Berlin Wall. Accordingly, he tried to respond fearlessly to the defining challenge of his presidency, if not his life, by improvising a heroic, existential narrative: he would be a fearless Churchill, not a pusillanimous Chamberlain. He got himself into the predicament so aptly articulated by Blight by trying to improvise Churchill's bravado in an age of assured destruction. Fearful and indecisive, he nevertheless continued to play the part of Churchill on the world stage. But simultaneously he privately succumbed to his worst fears by secretly improvising a classic Chamberlain script through the secret deal.

Blight's account of McNamara's fear is equally problematic. The secretary of defense, often characterized as the epitome of cool rationality, also acted in puzzling, if not contradictory, ways. During the first Ex Comm meeting on October 16, he expressed his apprehension with power and clarity: he urged that any attack on Cuba must occur *before* the Soviet missiles became operational, lest they be launched. Nevertheless, in a matter of days, he orchestrated plans to attack Cuba *after* the missiles were operational. As Trachtenberg explains:

> On October 16, he [McNamara] argued that an attack on Cuba, after any of the missiles were operational, would pose too great a risk: some of those missiles might . . . be launched, and this could lead to a thermonuclear holocaust. But by October 27—that is after the CIA had reported that some of the missiles . . . were indeed operational—McNamara declared that "we must now be ready to attack Cuba. . . . Invasion had become almost inevitable."[116]

Blight cites William James to make his case about the fear that tempered the Ex Comm. In order to explain how Kennedy and his associates got themselves into this fearful situation in the first place, he might have considered James's trenchant remark in *The Moral Equivalent of War*: "discussing the horror of war does no good; that's its main appeal." The appeal has little connection with noble ideals; wars—or nuclear crises—offer the perverse thrill of gambling for the ultimate stakes. Curiously, Blight suspects that ordinary Americans experienced this perverse exhilaration during the crisis. He suggests that the crisis may have given ordinary folk something akin to a thrilling roller coaster ride. But even though he claims that the Ex Comm was consumed by the terror that the situation was veering out of control—just like a roller coaster—he assures the reader that the Ex Comm did not experience such perverse exhilaration.[117]

Blight is especially moved by Kierkegaard's grasp of angst: each chapter begins with an aphorism penned by the troubled Dane. Perhaps Blight's grasp of subjectivity would be more nuanced and dialectical if he pondered another Kierkegaard jeremiad: "The purity of the heart is to desire one thing." Kierkegaard, of course, never accused fallen humanity of purity: it is our fate to be beset by contradictory passions.

Blight fails to account for the mystery of the crisis because his one-dimensional interpretation ignores the preconscious, processual, and contradictory dimension of subjectivity. He privileges conscious remembrance and neglects the tacit dimension of subjectivity. I am not advocating a psychohistory that purportedly explores the remote interstices of the unconscious. However, I am suggesting that subjectivity cannot be understood without reference to the preconscious. By "preconscious" I understand the tacit dimension of experience that operates just beneath conscious awareness, our second nature of which we are seldom aware.[118] For example, during most language practices, the rules of grammar are preconscious. Since grammar is ordinarily an innocuous subject, individuals can readily be made aware of their preconscious grammatical practices. To have a flair for the obvious, the Ex Comm discourse reveals that Kennedy and his advisers spoke English. Following long-habituated rules, they matched singular verbs with singular subjects. It strains credulity to imagine that these highly educated native speakers consciously strove to use proper English grammar—their linguistic practices were preconscious. No doubt, if the opportunity arose, they could easily explain the semi-intuitive preconscious rules of grammar operating just beneath the surface.

There is, of course, more to the preconscious than rules of grammar. Since crisis discourse has long been the lingua franca inside the Beltway, it is reasonable to suspect that, like grammar, crisis narratives operate just beneath the surface. To reiterate, these narratives are not merely static, cognitive frames that merely represent what is happening; they are resonant scripts that indicate *why* it is happening, and *what is expected* of an actor. Unlike grammar, however, actors have a profound existential investment in the narratives they improvise. They seem reluctant, or unable, to scrutinize the resonant crisis narratives that script their thoughts and deeds: perhaps Kennedy could not readily admit to himself or others that he was a would-be hero desperately trying to vindicate himself from the shame of appeasement. Perhaps it was even more unnerving for him to admit that, bedeviled by conflicting narratives, he was cast into liminality and paralyzed by indecision: unable to decide between being Churchill or Chamberlain, he tried to be both. This reading of Kennedy is—to say the least—arguable. But it is more dubious to presuppose that subjectivity is nothing but public representations of conscious activity.

Finally, Blight's approach to subjectivity is static rather than processual. Rather than explicating the narratives the Ex Comm improvised to interpret and resolve their predicament, Blight dwells upon an epiphenomenon: the fear that gripped the Ex Comm as they anticipated an unhappy ending to the story. But what was the story? Blight evidently tries to recapture subjectivity by decontextualizing and freezing a scene from the Ex Comm saga. It is as if we had a movie of those thirteen days: rather than running the film so that we can witness the action, he projects the last frames one at a time.

Despite his allusion to May and Neustadts' approach to critical oral history, Blight overlooks narrativity. It is essential to grasp the story that actors are preconsciously improvising. This story is seldom transparent, especially to the actors themselves. Interpretive inquiry has been shunned, at least in theory, due to the daunting problem of verification. Empirical claims can be replicated and publicly disconfirmed. No such luxury is available to those who would explicate subjectivity. The passage of time and declassification of diverse documents have done little to resolve contesting accounts of the look and feel of Kennedy's joust on the abyss. While Blight does not confront this nettlesome problem directly, he urges that "One rule, and one rule only, must always prevail: the psychological accounts of the thoughts, feeling, and actions must ring true to actors, psychologists, and ordinary people alike."[119]

Blight suggests that any interpretation not embraced by an actor must discounted. Seeking an actor's imprimatur, however, presents a host of difficulties. Which of the conflicting representations of an actor's subjective experience shall we endorse? (Indeed, shall we presuppose that actors are invariably aware of the forces motivating them?) The literature on the Cuban missile crisis reveals—to put it tactfully—pronounced differences between Kennedy's public representation of his intentions and his private pronouncements. In public he urged that he had to act because Soviet missiles dramatically increased the threat to the survival of the continental United States and to all of North America. In private, however, he determined that this was not the case, and that the problem was more of a symbolic confrontation with profound personal and political ramifications. As a pundit once observed, there are always two reasons for things: very good reasons and the real reasons. If we must rely upon an actor to validate our interpretations, do we rely upon the very good reasons expressed in public, or do we presuppose that the real reasons are articulated in private? At the risk of being accused of undue cynicism, I believe it is not inconceivable that political actors are in the habit of deceiving others—and themselves.

Despite his considerable psychological acumen, Blight does not consider the rich and provocative literature on self-deception. Thinkers as diverse as Freud and Sartre posit self-deception as *the* defining feature of our subjective predicament. And, turning to crises explicitly, Lebow aptly highlights an aphorism from Goethe: "We are never deceived, we deceive ourselves."[120]

Because actors are often dissembling with the public and with themselves, and because they do not always grasp the essence of their decisions, we can seldom rely upon them to validate our interpretations. The next chapter discusses the daunting problem of verification. Suffice it to say here that in addition to fitting the facts that are known and yet to be discovered, an interpretation should be consonant with a more nuanced, dialectical understanding of subjectivity.

Most analysts adopt a hermeneutics of suspicion. Nixon's account of Watergate and Reagan's rendition of Granada are seldom accepted at face value. It is surprising that Blight uncritically accepts McNamara's recollection of his subjectivity. Steinbruner was right: we must somehow tell actors what they are not prepared to hear about things they believe they already understand.

In sum, the competition embraces diverse perspectives. Long dominated by political realists, the study of crisis prevention and management has been enriched by students of bureaucratic politics, and by cognitive and psychological approaches to political inquiry. However, these contending approaches have one thing in common: what Jim George calls "the significant albeit silenced issue in international relations—interpretation."[121] Regardless of theoretical professions, analysts are not mere ciphers noting what is said and done; they superimpose meaning upon cryptic texts and symbolic performances deemed worthy of attention. As the philosopher Charles Cooley wrote long ago: "Records of behavior without interpretation are like a library of books in a strange tongue. They . . . mean nothing until they find their goal in other minds."[122]

Much like ethnographers, analysts invoke favored narratives to interpret crisis texts and performances—these narrative often become "data." (Indeed, crisis analysts are not the only ones who confuse interpretations of reality with reality.) The contending schools of crisis analysis author different stories about what we already know. Anthropologist Edward Bruner's gloss on ethnography seems applicable to investigations of the exotic crisis culture inside the Beltway:

> It is not that we initially have a body of data, the facts, and we then must construct a story or theory to account for them. Instead . . . the narrative structures we construct are . . . primary narratives that establish what is to count as data.[123]

However, since analysts are unaware of the interpretive dimension of their praxis they seldom give sufficient weight to the unavoidably tendentious nature of their interpretations and to a host of other related problematics. Like other academics, we tend to believe everything we think. The time has come for an avowedly interpretive, self-reflective approach to crisis inquiry.

NOTES

1. Clifford Geertz, *Local Knowledge* (New York: Basic Books, 1983), 151.
2. Edward M. Bruner, "Ethnography as Narrative," *The Anthropology of Experience,* Victor W. Turner and Edward M. Bruner, eds., (Urbana: University of Illinois Press, 1986), 141.
3. Murray Edelman, *Constructing the Political Spectacle* (Chicago: University of Chicago Press, 1988).
4. Richard Shusterman, "Beneath Interpretation," in *The Interpretive Turn,* David R. Hiley, James F. Bohman, and Richard Shusterman, eds., (Ithaca: Cornell University Press, 1991), 102.
5. Ernest Cassirer, *An Essay on Man* (Garden City: Doubleday Anchor, 1956), 43.
6. Mark Poster, *The Mode of Information* (Chicago: University of Chicago Press, 1990), 6.
7. Richard Betts, *Nuclear Blackmail and Nuclear Balance* (Washington: Brookings Institution, 1987), 116.
8. Theodore Sorensen, "Kennedy Vindicated," in *The Cuban Missile Crisis*, Robert Divine, ed., (Chicago: Quadrangle Books, 1971), 208.
9. Northrop Frye, *The Great Code: The Bible and Literature* (Toronto: Academic Press, 1981), 227.
10. See James Blight's discussion of Schelling in his *The Shattered Crystal Ball* (Lanham: Rowman & Littlefield Publishers, Inc., 1992), 109.
11. Robert S. McNamara, *In Retrospect* (New York: Times Books, 1995), 337–338.
12. Quoted in Blight, 82.
13. Robert S. McNamara, "The Military Role of Nuclear Weapons," *Foreign Affairs* (Fall 1983): 68.
14. See Ron Hirschbein, "A Suspicious Look at Nuclear Deterrence," in *On The Eve of the 21st Century,* William C. Gay and T. A. Alekseeva, eds., (Lanham: Rowman & Littlefield, 1994), 85–104; also see Hirschbein's *Newest Weapons/Oldest Psychology: The Dialectics of American Nuclear Strategy* (New York: Peter Lang, 1991), 82–95.
15. Marc Trachtenberg, "The Influence of Nuclear Weapons in the Cuban Missile Crisis," in *Nuclear Diplomacy and Crisis Management* Sean Lynn-Jones, Steven Miller and Stephen van Evera, eds., (Cambridge: MIT Press, 1990), 266.
16. Gayle L. Ormiston and Alan D. Schrift, *The Hermeneutic Tradition* (Albany: State University of New York Press, 1990), 5.
17. Michel Foucault, "The Order of Discourse" in *Language and Politics,* Michael Shapiro, ed., (New York: New York University Press), 112.
18. Thomas Kuhn, "The Natural and the Human Sciences," in *The Interpretive Turn*, David R. Hiley, James F. Bohman, and Richard Shusterman, eds., (Ithaca: Cornell University Press, 1991), 21.
19. David Samuels, "The Call of Stories," *Lingua Franca* (May/June): 1995, 35–36.
20. J. David Singer, "The Behavioral Science Approach to International Politics: Payoffs and Prospects," in *International Politics and Foreign Policy*, James N. Rosenau, ed., (New York: Free Press, 1969), 67.
21. Richard Ned Lebow, *Between Peace and War: The Nature of International Crises* (Baltimore: Johns Hopkins University Press, 1981), 13.
22. Richard Ned Lebow, "Domestic Politics and the Cuban Missile Crisis: The Traditional and Revisionist Interpretations Reevaluated," *Diplomatic History* (Fall 1990): 471–492.

23. Richard Ned Lebow and Janice Gross Stein, *We All Lost the Cold War* (Princeton: Princeton University Press, 1994).

24. Robert O. Keohane, *International Institutions and State Power* (Boulder: Westview Press, 1991), 158.

25. Ibid.

26. Geertz, *The Interpretation of Cultures* (New York: Basic Books, 1973), 7.

27. Keohane, 37.

28. Ibid., 159.

29. Samuels offers a telling account of this problematic in "The Call of Stories."

30. Bruner, 153.

31. Graham Allison, *The Essence of Decision: Explaining the Cuban Missile Crisis* (Boston: Little, Brown, 1971), 38.

32. Thomas Kuhn, *The Structure of Scientific Revolutions,* 2nd ed. (Chicago: University of Chicago Press, 1970), 109.

33. McGeorge Bundy, *Danger and Survival* (New York: Random House, 1988), 392.

34. Kenneth Burke, *Permanence and Change,* rev. ed., (Los Altos: Hermes Publications, 1954), 20.

35. Hannah Arendt, *The Human Condition* (Chicago: University of Chicago Press, 1958), 192.

36. James Fentress and Chris Wickham, *Social Memory* (Oxford: Blackwell, 1992), vii.

37. Samuels, 37.

38. Stephen E. Ambrose, *Nixon,* vol. 2 (New York: Simon and Schuster, 1989), 10.

39. Ibid., 13–17.

40. Richard Nixon, *In the Arena* (New York: Simon and Schuster, 1990), 79.

41. Anatoly Dobrynin, *In Confidence* (New York: Times Books, 1995), 76.

42. Bruce Mazlish, *Kissinger: The European Mind in American Foreign Policy* (New York: Basic Books, 1976), 11.

43. Michael J. Shapiro, *Reading the Postmodern Polity* (Minneapolis: University of Minnesota Press, 1992), 44.

44. Victor Turner, *Dramas, Fields and Metaphors* (Ithaca: Cornell University Press, 1971), 17

45. Quoted in Geertz, *The Interpretation of Cultures*, 13.

46. Keohane, 35.

47. See Jack Levy's discussion of the realist paradigm in his "The Causes of War: A Review of Theories and Evidence" in *Behavior, Society and Nuclear War,* vol. 1, Philip Tetlock, Jo Husbands et al. (New York: Oxford University Press, 1989), 224–228; also see the critique of realism in Chapter 3 of *International Institutions and State Power.*

48. Henry Kissinger, *Diplomacy* (New York: Simon and Schuster, 1994).

49. See, for example, Reinhold Niebuhr, *Moral Man and Immoral Society* (New York: Scribners, 1933).

50. Cited by Holsti in "Crisis Decision Making," in *Behavior, Society and Nuclear War,* vol. 1, Philip Tetlock, Jo Husbands et al, (New York: Oxford University Press, 1989), 16.

51. Quoted in Murray Edelman, *The Symbolic Uses of Politics* (Urbana: University of Illinois Press, 1985), 164.

52. Ole. R. Holsti, *Crisis Escalation War* (Montreal: McGill-Queen's University Press, 1972), 23.

53. Jim George offers a penetrating critique of realist assumptions in his *Discourses of Global Politics: A Critical (Re)Introduction to International Relations* (Boulder: Lynne Rienner, 1994).

54. Hans J. Morgenthau, *Politics Among Nations: The Struggle for Power and Peace* (New York: Alfred Knopf, 1960), 10.

55. George, 92.

56. Ibid., 53.

57. Robert Jervis, *Perception and Misperception in International Politics* (Princeton: Princeton University Press, 1976), 19.

58. Allison, 12.

59. Raymond Garthoff, *Reflections on the Cuban Missile Crisis* (Washington: Brookings Institution, 1987), 157.

60. Bundy, 452.

61. McNamara, *In Retrospect,* 341.

62. As of this writing, McNamara's most recent pronouncement was during his Founder's Day speech at the University of California, Berkeley, April 13, 1996.

63. Quoted by Lebow, *Between Peace and War*, 298.

64. Bundy, 412–413.

65. Turner, *Dramas, Fields and Metaphors*, 38.

66. Reinhold Niebuhr, *Moral Man and Immoral Society.*

67. Arnold Wolfers, "'National Security' as an Ambiguous Symbol," in *Classics of International Relations*, John A. Vasquez, ed., 3rd. ed., (Upper Saddle River, N. J.: Prentice Hall, 1996), 150.

68. Robert Jervis, *The Logic of Images in International Relations* (Princeton: Princeton University Press, 1970), 178–179.

69. Allison, 3.

70. Ibid., 248.

71. Ibid., 181.

72. Ibid., 162.

73. Graham Allison and Morton Halperin, "Bureaucratic Politics: A Paradigm and Some Policy Implications," in *Classics of International Relations*, John A. Vasquez, ed., 3rd. ed., (Upper Saddle River, N. J.: Prentice Hall, 1996), 176.

74. Allison, *"Bureaucratic Politics,"* 190.

75. Ibid., 206–207.

76. Ibid.

77. Ibid., 1.

78. Ibid., 192–194.

79. Ibid., 39.

80. Lawrence Chang and Peter Kornbluh, *The Cuban Missile Crisis 1962* (New York: New Press, 1991), xv–xix.

81. I first learned of these secret negotiations in an interview with Raymond Gartfhoff (a State Department adviser to the Ex Comm) at the Brookings Institution on May 9, 1990; Anatoly Dobrynin discusses this "secret channel" *In Confidence*, 71–95.

82. Bundy, 432.

83. Not surprisingly, the substance of Robert Kennedy's meeting is of enduring interest. Allison claims that Kennedy issued an ultimatum, and analysts such as Alexander George concur. Blight, however, is among those who disagree. Based upon a recently declassified document from Dobrynin, Lebow offers the following interpretation: Kennedy de facto issued an ultimatum during his secret meeting, which de jure was treated as a request for a cooperative settlement by Dobrynin, but not by Khrushchev. Given the remarkable ambivalence and equivocation of the encounter, it appears to me that, immersed in liminality, grasping at straws, Kennedy simultaneously issued an ultimatum *and* a conciliatory secret deal—it's a matter of interpretation.

84. Bundy, 432.

85. Cited by Holsti in "Crisis Decision Making," 65.

86. Cited by George, 22.

87. Robert Jervis, *Perception and Misperception in International Politics* (Princeton: Princeton University Press, 1970, 5.

88. See Part II of Ibid.

89. Thomas Kuhn, *The Structure of Scientific Revolutions* (Chicago: University of Chicago Press, 1962).

90. Hirschbein, *Newest Weapons/Oldest Psychology.*

91. Jervis' earlier work, *The Logic of Images in International Relations* (Princeton: Princeton University Press, 1970), offers insight into impression management through the construction of images, posturing and other modes of symbolic performance. He demonstrates that international relations are about "threatening on the cheap": a pirouette of dissembling words and deceptive gestures. The perceptive study reads like an inquiry into semiotics—the creation, transmission and reception of meaning. Wedded to his paradigm, however, Jervis embeds his analysis in the conceptual apparatus of cognitivism; therefore he gives insufficient weight to folly and self-deception.

92. Jervis, *Perception and Misperception, 5.*

93. Barbara Tuchman, *The March of Folly* (New York: Alfred Knopf, 1984); curiously, during the Cuban missile crisis, President Kennedy urged his associates to read Tuchman's *Guns of August*, a study of the irrational factors that precipitated World War I. For reasons that should be clear at this point, I do not share Tuchman's view that Kennedy and the others acted prudently during the Crisis.

94. Cited by Murray Edelman in *The Symbolic Uses of Politics* (Urbana: University of Illinois Press, 1985), 30.

95. Jervis, *Perception and Misperception,* 121–122.

96. Lebow, *Between Peace and War,* 154–155.

97. See Lebow and Steins' discussion of the incident, 341.

98. Geertz, *Interpretation of Cultures,* 13.

99. Lebow, *Between Peace and War,* 10–11.

100. Jervis, *Perception and Misperception,* 35.

101. Ibid., Chapter 4.

102. Ibid., 217.

103. Ibid., 218.

104. See Hirschbein's "Support Our Tropes: A Critique of Persian Gulf Discourse," *The Eye of the* Storm, Lawrence F. Bove and Laura Dunham Kaplan, eds., (Amsterdam: Rodopi, 1995).

105. Lebow, *Between Peace and War, 298.*

106. Cited by Clifford Geertz in "Learning with Bruner" in *New York Review,* April 10, 1997, 23.

107. Ibid., 22.

108. Blight, 174.

109. Ibid., 90.

110. Blight calls critical oral history applied phenomenology. I suspect that many philosophers would find this usage peculiar since philosophic phenomenology deals with the a priori processes of experience. In any case, Blight's method seems more hermeneutic than phenomenological.

111. James Blight and David Welch, *On The Brink: Americans and Soviets Reexamine the Cuban Missile Crisis* (New York: Farrar, Straus, & Giroux/Hill and Wang, 1989).

112. Blight, *Shattered Crystal Ball,* 79.

113. Ibid., *10.*

114. Ibid., 37–38.

115. Ibid., 98; Blight had the opportunity to interview certain Ex Comm members and their families at conferences he helped organize; he indicates that the woman he interviewed wishes to remain anonymous.

116. Trachtenberg, 260-261.

117. Blight, *The Shattered Crystal Ball*, 28–29.

118. See for example Michael Polanyi's account of tacit knowledge in his *Personal Knowledge* (London: Routledge, 1958).

119. Blight, *The Shattered Crystal Ball*, 89.

120. Lebow, *Between Peace and War*, frontispiece.

121. George, 146.

122. Cited by Robert Prus in *Symbolic Interaction and Ethnographic Research* (Albany: State University of New York Press, 1996), 48.

123. Edward Bruner, "Ethnography as Narrative," in *The Anthropology of Experience* (Urbana: University of Illinois Press, 1986),143.

CHAPTER 2

A HERMENEUTIC PRIMER

A physicist friend of mine once said in facing death he drew some consolation
from the reflection that he would never again have to look up the word "hermeneutics" in the dictionary.

—Steven Weinberg[1]

Despite the fact that in practice, crisis inquiry is decidedly interpretive, the term
"hermeneutics" is not (to understate the case) a commonplace in international relations discourse. Curiously, however, despite—or perhaps because of—their interpretive practices, analysts are reluctant to represent themselves as interpreters,
let alone hermeneuticists. As Geertz remarks:

> Many of them [social scientists] have taken an essentially hermeneutic—or, if
> that word frightens, conjuring up images of biblical zealots . . . and Teutonic
> professors, an "interpretive"—approach to their task.[2]

Given the esoteric nature of the term—and the bad press—it will not suffice
to assure the reader that since this book is, in effect, an essay in hermeneutics,
his/her curiosity will be sated in due course. My predicament is illustrative; it is
a quandary confronted by anyone struggling to understand the unfamiliar. In trying to define hermeneutics to the uninitiated, I am caught in what hermeneuticists call the "hermeneutic circle": in order to understand the particular, one must
understand the general; but in order to understand the general, one must grasp
the particular. (To cite Geertz's illustration, how can we grasp the meaning of a
baseball glove unless we understand the game? But how can we understand the
game without understanding the apparatus?) Turning directly to the paradox that
vexes this study, in order for the reader to understand my novel take on crises
he/she should understand hermeneutic inquiry. However, in order to understand
such inquiry, he/she should have an a priori grasp of my reading of crises. How
is this paradox to be resolved?

The answer seems obvious—with difficulty. As Geertz argues, anyone who struggles to render the unfamiliar familiar travels in hermeneutic circles. The dialectical movement between the particular and the general reflects the "inner conceptual rhythm" of ethnography—or of crisis explication:

> Hopping back and forth between the whole conceived through the parts . . . and the parts conceived through the whole . . . we seek to turn them, by a sort of intellectual perpetual motion, into explications of one another. . . . All this is the familiar trajectory of what Dilthey called the hermeneutic circle. . . . It is central to ethnographic interpretation, and thus to the penetration of other people's thought, as it is to literary, historical, philological, psychoanalytical, or biblical interpretation.[3]

Perhaps understanding the unfamiliar is not as daunting as it appears. The paradox of the hermeneutic circle can be likened to Zeno's paradox. The mathematical difficulties that bedeviled the ancient Greek do not prevent us from going from point A to point B. And, despite our encapsulation in hermeneutic circles and the attendant philosophic difficulties, children understand baseball, and adults—with considerably more effort—can better understand foreign cultures without benefit of clergy, Teutonic philosophers, or other hermeneuticists. What's the secret? As we shall see, narrative—storytelling—is the key to the paradox. The unfamiliar is rendered intelligible through this virtually universal conceptual strategy: we liken the unfamiliar present to a familiar story of the remembered past. To be sure, the project of this study—explicating the crisis narratives that actors read into situations—cannot bestow a consummate, irrefutable grasp of a particular crisis—let alone crises in general. However, our understanding of crisis construction, management, and remembrance is enhanced by exploring the interpretive, authorial and performative practices of political actors. Put succinctly, we must come to grasp the crisis narratives actors invoke, author, and improvise in order to restore the status quo ante.

To reiterate, a hermeneutic approach does not involve mind reading. It does, however, presuppose that we can read an actor's culture—his intersubjective experience—through his texts and performances. In order to outline the contours of this hermeneutic approach to crisis inquiry, this chapter is divided into three sections: (1) the presuppositions of hermeneutic inquiry; (2) an illustrative example of the strengths and weaknesses of such inquiry; (3) a gloss on the problematic of hermeneutic inquiry—judging contesting interpretations.

PRESUPPOSITIONS

> [Language] is the game in which we are all participants. None less so than any other. Each of us is "it," and it is always our turn. . . . When at last we have got to the bottom of something which seemed to us strange and unintelligible, when we have managed to accommodate it with our linguistically ordered world, then everything falls into place.
>
> —Hans-Georg Gadamer[4]

My approach is indebted to the cultural hermeneutics of interpretive anthropologists such as Turner and Geertz—an interpretive method used to explicate crises at other times and places. This spin on hermeneutics suggests that a crisis begins with a predicament in which "*an* experience" disrupts facile routines. Given the symbolic turn in international relations, texts and performances—not obdurate facts—precipitate such disruptions. Actors improvise predictable strategies for resolving the predicament—they mass the tropes. For a variety of personal and political reasons, actors are captivated by certain metaphorical crisis narratives. These narratives render a cryptic text intelligible by likening it to a resonant crisis narrative of the remembered past. They also prescribe what must be done and what genre of social drama must be improvised for an actor to attain his/her preconceived destiny by resolving the crisis. Finally, this approach prescribes a method for gaining access to an actor's crisis narratives. These ancient narratives are reincarnated in the data of this inquiry—an actor's texts and performances.

In articulating the presuppositions that inform this study, I explore the predicament of political actors; their strategy for resolving this predicament; and my methodological strategy for understanding their struggle.

Predicament

Life is not always easy for political actors cursed by Hermes. They are thrown into a world in which friend and foe alike play language games by authoring cryptic texts. Life would be easier if they confronted unmistakable threats, but actors seldom directly observe objective events; they interpret signals and messages, and respond in kind. While academics may engage in mathematical modeling and game-theoretic exercises, the texts and performances that beset actors are not unequivocal expressions akin to mathematical propositions. Of course, life would also be easier if these texts and performances were utterly unintelligible, something akin to extraterrestrial gibberish: in this situation actors could simply resign themselves to the hopelessness of deriving meaning from political discourse. However, like the rest of us, they occupy the vast territory in between. This unbounded and variegated world of lived experience is a realm of ambiguous expressions relentlessly subject to contesting interpretations. In other words, the world of lived experience is neither transparent nor impenetrable: it is an opaque world rendered intelligible by reading arguable meanings into and out of texts. Kenneth Burke's observation about the predicament of human existence is applicable to those charged with interpreting and managing international relations:

> The problems of existence do not have one fixed, unchangeable character, like the label on a bottle. They are open to many interpretations—and these interpretations in turn influence our selection of meanings.[5]

Actors, of course, are not constantly bedeviled by the problems of existence. On the contrary, much of their time is spent perfunctorily scanning briefs and engaging in obligatory ceremonial performances. As long as life runs its expected course, there is little need to question one's existence. However, as Turner suggests, certain experiences are epiphanic. His account of such experience is based upon a series of presuppositions. He presupposes that, in order to interpret social action, we must somehow come to appreciate an actor's inner lived experience. While analysts may attempt to represent this experience as observable behavior or atomistic perceptions, actors—to invoke ordinary usage—do not have behavior or perception; they have experiences. He distinguishes between mere experience—the passive endurance and acceptance of events—and *an* experience, the disruption of routine that begins with shocks of anguish or ecstasy.[6] Turner aptly refers to such experiences as transformative experiences—experiences that stand out in stark relief from mundane experience.

> Each of us had certain "experiences" which have been formative and transformative, that is, distinguishable, isolable . . . external events and internal response to them such as initiations into new lifeways . . . [or] a cause celebre such as . . . Watergate, the Iranian hostage crisis, or the Russian Revolution.[7]

Anthropologist Roger Abrahams offers a further distinction useful in crisis explication. Certain transformative experiences are anticipated, even planned. For example, actors may anticipate their inner response to extraordinary events such as inaugurations or resignations. Since such events are orchestrated, well-prepared actors know what to expect and what is expected—they are generally on their best behavior. However, other transformative experiences are unexpected. Caught by surprise, actors are capable of uncharacteristic folly.[8] Indeed, Kennedy, Nixon, and Kissinger anticipated—even welcomed—crises; unfortunately, they seldom got the ones they wanted.

During these unwanted episodes, well-chosen—or poorly chosen—words disrupt routine existence by throwing actors into ambiguous situations that call their very identity into question.[9] For example, it seems that Kennedy had such a transformative experience when he learned of the missiles.[10] Bundy's revelation disrupted Kennedy's smooth, habituated existence; he could no longer operate on automatic pilot, so to speak. Given the surplus meaning Kennedy attached to Soviet actions, the missile deployment undermined his self-image and called his preconceived destiny into question. With Heidegger he learned that, "The world as world is only revealed to me when things go wrong."[11]

Thrown into a situation in which things went wrong, Kennedy of course wanted to know what was happening. These cognitive needs were satisfied easily: obviously, the Soviets (or so it appeared at the time) secretly installed forty-two strategic nuclear weapons in Cuba.[12] Kennedy, of course, did not live by cognition alone. The situation demanded what Habermas calls "communicative competence." He needed to construct and promote an interpretation of events that would do the following:

1. Fulfill his teleological need: Compelled to make sense of the situation, he asked, What was the point of Khrushchev's action?

2. Respond to his normative exigencies by prescribing what must be done: How must he act to express and valorize his interpretation?

3. Facilitate the dramatic enactment of his preconceived destiny: What script and dramatic gestures were essential for him to be remembered as a profile in courage?[13]

Accordingly, Kennedy became an interpreter, author, and performer. In a phrase, he wanted to understand and to be understood. As an interpreter, he asked, "What's the story: why is Khrushchev doing this to me?" As an author and performer he (like Shakespeare's benighted Prince of Denmark) wanted to tell his story. The script was not legislated by the transformative experience itself. As Turner explains, interpreting, authoring, and performing are processes governed by an a priori conceptual strategy: "Dilthey saw such experiences as having a . . . processual structure—they are 'processed' through distinguishable stages."[14] These predictable stages may be represented as a conceptual strategy.

Strategy

If we regard narrative ethically, as the supreme instrument for building 'values' and 'goals,' . . . which motivate human conduct into situational structures of 'meaning,' then we must concede it to be a universal cultural activity, embedded in the very center of the social drama, itself another cross-cultural and trans-temporal unit in social process.

—Victor Turner[15]

The process begins, as Geertz suggests, by inscribing transformative experiences into texts. This inscription renders the world more tractable by reducing pulsating, evanescent experience to a frozen inscription. As he explains, inscription fixes meaning: "When we speak, our utterances fly by as events like any other behavior; unless what we say is inscribed in writing . . . it is as evanescent as what we do."[16]

Accordingly, non-written observations and interpretations of international events are reduced to writing and communicated as texts. In order to interpret such inscriptions—to offer yet another refrain of the Goldberg Variation—actors appropriate narratives from their life and culture and read the script into the text. Indeed, the research of Turner and Geertz confirms a widely held philosophic view: storytelling is the favored mode of making sense of the unfamiliar.

Evidently, the discovery of narrativity was *an* experience for Turner. It prompted him to act in a manner decidedly out of character for his profession—he hazarded a cultural universal. Based upon his outdoor knowledge and reflection, he claimed that at virtually every time and place, humans interpret their experience and express their preconceived destiny through culturally transmitted narratives. Geertz shares this perspective. As he explains, narratives offer an unproblematic way of understanding so deeply embedded in consciousness as to be virtually invisible. They conveniently plot enigmatic situations by arbitrarily assigning a beginning, climax and resolution to the event.

Turner and Geertz reconfirm much of the influential indoor reflection on the role of narrativity in interpreting experience. Walter Fisher's study of narrativity cites Alasdair MacIntyre with approval:

> Man is in his actions and practice, as well as in his fictions, essentially a story-telling animal; [accordingly] enacted dramatic narrative is the basic and essential genre for the characterization of human actions.[17]

Apparently, Gregory Bateson is so moved by his discovery of narrativity that it is only a slight exaggeration to suggest that his claims surpass the hyperbolic: "If I am at all fundamentally right in what I am saying, then *thinking in terms of stories* must be shared by all mind or minds, whether ours or those of redwood forests and sea anemones."[18] Fortunately, exploring the inner lives and significative systems of the denizens of the forest and the sea is beyond the scope of this inquiry. My aim is more modest: gaining entry into the conceptual strategies American actors improvise in response to certain unexpected, transformative experiences. Actors appropriate narratives from their life and culture in order to get a handle on such experiences.

A survey of the narrativity literature (a dominant influence in the humanities and a growing trend in social inquiry) reveals that narratives play a profound and variegated role in understanding the world, and in being understood. Storytelling: imposes meaning, prescribes values, and scripts performance. Yet, as I have suggested, narratives are often preconscious, or, in Berlin's words, "semi-intuitive." Specifically, narratives mitigate puzzlement by imposing a storyline that imposes a beginning, development, climax, and resolution upon transformative experience. Action is defined in terms of central characters, roles, and performances. The storyline is remarkably impervious to unexpected or contradictory developments. As Burke suggests, narratives offer answers to the questions posed by transformative experiences:

> They are *strategic* answers, *stylized* answers. . . . These strategies size up the situation, name their structure and outstanding ingredients, and name them in a way that contains an attitude toward them.[19]

Specifically, crisis narratives are conceptual strategies for interpreting ambiguity and for restoring the status quo ante. And, as Burke suggests, the repertoire of crisis narratives is limited to the stock on hand. (To reiterate, I contend that the crises explicated in this inquiry were constructed and promoted in accord with two ancient narratives—the existential and the clinical.) In any case, the crisis narratives invoked initially to interpret a text or performance are drawn from the hallowed secondary sources of the past. Unfortunately, political actors seldom have the time or the inclination to understand the present in its own right. As Berlin cautions, judicious judgment requires a statesman "to understand a particular situation in its full uniqueness, the particular men and events and dangers, the particular hopes and fear which are actively at work in a particular place at a particular time."[20]

Just as generals are invariably fighting the last war, actors are managing the previous crisis. In other words, crisis construction is a conceptual strategy that makes sense of an unfamiliar present by likening it to a familiar remembered past. For Turner there is something familiar about this conceptual strategy: he concludes that at every time and place he investigated, individuals responded to transformative experiences by summoning up precedents from the conscious or unconscious past. Despite our Enlightenment pretensions, we are much like our ancestors: we invoke ancestral authority to interpret and resolve dangerous uncertainty. (As we have seen, a variety of influential analysts, such as May and Jervis, provide numerous examples.) However, as Turner stresses, our invocation of the past is far from consistent: we often attempt to get a handle on the present by conjuring up mixed—if not conflicting—metaphors. According to Turner, the conflict is played out in the social dramas we call crises.[21] (As I argue in the next chapter, Kennedy's crisis management was reckless and indecisive because he simultaneously labored under crisis narratives improvised by Churchill and Chamberlain.)

However, before we turn to these dramas—morality plays that offer a pretext for the improvisation of an actor's preconceived destiny—it is essential to explore the role of historical metaphors in crisis construction, management, and remembrance. Turner expresses the guiding concept of his interpretive inquiry when he writes: "Social actions acquire their form through the metaphors in their actors' heads."[22] Metaphorical constructions are so subtle and pervasive that it is tempting to define metaphors by likening them to something else. Resisting this temptation for the moment, I turn to Turner's account of metaphor, an account indebted to several recent philosophers. Citing Max Black, he defines metaphor as an analogical strategy that compares a primary subject to a derivative subject. Kennedy, for example, likened his situation to the predicament his predecessors faced in the 1930s: an intractable, unscrupulous enemy threatened the peace. Such constructions, of course, are misleading: they exaggerate similarities and conceal differences between past and present. Kennedy was captivated by the Munich Syndrome. Like the rest of his generation, he overlooked differences between the Nazis and the Communists. However, unlike many of his contemporaries, he *knew* that the nuclear age changed everything—but he was reluctant to believe it.

The metaphorical narratives used to interpret transformative experience resemble scientific paradigms—but, to be sure, we must be wary of being seduced by facile analogies! In Turner's telling phrase, science begins with metaphor but ends with algebra. However, the metaphors that govern social life are embraced as long as they meet our subjective needs. Unlike scientific paradigms, metaphorical narratives are not ultimately subject to empirical disconfirmation. They become self-certifying myths because they satisfy an actor's interpretive, authorial, and performative needs. The ancient root metaphors that inform popular drama persist because they celebrate a saga of virtually universal appeal—a heroic story with a happy ending. In other words, unlike scientific paradigms, root metaphors are icons that convey sacred narratives. Paradigms present images of unchanging physical laws, while root metaphors provide venerable catechisms that instruct the faithful on the ritualistic dramas necessary for atonement and salvation. Most important, paradigms do not change reality. Whether the universe is viewed as an organism or a machine, the missiles were in Cuba. Root metaphors, however, can and do change social reality. Kennedy's dramaturgic image of himself and his calling did not, of course, alter the physical reality of the missiles in Cuba, but it did determine his understanding of and response to the episode.

Taken as a whole, the literature suggests that metaphorical narratives offer an extraordinary advantage in interpreting the world: they resolve the paradox of the hermeneutic circle. As Edward Bruner explains:

> As we can only enter the world in the middle, in the present, then stories serve as meaning-generating interpretive devices which frame the present within a hypothetical past and an anticipated future.[23]

In other words, a narrative is a gestalt that represents the particularity of the present as part and parcel of a familiar story stretching from a comprehended past to an anticipated future. Bruner suggests that:

> [A] Story . . . has a remarkable dual aspect—it is both linear and instantaneous. On the one hand, a story is experienced as a sequence, as it is being told or enacted; on the other hand, it is comprehended all at once—before during and after the telling.[24]

These grand narratives are often referred to as metanarratives because they allegedly reveal *the* story about a text, a story that marginalizes or eclipses competing accounts. Cast in this perspective, a crisis narrative is a metanarrative represented as the only possible interpretation of a text. It is, of course, logically possible to entertain contesting stories about an ambiguous text. And given the dangers of promiscuously reading crisis narratives into diverse situations, analysts understandably exhort those inside the Beltway to live with doubt by embracing the ambiguities of international life. However, for the most part, this is not a real, historic possibility for actors with little enthusiasm for traveling in hermeneutic circles. There is considerable speculation as to why actors are unnerved by ambiguity. Perhaps it reflects the human condition or actors' inflated views of their abilities. Or could it be that those responsible for momentous decisions must convince themselves that they and their actions are indispensable? In any case, once an actor construes a text or performance as a crisis, it is unlikely that he will entertain other possibilities. Indeed, it would be difficult to find examples of an actor recanting by allowing that an episode was actually a chronic problem he could live with rather than an acute crisis demanding immediate, perilous resolution.

A crisis, of course, is not merely a scholarly interpretation of a text or performance, nor is it simply a plot for escaping the hermeneutic circles etched by a volatile international realm that seldom remains familiar. It is a form of self-expression. As Geertz argues, it is through such performative self-expressions that people author themselves. A crisis, then, is a pretext for making a scene—for improvising a drama to which "attention must be paid."[25] Turner refers to such dramas as "social dramas." These public, highly symbolic theatrics are construed as a test of will, a pretext for the improvisation of cherished metaphorical narratives. As Turner explains, life is a series of transitional dramas in which

> Subjects move, as Lloyd Warner has put it, from "a fixed placental placement within his mother's womb, to his death . . . and final containment in his grave as a dead organism—punctuated by a number of critical moments of transition which all societies ritualize . . . with suitable observances to impress the significance of the individual and the group on living members of the community"[26]

I cannot deal with the full import of this eschatological reference. I am concerned with those critical moments Turner refers to as "life-crisis dramas": rites of passage that result in either status elevation or failure and defeat. Such dramas are not limited to the primitive and exotic. They are also, in Abrahams' words, the holy practice of secular humanism: the ritualizing construction and consecration of the self. Just as a tribesman must complete a heroic journey to become a chieftain, so a politician must endure a rite of passage to be enshrined as a statesman. Abrahams quotes Goffman's aphorism: "Many gods have been done away with, but the individual himself remains a deity of great importance."[27]

As Turner recognized, social dramas in which individuals struggle to immortalize themselves are improvised in high places in the overdeveloped world:

> If it is a social drama involving two nations in one geographic region, escalation could imply a stepwise movement toward antagonism across the dominant global cleavage between communist and capitalist camps.[28]

However, as an anthropologist, he restricts his account of social dramas to other times and places. And yet, his ability to see the histrionic in history offers a rich, untapped source for understanding the crises that emerge from dominant global cleavages. True, Turner's depiction of the early and late stages of a dramatic crisis is rather unremarkable. Like most analysts, he recognized that crises are precipitated by a symbolic breach of some crucial understanding, and that unless the breach is redressed, the crisis escalates. And, to be sure, crises are resolved by mustering words or weapons to reestablish the status quo ante. However, his remarkable account of liminality offers extraordinary insight into the determinative middle phase of existential crises such as Kennedy's rite of passage from the playboy son of Joe Kennedy to the daring king of Camelot.

Turner expresses his indebtedness to anthropologist Arnold van Gennep, who coined the well known phrase "rite of passage." However, Van Gennep's profound and heuristic account of liminality—the harrowing transitional phase in such rites—is an esoteric notion familiar only to those initiated into the anthropological lore. This is unfortunate because this fertile notion presents intriguing possibilities for enhancing our understanding of what it is like to endure a nuclear crisis. Therefore, a brief excursion into anthropological esoterica seems justified.

According to Van Gennep, rites of passage are marked by three phases: separation, transition, and incorporation.[29] For example, the passage from tribesman to chieftain is characterized by carefully prescribed ceremonies that separate the would-be leader from his community and subject him to unnerving rites of transition. These rites place the initiate in an alien environment, and subject him to disorienting trials and painful humiliations. During this transition the world no longer makes sense; in effect, he becomes a stranger to himself, lost in a world he neither understands nor controls. Bereft of cherished stories to make sense of the world, he endures liminality.

Of course, in traditional cultures the elders perform highly stylized, sacred rites to reincorporate the initiate into the society as chieftain—the outcome is known. However, as many have noted, secularized societies such as the United States lack venerable, carefully prescribed passages. A politician who wants to be immortalized as a statesman is on his own—the outcome is unknown. There is no explicit, carefully prescribed heroic journey to complete; and no authoritative council of elders bestows its imprimatur upon the successful sojourner. (Kennedy, with considerable help from the guardians of his legend, managed to immortalize himself as a jaunty, youthful statesman; the verdict is still out on Nixon and Kissinger.)

While, as Turner suggests, every crisis has a phase in which people mask their emotions by pretending nothing is wrong, life-crisis rites are marked by an interlude in which the initiate is, in Turner's memorable phrase, "betwixt and between metaphors." In other words, the initiate is abandoned and thrown into a situation outside the periphery of everyday life, a predicament with none of the attributes of past or future stages. (A distraught Vietnam combat veteran recalled this predicament when he lamented, "I had no metaphors, just reality.") What Turner calls the mysterious, fearful darkness of liminality renders robust individuals weak and exquisitely vulnerable.

Turner, of course, evokes further anthropological imagery to describe this fateful transition. He explains that a liminal transition is a no-man's land between and betwixt metaphors, in which initiates are neither here nor there; they are cast into a milieu "detached from mundane life and characterized by ambiguous ideas, monstrous images, sacred symbols, ordeals, humiliations, esoteric and paradoxical instructions."[30]

Perhaps Nietzsche experienced liminality writ large when he inscribed the transition from sectarian to secular society in his obituary for God. There was no encomium, just a lamentation about being adrift in a world with no horizon—a realm with no lights or omens. And more recent existentialists such as Teilhard de Chardin offer more personal accounts of liminality that might well serve as a gloss on Kennedy's tribulations during the Cuban missile crisis:

> For the first time in my life . . . I took the lamp and, leaving the zone of everyday occupations and relationships where everything seems clear, I went down into my inmost self, to the deep abyss whence I feel dimly that my power of action

emanates. At each step of the descent a new person was disclosed within me of whose name I was no longer sure, and who no longer obeyed me. And when I had to stop my exploration because the path faded from beneath my steps, I found a bottomless abyss at my feet, and out of it came—arising from I know not where—the current which I dare to call my life.[31]

Barring unforeseen complications, liminality is resolved for the tribal initiates when they are reincorporated into the culture in their new roles. Unfortunately, social dramas do not always have a happy ending in American society: liminality can lead to chaos and disaster. In their role as architects of the Vietnam War, former Ex Comm members struggled to improvise the metaphorical narratives that supposedly led to the triumphant resolution of the Cuban missile crisis.[32] In so doing, they threw combatants into the absurdity so well depicted in *Apocalypse Now*; all too many veterans have yet to find their bearings, let alone new metaphors.

This is not to suggest that liminality invariably leads to disaster in American society. In Turner's words: "Liminality can . . . be described as fructile chaos, a storehouse of possibilities . . . a striving after new forms and structures, a gestation process of modes appropriate to postliminal existence."[33] Liminality can give birth to new metaphors. As we shall see, a liminal interlude during the Cuban missile crisis engendered a new strategy. Kennedy and his associates found themselves betwixt and between metaphors—neither here nor there. As they framed their choices, the old metaphor of massive retaliation was decidedly dangerous in the nuclear age; and the thought of public negotiations evoked images of the feckless Chamberlain. The dilemma gave birth to the gradual escalation metaphor: a strategy designed to give an adversary the time and incentive to back down by escalating a crisis in incremental, carefully calibrated steps. As Bruner explains, these incipient metaphors begin as personal narratives, but— when improvised by elites—they become transformed into collective narratives.[34] This metamorphosis often scripts a would-be hero's legendary journey.

The foregoing gloss on the Cuban missile crisis raises pivotal methodological concerns: How can we gain access to an actor's metaphorical crisis narratives, and to those improvisations known as social dramas? And how can we come to better appreciate the liminal transitions in such dramas? And what are we to say about the invariably contesting responses to these questions? Both Turner and Geertz realize that—despite their interpretive practices—many colleagues view interpretive inquiry as mind reading or divination. Turner realizes that it may appear to others that he seeks magical insight into the inner life and conceptual world of others.

If one had the science-fiction means of penetrating into the minds of . . . actors, one would undoubtedly find . . . at almost any endopsychical level existing between the full brightness of conscious attention and the darker strata of the unconscious a set of ideas, images, concepts, [in a phrase, metaphorical narratives]. . . . These are models of what people believe they do, believe they ought to do, or would like to do.[35]

Turner does not believe in magic. The choice is not between positivism and divination. The interpretive struggle involves reading an actor's culture, not his mind, by accessing the preconscious realm betwixt and between self-serving conscious representations of the self and unconscious, undifferentiated instincts—a realm of more concern to the Freudians than to the rest of us. Avowedly interpretive accounts of crises cannot be built upon the sturdy foundation of physics, but neither should they be dismissed as repartee. Such interpretations invoke the insights of the humanities to make better sense of texts and performances.

Method

Many social scientists have turned away from a laws and instances ideal of explanation toward a cases and interpretations one, looking less for the sort of thing that connects planets and pendulums and more for the sort that connects chrysanthemums and swords.

—Clifford Geertz[36]

In order to contribute to the resolution of the questions that inform this study —the issues of crisis construction, management, and remembrance—I rely upon a simple procedure beset by complex difficulties. *After explicating vintage Kennedy, Nixon, and Kissinger crisis narratives found in their respective texts, I examine their performances to determine whether they improvised these narratives at critical junctures.* There is no difficulty locating such texts. Fortunately—for purposes of explication—these actors were consumed by crises. They wrote voluminously about what they took to be crises; indeed, their texts are concerned with little else. Perhaps Kundera understands why this is so:

We are all writers. The reason is that everyone has trouble accepting the fact that he will disappear unheard of and unnoticed in an indifferent universe, and everyone wants to make himself into a universe of words before it's too late.[37]

Kennedy, Nixon, and Kissinger did not fade from the political scene unnoticed; their wish was granted—they are remembered by their crises. Who can think of Kennedy without recalling the Cuban missile crisis? And surely Nixon and Watergate are linked inextricably in our collective imagination. Likewise, the redoubtable Kissinger shuttled from one crisis to another. The difficulty lies in interpreting the universe of words and deeds authored and improvised by these actors. I attempt to distill the notion of "crisis" that informs works such as *Why England Slept, Six Crises,* and *Diplomacy.* Likewise, relying upon my interpretation of the historical record, I attempt to show that these works foretold defining Kennedy, Nixon, and Kissinger crises. This is more than retrospective. I am, in effect, predicting that we can determine what will be construed as a crisis—and what will be disregarded—by explicating the archetypal crises narrated in an actor's texts.

I am not—to say the least—supremely confident about the interpretations I hazard. I am well aware that the interpretive process is self-confessional, and that

I am reading much into an actor's thoughts and deeds. With Isaiah Berlin, I hold social phenomenon such as crises are generated by "a complicated network of relationships involving every form of human intercourse, more and more insusceptible to tidy classification, more and more opaque to the theorist's vision."[38] But I am convinced of one thing: my interpretations will not be enshrined as *the* definitive, irrefutable take on these texts and deeds. I suspect that even if crises become a relic of the past, interpretations of these events will proliferate— Montaigne was right. This realization confronts us with a problematic of any interpretive inquiry: how are we to judge among contesting interpretations?

Turner's explication of the legendary life crisis of Thomas Becket illustrates the strengths and liabilities of cultural hermeneutics. Accordingly, I begin with his account of this saga. He develops a plausible, even compelling, account of actions that seem ineffable to the competition—Becket's martyrdom. Of course, not all scholars embrace Turner's interpretation; with Montaigne, he realizes that there is no end to interpretation. If Kennedy's, Nixon's, and Kissinger's wishes are granted, like Becket, their lives and crises will be the subject of disputation a thousand years hence.

In any case, as philosopher James Bohman observes, the importance, if not the inevitability, of interpretation is finally being recognized in disciplines that formerly eschewed humanistic approaches to inquiry. But ironically

> The more . . . interpretive disciplines proclaim the importance of interpretation in all of inquiry, the less there is agreement about what it is, what interpretive practices presuppose, and how to judge interpretive success and failures.[39]

Therefore, this methodological discussion concludes by addressing a problem that preoccupies those involved in indoor hermeneutics: How are we to judge among contesting interpretations?

CULTURAL HERMENEUTICS IN ACTION: TURNER'S ACCOUNT OF BECKET

> It is here, I think, that the social drama approach . . . can be shown to be a useful tool for . . . estimating the significance of general propensities in specific situations. Indeed, the Becket case lends itself almost too readily to treatment by the social dramatistic technique. Becket's public life was nothing if not dramatic, full of strong situations.
>
> —Victor Turner[40]

In order to illustrate the approach that informs this inquiry, I indulge in a brief historical interlude that harkens back to the year 1170. Thomas Becket, it may be recalled, was Archbishop of Canterbury, and, for a time, closest friend of his sovereign, Henry II. Not surprisingly, he became Henry's chancellor. However, rather than allow Henry to rule the church, he invited his own martyrdom.

The competition would have difficulty interpreting this seemingly puzzling behavior. Surely Becket was not a rational actor as the term is ordinarily understood: he did not cherish his survival above all else. On the contrary, although given abundant opportunities to recant, he did not. Further, Becket did not suffer from impediments to accurate cognitive processing: he knew full well that the king would not permit him to live once he refused the royal demands. Allison, for example, would have difficulty explaining the essence of Becket's decision. The political bureaucracy (represented by the aristocracy) and the ecclesiastical bureaucracy (personified by the pope) urged Becket to comply with the king's demands. Indeed, even the expectation of painful death did not persuade the archbishop to alter his course. Evidently, he did not dread extinction; he embraced it.

Given these difficulties, Turner advocates searching for the root paradigms (metaphorical narratives) that prescribed defiance and martyrdom. According to Turner, just as DNA determines human physiology, so root paradigms determine responses at critical junctures. These metaphorical narratives emerge from the preconscious when humans are forced to choose. Therefore, in order to make sense of Becket's martyrdom, Turner seeks cultural models in the minds of the actors, which he calls root paradigms:

> Paradigms of this fundamental sort reach down to the irreducible life stances of individuals, passing beneath conscious prehension to a fiduciary hold on what they sense to be axiomatic values, matters literally of life or death.[41]

Turner's search begins with the abundant biographical and historical accounts of Becket's tribulations. And, as he recognizes, it also relies upon the interpretive metaphors residing in his head. Turner's narrative is a saga of the dialectical interplay of mixed metaphors. He recounts the contradictory forces that beset the relationship between the sovereign and the archbishop, and the contradictory forces within the actors themselves. For example, while daring Becket to defy him, the king made overtures of friendship. Becket too, was ambivalent: he responded to the overtures only to insist that no compromise was possible.

Both men lived with these contradictions for a time: Becket accommodated the king's imperious demeanor, and countenanced the bullying and humiliations visited upon him. Though increasingly impatient, the king tolerated his friend's insubordination. Eventually, Henry insisted that only he should govern church and state. Becket broke with the king, resigned the chancellorship, and traded the pleasure of his sumptuous life at court for poverty, ruination, and untimely death. Turner interprets this transition as an initiation into Becket's root metaphor, a narrative that emerged when the archbishop's back was against the wall—Christian martyrdom:

> To an anthropologist the whole extraordinary business of Becket's life and death . . . takes on the stylized character of an initiation ceremony—an initiation into the status of martyr. . . . This pattern, stamped on the real events of history by a primary process at first unpent by royal edict but afterward governed by its own

inner law, took the . . . shape of the martyr's way . . . the glorious goal of the martyr's crown, to be won by a painful death rather than by a meritorious life.[42]

In the midst of this journey to martyrdom and sainthood, Becket—to continue Turner's narration—was cast into liminality. He believed he had embarked upon a righteous path by preserving the integrity of the church. Yet, he was reviled by the king, abandoned by his allies, and mortally threatened by savage noblemen. Estranged from his worldly life in the highest circles of church and state, betwixt and between metaphors, he endured the dark night of the soul in his humble abbey: in Turner's words, "a liminal place if ever there was."[43]

However, his time in his existential wilderness proved fruitful: a root metaphor emerged that would consume Becket's life with incendiary passion. As Turner explains:

It was in these circumstances [of abandonment and persecution] that courage came back to Becket from the paradigm glowing redly in his mind, the *via crucis* pattern of martyrdom.[44]

According to Turner, Becket emerged from liminality as the initiated Defender of the Faith. In so doing, he emulated the exemplar of Christian martyrdom, St. Stephen—an early believer murdered for defending the church against pagan Rome. Turner's evidence is circumstantial but intriguing. Becket left his refuge for St. Stephen's Chapel, and celebrated St. Stephen's Mass out of season. After the Mass, he literally bore his own cross before the king. Combative, yet serene—or so the legend goes—he steadfastly refused to comply with Henry's decrees.

Decidedly ambivalent, so to speak, the king allowed Becket to escape his wrath, at least for a time. As Turner explains: "It is hard to separate love from hate in the relationship between these two men, and harder to define the nature of either."[45] Eventually, however, the king prevailed upon his knights to commit the infamous murder in the cathedral. As Turner notes, Becket's final moments are portrayed in contradictory ways in literature and art. This is as it should be:

Becket became himself a powerful, "numinous" symbol precisely because, like all dominant or focal symbols, he represented a coincidence of opposites . . . a tension between opposite poles of meaning. Becket was at once lion and lamb, proud and meek.[46]

In recounting Turner's explication of Becket, I am not suggesting that recent American leaders should be likened to Becket: I am not proposing the canonization of Richard Nixon, nor am I urging that twentieth century politicians are governed by visions of martyrdom, although the thought crossed my mind in considering Kennedy's bravado during his defining life crisis. (As Robert Smith Thompson notes, photographers were on hand when the president and Mrs. Kennedy attended Mass at St. Stephen the Martyr Church in Georgetown during the crisis. As the Becket and Kennedy legends suggest, narratives of martyrdom have virtually universal resonance.)[47] Rather, I am suggesting that crises are about the invocation and improvisation of mixed metaphors. Explicating these metaphors is—to say the least vexatious. In a satirical piece entitled, "No Smoking Gun," Alexander Cockburn invites us to imagine how the Becket saga might be depicted by today's "spin doctors."

What would occur today if a small Canterbury newspaper claimed that witnesses heard the king insist that his noblemen must rid him of the meddlesome priest? Relying upon "credible deniability," surely the British Secret Service would dismiss the claim as "almost certainly disinformation, either from the French court or from the papacy." And, naturally, Henry's press secretary would insist that Becket, "was not only a very great man but a close personal friend with whom there had been quarrels . . . which have long been settled." And lambasting one of his favorite targets—the popular press—Cockburn imagines that the *Los Angeles Times* would editorialize that for the Canterbury paper's claim to be true, "There would have to be a 'smoking gun,' in the form of sworn statements from the assassins about the King's request, or a facsimile of any written orders by Henry II demanding Becket's death."[48] In the absence of such a "smoking gun," how shall we evaluate contesting interpretations of recent crises?

JUDGING CONTESTING INTERPRETATIONS

> What if . . . there is no such thing as a theory of interpretation? Does it follow that we are no longer in a position to understand what we read? Or is it rather the case that hermeneutical theories make such understanding impossible?
> —Stanley Rosen[49]

While, to be sure, the practitioners of outdoor hermeneutics defend their interpretations against the competition, apparently it is the devotees of indoor hermeneutics who are preoccupied with the theoretic difficulty that concerns us here—evaluating contesting interpretations. As Rosen concludes, a review of the literature suggests that the problem is far worse than Montaigne imagined: because diverse interpretations abound, theories—and metatheories—of interpretation proliferate.[50] There is probably more dispute about theories of interpretation than about the various contests between particular interpretations themselves. As Rosen complains:

> Reading is for us today no longer a pleasure . . . it is a problem. . . . The sophisticated professor cannot read a page without methods and antimethods. Parasitic upon texts notorious for their obscurity is a thicket of revised doctoral dissertations, praised or blamed by reviewers.[51]

Given this situation, it is futile to enter into the fray by embracing one of the many partisan theories of interpretation. Quite obviously, authors and readers can still communicate despite the lack of solidly grounded interpretive theory. Specifically, we can attain a better understanding of particular crises without the imprimatur of a venerable theory of interpretation. Second, defending my favored—albeit controversial—theory of interpretation would be futile and distracting: rather than defending my interpretation of particular actors and crises, I would be defending an esoteric and dubious theory of interpretation. And rather than arguing about particular crises, I would be struggling to convince the more extreme postmodernists (who hold that all interpretation is fictive) that one interpretation can be better than another.[52] I would rather expend my efforts trying to convince the competition that they, too, are interpreters, and that their interpretations would be enhanced by giving the proper place to the role of metaphorical narratives in getting a handle on crises.

This is not to suggest that I am indifferent to the problematic posed by the seeming inevitability of contesting crisis interpretations. On the contrary, I presuppose four criteria for evaluating these interpretations. Given the theoretical acrimony, I doubt that I could persuade those with contrary beliefs to adopt my presuppositions. (For example, I am not sure how I would persuade the more extreme postmodernists that interpretations should be internally consistent, and that they should fit the facts.) I offer a straightforward response to the problematic posed by evaluating diverse interpretations: I simply articulate what I regard as appropriate criteria for judging crisis interpretation. This articulation is far from definitive, but it does reveal the first principles that I would like to believe inform my interpretive strategy.

My interpretive efforts are guided by four criteria. The first two are widely accepted epistemological standards for judging virtually any explanation or interpretation—they can be dispatched quickly. However, since (as I have emphasized) interpretation reads meaning into events, the interpreter confronts controversial semiotic issues.

1. *Coherence.* Interpretation should not be self-contradictory; it should be internally consistent. It must be remembered, of course, that it is we who supply the inner coherence of understanding, not the events themselves. (Indeed, as I note below, I presuppose that personal and social reality are about the interplay of contradictory forces.) In any case, I am simply urging the obvious: we should not contradict ourselves. (For example, it is one thing to have a dialectical understanding of human reality; it is quite another to simultaneously claim that reality is contradictory *and* that it is non-contradictory.) Coherence, of course, does not suffice. The most bizarre conspiracy theories are seamless and consistent—that's their main attraction.

2. *Correspondence.* Accordingly, an interpretation must fit the facts known and those discovered. There is, of course, no immaculate perception: our interpretive scheme determines the facts we privilege and those we dismiss or ignore. Nevertheless, an interpretation should account for the facts adduced by competing schemes—it must, as I have stressed, be on target. In a phrase, comprehensiveness is a virtue. (I would like to think that my inquiry offers a robust interpretation of Kennedy's defining crises, and of Nixon's and Kissinger's crises and non-crises.)

To be sure, since events such as crises are thickly described, it is often difficult to distill fact from interpretation. (Is it a thin or a thick description, for example, to claim that Kennedy experienced intense political pressure to appear tough on Cuba?) Given such difficulties, I resort to the extreme examples favored by philosophers struggling to make a point: an interpretation that narrates Abraham Lincoln's role in advising Khrushchev is counterfactual. But as we shall see in the next chapter, there is no need to resort to extremes. Recently discovered facts about the Cuban missile crisis cry out for interpretation. These events include: Robert Kennedy's numerous secret meetings with Anatoly Dobrynin; the president's secret meeting with his most trusted advisors after the last Ex Comm meeting; and the secret deal that resolved the crisis.

3. *Context*. Contextualizing a text or performance is the heart and soul of the interpretive inquiry; and, as Geertz recognizes, it is also the most vexing:

> The besetting sin of interpretive approaches to anything is that they tend to resist . . . conceptual articulation and thus to escape systematic modes of assessment. You either grasp an interpretation or you do not, see the point of it or you do not, accept it or you do not.[53]

While the process of contextualizing can be described, the success of the endeavor itself is a matter of highly subjective interpretation, as Geertz suggests. Contextualizing a crisis clearly involves embedding it in a historical, cultural, and political milieu; and it also involves coming to appreciate an actor's lived experience and conceptual imagination. But what we ultimately crave is *an* experience, the Holy Grail of interpretive inquiry: an epiphany, an ultimate "Aha!" experience when suddenly everything comes together and makes sense. But there seldom is—to invoke my overused metaphors for the last time—a smoking gun or a bull's-eye. Those of us who interpret crises settle for much less. Our exegetical efforts are rewarded only by an occasional insight that brings a few things together. The essence of such insights remains elusive and ill-defined—"I know it when I see it!"

Like most analysts, I have had these intimations of insight. For example, like many colleagues, I struggled to make sense of the fact that Khrushchev sent Kennedy two seemingly inconsistent missives. The first proposed a congenial settlement of the crisis: the Soviets would remove the missiles if the United States promised not to invade Cuba. However, the next day Kennedy received a more strident tract in which Khrushchev insisted that the United States must remove its missiles from Turkey. An interview with Raymond Garthoff of the Brookings Institution put these events in context. He revealed that Robert Kennedy met secretly with Dobrynin just after the first letter was received, and proposed the missile trade. Dobrynin corroborates this account, and indicates that he communicated the proposal to his superiors. Khrushchev quickly changed his demands to get the best possible deal.[54]

In any case, contextualizing is more art than science. As we have seen, scientific explanation involves subsuming particular events under mechanical-causal laws. Context is irrelevant—at least in textbook applications of classical physics. For example, in any culture the behavior of falling objects is explained by the laws of gravity—context is irrelevant. However, in practicing the art of crisis interpretation we must be attentive to a variety of personal, cultural and histori-cal contexts, for we seek the culturally transmitted narratives that guide the con-struction, management and remembrance of a crisis. (A crisis in Ethiopia precip-itated by civil war differs markedly from a crisis precipitated by a symbolic per-formance that poses no threat to national survival or identity.)

Despite the symbolic turn in international relations, crisis interpretation is not an arcane art. As Geertz stresses:

> The whole point to a semiotic approach to culture . . . is to aid us in gaining access to the conceptual world in which our subjects live so that we can, in some extended sense of the term, converse with them.[55]

This project is akin to better understanding another culture. To be sure, given our preexisting sensibilities, we cannot become natives. But surely our under-standing is enhanced by speaking their language and by grasping their concep-tual world—a realm of narratives and improvisations. This understanding, of course, is tentative and incomplete. Geertz's admonition about the art of ethno-graphy applies to those of us who read meaning into and out of the texts and performances authored by exotics inside the Beltway:

> [The problem is to] steer between overinterpretation and underinterpretation, reading more into things than reason permits and less into them than it demands. Where the first sort of mistake, telling stories only a professor can believe, has been much noted . . . the second, reducing people to ordinary chaps out, like the rest of us, for money, sex, status and power . . . has been much less so. . . . We are surrounded . . . neither by Martians nor by less well got-up editions of our-selves.[56]

I suspect that those inside the Beltway are ordinary chaps in that their lives are beset by contradictions. However, to paraphrase F. Scott Fitzgerald, elites are different: they are bedeviled by the peculiar contradictions that vex those trying to make history.

4. *Dialectical presuppositions.* In interpreting an event, analysts invariably read their preconceptions into the text. As Habermas observes:

> Hermeneutical understanding cannot enter into a question without prejudice; on the contrary, it is unavoidably biased by the context in which the understanding subject has first acquired his schemata of interpretation.[57]

Such bias cannot be escaped; it can only be acknowledged. For example, we must presuppose one of two things about the self: it is invariably static and co-herent, or it is beset by the dialectical interplay of contending forces. The com-petition assumes the former. Realists offer the clearest case when they presup-pose that decision-making is the unitary outcome of rational actors. Curiously, Allison argues that the decision-making process is often the outcome of bureau-cratic competition, but he does not consider the possibility that actors themselves may not be of one mind. (Freudians—and others who eschew reductive approaches to the self—might suggest that Allison's bureaucratic politics is writ small in the struggles between conflicting forces within an actor's personality.)

Likewise, cognitive approaches presuppose that actors are unitary selves governed by an overarching motive—the will to truth. Jervis' gloss on Nixon's behavior during his Watergate crisis provides a quintessential example:

> Thus if we did not know better it would be tempting to argue that the contradictory and erratic behavior displayed by Richard Nixon in Watergate . . . shows that "Nixon" is not a single individual at all, but rather a title for the set of behaviors that are produced by the interaction of conflicting entities, each pursuing its own narrow interests in ignorance of or indifference to any wider goals of the "general Nixon interest."[58]

Given my dialectical bias, I do not know better. With playwright Friedrich Durrenmatt I contend that, "He who exposes himself to the paradoxical exposes himself to reality."[59] I interpret "Nixon" as a struggle between two personas: the low tragedy of Willy Loman, and the high tragedy of Richard III. (Chapter 4 depicts the eventual triumph of the hapless salesman in Nixon, the persona that wanted to be "well-liked.")

Similarly, Blight (as we have seen) develops a one-dimensional account that reduces Kennedy and his trusted advisers to prudent men overwhelmed by nuclear angst. To reiterate, this dimension must be given proper weight. But could it be that another dimension of Kennedy's personality—his insatiable desire to inscribe himself in history as a profile in courage—got him into the fearful predicament in the first place?

As Turner suggests, political actors are vexed by such mixed metaphors, indeed, they *are* mixed metaphors. Unaware of these irreconcilable, contesting, preconscious narratives operating just beneath the surface, their life-crises are often initiations into liminality. He concludes:

> Men . . . heavily involved in jural-political, overt and conscious structure are not free to mediate and speculate on the combinations and oppositions of thought; they are themselves too crucially involved in the combinations and oppositions of social and political structure and stratification. . . . But in ritual liminality they are placed . . . outside the total system . . . transient, they become men apart. . . .[60]

Kennedy may have recognized his conflicted nature; perhaps he was haunted by the ever-present danger that something might snap. James Reston reported that during the height of the civil rights demonstrations in the summer of 1963, Kennedy allowed that he was besieged by problems on every side. He astonished an audience by reciting a Shakespearean lamentation:

> The Sun's o'ercast with blood: fair day, Adieu!
> Which is the side that I must go withal?
> I am both; each army hath a hand;
> And in their rage, I having hold of both,
> They whirl asunder and dismember me.[61]

NOTES

1. Steven Weinberg, "Sokal's Hoax," *The New York Review*, August 8, 1996, 11.

2. Clifford Geertz, *Local Knowledge* (New York: Basic Books, 1983), 21.

3. Ibid., 69.

4. Hans-George Gadamer, "Rhetoric, Hermeneutics, and the Critique of Ideology: Metacritical Comments on *Truth and Method*," *The Hermeneutics Reader*, Kurt Mueller-Vollmer, ed., (New York: Continuum, 1989), 284.

5. Kenneth Burke, *Performance and Change* (Los Altos: Hermes, 1954), 10.

6. Victor Turner, "Dewey, Dilthey, and Drama" in *Anthropology of Experience*, Turner and Edward M. Bruner, eds., (Urbana: University of Illinois Press, 1986), 35.

7. Ibid.

8. Roger D. Abrahams, "Ordinary and Extraordinary Experience," in *Anthropology of Experience*, Turner and Edward M. Bruner, eds., (Urbana: University of Illinois Press, 1986), 63.

9. Those with philosophic background will recognize that my analysis of disruption is indebted to Heidegger; Zygmunt Bauman offers an accessible account of this Teutonic philosopher in his *Hermeneutics as Social Science* (New York: Columbia University Press, 1978), Chapter 7.

10. McGeorge Bundy, *Danger and Survival* (New York: Random House, 1988), 414. Bundy notes that perhaps the president did not use all of these oft quoted words in his response, but—according to Bundy—"there is nothing wrong with the music."

11. Quoted by Bauman, 156.

12. In 1992 McNamara learned that the Soviets had 162 nuclear warheads in Cuba; see his account in *In Retrospect* (New York: Times Books, 1995), 341.

13. See Walter R. Fisher's account of Habermas and his insightful exploration of narrativity in his *Human Communication as Narration: Toward a Philosophy of Reason, Value, and Action* (Columbia: South Carolina University Press, 1987), 91.

14. Turner, "Dewey, Dilthey, and Drama," 35.

15. Victor Turner, "Social Dramas and Stories About Them," *Critical Inquiry* 7 (1980): 141.

16. Geertz, *Local Knowledge,* 31.

17. Fisher, 58.

18. Quoted by Fisher, 65.

19. Burke, 12–14.

20. Isaiah Berlin, "On political Judgment," in *New York Review*, October 3, 1966, 27.

21. Turner, "Dewey, Dilthey, and Drama," 35–36.

22. Victor Turner, *Drama, Fields and Metaphors,* 13.

23. Bruner, "Introduction," 18.

24. Bruner, "Ethnography as Narrative" 153.

25. Geertz, "Epilogue" in *Anthropology of Experience*, Turner and Edward M. Bruner, eds., (Urbana: University of Illinois Press, 1986), 373.

26. Turner, *The Ritual Process* (Chicago: Aldine Company, 1969), 168.

27. Abrahams, 45–46.

28. Turner, *Dramas, Fields and Metaphors*, 38.

29. Arnold Van Gennep, *The Rites of Passage* (Chicago: University of Chicago Press, 1960), 10–11, 65–115.

30. Turner, "Dewey, Dilthey and Drama," 41.

31. Pierre Teilhard de Chardin, *The Divine Milieu* (New York: Harper & Row 1960), 6. I wish to thank my former research assistant, Diane Welch, for calling de Chardin's observation to my attention.

32. See McNamara's confession regarding his reliance upon misleading metaphors in *In Retrospect.* In Chapter 3, I argue that gradual escalation doctrine was one of the most destructive strategies that emerged during a liminal phase of the Cuban missile crisis; it became the template for American conduct of the Vietnam war.

33. Turner, "Dewey, Dilthey and Drama," 42.

34. Bruner, "Ethnography as Narrative," 143.

35. Turner, "Dewey, Dilthey and Drama," 36.

36. Geertz, *Local Knowledge,* 19.

37. Milan Kundera, *The Book of Laughter and Forgetting* (New York: Penguin, 1987), 106.

38. Quoted by Kenneth Baker in "Ideas as an Unpredictable Force in History," in the "Book Review," *San Francisco Examiner & Chronicle* (May 25, 1997): 10.

39. James Bohman, "Introduction," in *The Interpretive Turn,* David Hiley et al. eds. (Ithaca: Cornell University Press, 1991), 1.

40. Turner, *Dramas, Fields and Metaphors,* 61–62.

41. Ibid., 64.

42. Ibid., 72.

43. Ibid., 87.

44. Ibid., 84.

45. Ibid., 96.

46. Ibid., 88–89.

47. Robert Smith Thompson, *The Missiles of October* (New York: Simon and Schuster, 1992), 248.

48. Alexander Cockburn, "No Smoking Gun," *The Nation,* (December 23, 1996), 8.

49. Stanley Rosen, *Hermeneutics as Politics* (Oxford: Oxford University Press, 1987), 142.

50. See, for example, G. B. Madison's account of the metatheoretic debate between Hirsch and Gadamer in his *The Hermeneutics of Postmodernity* (Bloomington: Indiana University Press, 1990), Chapter 2.

51. Rosen, 144.

52. Pauline Rosenau offers an adroit account of postmodernism and its attendant controversies in her *Post-Modernism and the Social Science* (Princeton: Princeton University Press, 1992); esp. Chapter 1.

53. Clifford Geertz, *Interpretation of Cultures* (New York: Basic Books, 1973), 24.

54. Interview with Raymond Garthoff at the Brookings Institution, August 1989. Anatoly Dobrynin, corroborates many of Garthoff's claims in *In Confidence* (New York: Times Books, 1995), 84–88.

55. Geertz, *Interpretation of Cultures,* 24.

56. Geertz, *Local Knowledge,* 16.

57. Jürgen Habermas, "On Hermeneutics' Claim to Universality" in *The Hermeneutics Reader,* in Kurt Mueller-Vollmer, ed., (New York: Continuum, 1989), 296.

58. Robert Jervis, *Perception and Misperception in International Politics* (Princeton: Princeton University Press, 1976), 24.

59. Friedrich Durrenmatt, *The Physicists* (New York: Grove Press, 1984), 86.

60 Turner, 64.

61. Reported by James Reston in the *New York Times,* November 23, 1963, 1. These lines are from *The Life and Death of King John, III, i.*

CHAPTER 3

THE ESSENCE OF INDECISION

The essence of ultimate decision remains impenetrable to the observer—often, indeed, to the decider himself. . . . There will always be the dark and tangled stretches in the decision-making process—mysterious even to those who may be most intimately involved.

—John F. Kennedy[1]

This is not the first account of the Cuban missile crisis, and surely it is not the last. The "missiles of October" spawned a cottage industry that flourishes to this day. The output is impressive: countless articles and books, televised docudramas, and various plays. While the popular media mass produce the Kennedy legend, hand-crafted pieces put different spins on the episode. The output is so voluminous that it evokes backlash such as E. A. Cohen's "Why We Should Stop Studying the Cuban Missile Crisis." Clearly, there is no end to interpretation. Like any commentator on international crises, I would be remiss if I did not discuss those waning fall days in 1962, a time when—to paraphrase Nietzsche—the world stared at the abyss and the abyss stared back.

But what can yet another discussion contribute to the literature? Have we not reached the fin de siècle of Cuban missiles crisis studies? Has it not all been said? It should be clear to any writer that he or she will not pen *the* enduring account of the mother of all crises. Such an account would close the doors on our cottage industry, the guild in which we labor as apprentices or journeymen— layoffs are unwelcome. Such worries, of course, are impurely academic. Since we are quarrelsome interpreters of the Ex Comm's contesting interpretations, there is little danger of lasting consensus. I join the fray by developing a novel account of the construction, management, and remembrance of the Cuban missile crisis. I have three concerns:

Why did Kennedy make a crisis move? I contend that the missiles posed a *problem* for Kennedy's international bargaining reputation and domestic political situation; but the *crisis* was with himself—it was his dark night of the soul. In the aftermath of a series of foreign policy defeats, he construed the missiles of October as the ultimate test of his authenticity: Would he be remembered as a Churchill or a Chamberlain?

How should Kennedy's crisis management be evaluated and interpreted? I argue that—not unlike his handling of the Bay of Pigs debacle—his management of the Cuban missile crisis was indecisive. Relying upon recent information, I show that Kennedy quickly escalated the crisis to the point where he and his brother believed that nuclear war was imminent; and yet, his private negotiations (his brother playing the part of Hermes) with the Soviets culminated with the secret deal—a capitulation to Khrushchev's demands. The confusion climaxed in Robert Kennedy's "Black Saturday" meeting with Dobrynin in which it appears that he simultaneously gave the ambassador an ultimatum (which was not to be represented as an ultimatum to Khrushchev) and acquiesced to the secret deal (an arrangement kept secret from most of the Ex Comm, Congress, and the American people). I develop a highly speculative interpretation of these puzzling actions. Given the complexity of Kennedy's efforts at impression management, I narrate a strange and complex saga of cruel surprises, mixed metaphors, intractable dilemmas, and lapses into liminality and desperation. In the end, I entertain an ironic possibility: Was Kennedy's indecisiveness a blessing in disguise? Could it be that his vacillation frightened Khrushchev, prompting him to dismantle the missiles?

How is the crisis remembered? The guardians of the Kennedy legend enshrine the crisis as the brief, shining moment of Camelot. The young leader jousted on the abyss, didn't give an inch, and miraculously emerged alive. The impact of the legend on popular culture is ubiquitous but relatively harmless: likening a celebrity such as Roseanne Barr to Kennedy because she went "eyeball to eyeball" with an adversary and didn't blink first is nothing worse than poor journalism; and paying fabulous sums for anything touched by the Kennedys is merely poor taste. However, as several Ex Comm members recognize, the impact of the crisis on the formulation and execution of American foreign policy is profound and pernicious: the remembered crisis encouraged a Soviet arms race and served as the template for American nuclear strategy, the Indochina War, and other crises such as Desert Shield.

WHY DID KENNEDY MAKE A CRISIS MOVE?

> He well knows what snares are spread about his path. . . . But he has put to hazard his ease, his security, his interest, his power, even his . . . popularity. . . . He is traduced and abused for his supposed motives. He will remember that obloquy is a necessary ingredient in the composition of all true glory. . . . He may live long, he may do much. But here is the summit. He never can exceed what he does this day.
>
> —Edmund Burke's eulogy for Charles Fox, the frontispiece of
> *Profiles in Courage*[2]

Kennedy defined Soviet actions as a crisis because he likened the Soviet challenge to the ultimate existential crises indelibly etched in memory and inscribed in his texts—heroic sagas that reveal the truth about men and events. The plausibility of this interpretation is far from obvious. Accordingly, I begin by considering prevailing accounts of Kennedy's crisis move. Like most analysts, I adopt a hermeneutics of suspicion—a skepticism that prevents me from taking an actor's public representation of himself at face value. Therefore, I reject what I regard as the legendary account of Kennedy's crisis move, the position that Kennedy publicly enunciated—and privately rejected: namely, that the crisis was a provocative and unmistakable threat to the survival of the United States, if not the entire western hemisphere. I also evaluate more filigreed academic analyses that conclude that Kennedy was motivated by a variety of factors such as international and domestic political concerns. While these interpretations clarify Kennedy's international and domestic problems, they fail to account for the disproportionate risks he hazarded during his crisis.

The Legendary Account

The ultimate impact of the missile crisis was wider than Cuba. . . . Before the missile crisis people might have feared that we would use our power extravagantly or not at all. But the thirteen days gave the world—even the Soviet Union —a sense of American determination and responsibility.

—Arthur Schlesinger, Jr.[3]

Early on the evening of October 22, 1962, Kennedy enunciated the narrative that would attain canonical status in the American civic religion. In a speech seen and heard throughout the land, he claimed that, in a brazen and unprovoked move, the Soviets had secretly deployed missiles in Cuba.[4] Worse yet, these nuclear weapons undoubtedly threatened the entire western hemisphere. Kennedy claimed that "The urgent transformation of Cuba into an important strategic base . . . constitutes an explicit threat to the peace and security of all the Americas." [5]

The president assured the public that urgent action was required, and that it was being undertaken. He stressed that such actions:

. . . will not prematurely or unnecessarily risk the costs of worldwide nuclear war in which even the fruits of victory would be ashes in our mouth—but neither will we shrink from that risk at any time it must be faced.[6]

And this, legend has it, is precisely what the president did. He fearlessly jousted on the abyss, never retreated, and miraculously triumphed. The most compelling demythologizing is provided by the president himself and his principal advisers. In a retrospective he allowed that the Soviet provocation was not an explicit military threat; it was a decidedly symbolic confrontation. Preoccupied with impression management, Kennedy urged that mere appearances could undermine the bargaining reputation of American leaders:

[The Soviet deployment] was an effort to materially change the balance of power
. . . and they were planning to open to the world the fact that they had these
missiles so close to the United States; *not that they were intending to fire them*
[italics mine], because if they were going to get into a nuclear struggle they have
their own missiles in the Soviet Union. But it would have politically changed the
balance of power. It would have appeared to, and appearances contribute to
reality.[7]

The private Ex Comm meetings secretly recorded by Kennedy are more telling. During the first day of the crisis, Kennedy determined that the missiles were
not a strategic threat requiring urgent action. While he expressed concern about
the effect of Soviet actions on American bargaining reputation, he seemed fixa-
ted upon a concern that was not expressed publicly—domestic politics. At the
evening Ex Comm meeting on October 16 he observed:

It doesn't make any difference if you get blown up by an ICBM flying from the
Soviet Union or one that was ninety miles away. Geography doesn't mean that
much. What difference does it make; they have enough missiles [within Soviet
borders] to blow us up anyway.[8]

McNamara averred that a missile's destination is more important than its
origins; "a missile is a missile." They agreed that they confronted a political, not
a military, problem.[9] It is worth noting that, in retrospect, McNamara emphasizes
that the missiles were a symbolic, not a strategic, threat:

As far as I am concerned, it [Soviet missiles in Cuba] made *no* difference. . . .
What difference would the extra forty [missiles] have made to the overall balance? We had some five thousand strategic warheads as against their three hun-
dred. Can anyone seriously tell me that having 340 would have made any difference? The military balance wasn't changed. I didn't believe it then, and I don't
believe it now.[10]

Indeed, during a retrospective symposium on the crisis—the Hawk's Cay
conference—McNamara implied that no crisis existed:

[McNamara] I think the literature is simply wrong in reporting our concern about
the date on which the missiles would become operational.
[Nye] But if you felt that time was running out quickly. . . .
[McNamara] I didn't think time made any difference.
[Carnesale] But wait a minute. Time pressure is what makes a crisis. Now you're
telling us that there was not time pressure—so why was there a crisis? I don't
understand.[11]

Responding to an interjection by Allison, McNamara turned to another issue:
Carnesale's query was never answered. The question, however, remains: "So
why was there a crisis?" Why, indeed!

Prevailing Perspectives

The American government controls and selectively releases crucial information. Key former participants like . . . McNamara and Robert Kennedy provide rich recollections (including "doctored" memoirs) [that] can shape interpretations.
—Barton J. Bernstein[12]

Interpreting the crisis may be even more daunting than Bernstein suggests: not only do the key players disagree regarding salient issues, they accuse one another of dishonesty. For example, Pierre Salinger (Kennedy's press secretary) claims that the Kennedy administration had long-standing plans to invade Cuba in October 1962. But McNamara maintains that while he could understand Cuban and Soviet apprehension about such an invasion, there were no such plans. Salinger urges that McNamara's denial doesn't wash. "His insistence that the U. S. never intended to invade Cuba, either before or during the crisis, flies in the face of the facts."[13]

In any case, as of this writing, most influential accounts concur that a crisis occurred for two not unrelated reasons: American bargaining reputation and the Kennedy presidency were on the line. It appears that these were formidable concerns. However, understandable apprehension regarding international and domestic politics does not account for the apparent confusion and grave risks.

The concern with bargaining reputation was not misplaced. On two occasions in September 1962, the president vowed that offensive Soviet weapons would not be tolerated in Cuba.[14] Allowing the missiles to remain would undermine American credibility among friends and foes. NATO allies might well look askance at American commitments and assurances. Worse yet, Khrushchev might be emboldened to test American resolve in venues such as Berlin and Turkey.

It was also clear that Kennedy had to come to the aid of his party. It was no secret that just as Cuba played a pivotal role in the 1960 campaign, so it was also playing a decisive role in the unfolding 1962 congressional elections. The Bay of Pigs fiasco suggested that, contrary to campaign promises, Kennedy did not have the best solution to the Cuban problem. And strident Republican critics disputed frequent reassurances from the Kennedy administration that no Soviet missiles were being deployed in Cuba. As Kennedy quipped just after the discovery of the Soviet bases: "We've just elected Capehart [to the Senate] . . . and Ken Keating [the most outspoken Republican critic] will probably be our next president."[15] Apparently, Kennedy feared that he would be impeached if he could not compel Khrushchev to remove the missiles. In his *Thirteen Days,* Robert Kennedy recounts a private conversation with the president that seems to encapsulate their mutual concerns. The attorney general observed:

It really looks mean, doesn't it? But then, really there was no other choice. If they get this mean on this one in our part of the world, what will they do on the next? I just don't think there was any choice. . . . If you hadn't acted, you would have been impeached. The president thought for a moment and said, "That's what I think—I would have been impeached."[16]

Surely, Kennedy was not indifferent to these international and domestic political concerns. Yet there is much that is puzzling about the behavior of this ordinarily pragmatic politician. As Neustadt observed, the crisis marks a whole "new dimension of risk"[17] that seems to elude prevailing approaches to international politics:

1. Ambiguous political challenges do not necessarily precipitate crises, nor do unmistakable military threats, for that matter. For example, the deployment of American missiles in Turkey did not precipitate a Turkish missile crisis; and Western Europeans did make crisis moves when the Soviets deployed missiles minutes from their capitals. To be sure, the Soviets and Europeans did not appreciate being targeted by missiles in close proximity, but there was no crisis response, no sense of urgency and impending war. Leaders did not issue public threats and demands, blockade adversaries, or put their armed services on high alert or issue ultimatums.

The case of Charles de Gaulle is telling. Informed of the crisis—but not consulted—by ambassador Charles Bohlen, he intimated that a more seasoned American leader might have acted differently. According to the ambassador, de Gaulle averred that the French had long grown accustomed to threats from various continental powers—they could live with it. The general added, rather haughtily, that he understood that the United States had not had a comparable experience.[18]

And, turning to American experience, Kennedy's successors did not make crisis moves in response to certain dire military threats. For example, the Johnson administration did not promote a crisis when the Soviets deployed weapons much more formidable than the vulnerable land-based missiles of 1962—nuclear submarines. And, the next chapter tries to account for the fact that even a "quantum leap" in Soviet strategic capability did not prompt Nixon to make a crisis move. Why, then, did Kennedy's political problems become the most unnerving crisis of the Cold War? What was unique about Kennedy and his situation?

2. Why didn't Kennedy define his international and domestic political concerns as an endurable problem he could live with, rather than an intolerable crisis demanding urgent, perilous resolution? True, diplomacy might have failed, but why didn't he give it a chance? Why the haste? Some claim that he couldn't negotiate because Khrushchev deceived him. True. But Kennedy was no newcomer to political machinations: surely the author of *Why England Slept* and successful campaigner knew that candor was not the hallmark of politics. In any case, Kissinger was deceived by Soviet diplomats about the submarine base, yet he negotiated successfully with Dobrynin. Others suggest that the Cold War atmosphere militated against such patience.[19] Yet, despite (or because of?) the Cold War zeitgeist, Eisenhower allowed himself eighteen months to resolve the Suez situation privately and secretly despite overt nuclear threats to American allies.

3. Specifically, why did Kennedy reject the suggestions of Adlai Stevenson (his United Nations ambassador) and Charles Bohlen and Llewellyn Thompson (the Ex Comm's respected Sovietologists) to try secret negotiations before going

going public   turning point

public? As these advisers urged, secret diplomacy would give Khrushchev the opportunity to back down without public humiliation; moreover, it would allow Kennedy more flexibility. Khrushchev's speech writer, Fyodor Burlatsky, claims that he is virtually certain that had Kennedy followed this advice, the unnerving crisis escalation would have been prevented, and the conflict would have been resolved diplomatically[20]

4. It is a misnomer to characterize the crisis as the model of gradual escalation. Why did Kennedy rapidly escalate the confrontation? To be sure, he began by resisting the advice of the "hawks." According to Richard Rhodes, General Curtis LeMay (Air Force chief of staff) urged: "The Russian bear has always been eager to stick his paw in Latin American waters. Now we've got him in a trap, let's take his leg off right up to his testicles. On second thought, let's take off his testicles, too."[21]

Despite his apparent need to prove himself, Kennedy rejected such macho psychosis. What is more impressive, he also rejected the advice of more respected hawks (including his brother and Dean Acheson) to attack Cuba immediately. Initially he seemed to understand that rapidly escalating crises could careen out of control. He urged his associates to read Tuchman's *Guns of August* (a depiction of the misinterpretations and unforeseen circumstances that precipitated a war that no one wanted, World War I). Yet, in a not-so-gradual escalation, in thirteen days he dramatically increased the risk of thermonuclear war by going public; blockading Cuba; mobilizing the armed forces for an invasion of Cuba; placing the Strategic Air Command on an unprecedented state of alert (Defcon 2); and issuing an ultimatum to the Soviet ambassador.

5. Why did Kennedy decide to turn the confrontation into a public spectacle, a social drama to be resolved with great alarm and fanfare while the world watched? Surely going public made it more difficult for either side to compromise without public humiliation. Some claim that the impending congressional elections prompted Kennedy to come to the aid of his party by publicly teaching Khrushchev a lesson. However, many of the Ex Comm members were not personally vulnerable to electoral politics. Moreover, those who were, feared that the confrontation might last many months, and that an unresolved confrontation with the Soviets and Cubans would be a political liability. Only in retrospect is it possible to script the episode as a thirteen day social drama.

6. And, with Tuchman, Kennedy knew that naval engagements often escalate all too quickly into full scale war. Yet, despite his apprehension, he put the blockade in place. (Well aware that a blockade can be construed as an act—if not a declaration—of war, he euphemistically called the blockade a "quarantine.")

7. As a student of history who profited from reading Tuchman, Kennedy undoubtedly understood that subordinates get out of control in crisis situations, and that serious mishaps are virtually inevitable—things seldom go as planned. Yet he persisted.

8. What is most disturbing, the president directed his brother to issue an ultimatum to the Soviets: withdraw the missiles in twenty-four hours or face an

American attack. True, Robert Kennedy simultaneously offered the secret deal. Nevertheless, as the Kennedy brothers and their associates feared, such a move foments crisis instability: given a serious threat, a weaker adversary has the incentive to strike first.

9. Kennedy did not hazard such grave risks in other crises. During the Bay of Pigs episode he resisted considerable pressure to escalate by injecting American troops and aircraft. It is puzzling that he did not escalate this non-nuclear crisis, yet he escalated the much more fearful Cuban missile crisis despite apprehension about Soviet retaliation. And during the penultimate Berlin crisis of 1961, Kennedy threatened nuclear retaliation if the Soviets seized Berlin, but he did not turn the confrontation into a public spectacle, nor did he issue an ultimatum or place the Strategic Air Command on an unprecedented state of alert. On the contrary, he tolerated what many construed as a public defeat—the infamous Berlin Wall. Why, then, did he become so exercised by Cuba? We cannot read his mind, but perhaps we can read the texts that depict his crisis narratives.

Kennedy Crises: Theory and Practice

Even with the most accurate contemporary records which may be kept, I am still impressed, from personal experience as well as observation, with how difficult it . . . is to feel that we've ever gotten to the truth of any great historical controversy.

—John F. Kennedy[22]

Kennedy's two books narrate exemplary crisis metaphors; indeed, these texts *are* sagas of contending crisis metaphors.[23] His narration seems self-confessional. These didactic accounts of great men and their crises begin when aspiring statesmen—politicians called to greatness—are visited with cruel, unexpected calamities by foes, both foreign and domestic. But the ensuing crises are not about selfless jousts with fearsome foes. They are about a more formidable struggle, the defining crisis of one's life—the ultimate battle with the self.

For Kennedy, Cuba was not merely a concern, it was an obsession. In order to grasp his fixation, we must explicate the culturally transmitted metaphorical narratives that shaped and guided his actions. Simply put, what story was Kennedy enacting? These narratives are found in Kennedy's two crisis sagas that presaged the crises of his presidency: *Why England Slept* and *Profiles in Courage*. Could it be that he interpreted the cryptic texts and symbolic performances of his adversary in terms of the unforgettable crisis narratives of yesterday—a dangerous venture in a new age of assured destruction?

Kennedy's contesting selves emerge in the dramas in his texts. His romantic persona is enthralled with heroic morality plays in which steadfast courage conquers all. However, a careful reading reveals the persona of a pragmatic politician willing to compromise to make the best of a bad situation. His hubris is poignantly revealed in this dichotomy: he was loathe to publicly express, let alone embrace, his less grandiose self. (Perhaps the Socratic dictum needs postmodern updating—know thyselves!) Kennedy's personas are mixed and never reconciled. Struggling to define courage, he offers what could be construed as a gloss on the secret deal:

> We should not be too hasty in condemning compromise as bad morals. For politics and legislation are not matters for inflexible principles or unattainable ideals. Politics . . . "is a field where action is one long second best, and where the choice constantly lies between two blunders."[24]

But this celebration of supple, pragmatic courage is short-lived. A few pages later his ideal self prevails as he prescribes uncompromising courage for the Cold War, a Manichaean struggle in which compromise means surrender:

> And thus, in the days ahead, only the very courageous will be able to take the hard and unpopular decisions necessary for our survival in the struggle with a powerful enemy. . . . And only the very courageous will be able to keep alive the spirit . . . that gave birth to this nation, nourished it as an infant and carried it through its severest tests upon the attainment of its maturity.[25]

Kennedy had a problem with his bargaining reputation and domestic political situation; but he had a crisis because he took Khrushchev's actions personally. Vintage Kennedy crises are not about abstract, impersonal concerns. They are about a more formidable struggle, the defining event of his life—the battle between a pragmatic self willing to make the best of a bad situation and a heroic self bound for glory. He construed Khrushchev's challenge as his ultimate test: Could he be true to the best in himself? (Perhaps he was indecisive because he couldn't decide what was best in himself.) In any case, for Kennedy a crisis is not about self-sacrifice; it is about self-love. As if to paraphrase Nietzsche, Kennedy explains that those canonized in his texts were true to themselves amid cruel and unexpected adversity, and self-doubt: "precisely because they did *love themselves*—because each one's need to maintain his own respect . . . was more important to him than his popularity . . . because his faith that *his* course was the best one, and would ultimately be vindicated, outweighed his fear of . . . reprisal."[26]

Crises in Theory: A Hagionomy of the Courageous

> Churchill was his literary model as well. John Kennedy projected himself as a different kind of politician, one who not only read books . . . but wrote them. His two books, *Why England Slept* and *Profiles in Courage* (1955), were . . . bestsellers and owed a great deal to Churchill, as well as to [Arthur] Krock and to Ted Sorensen, respectively.
>
> —Richard Reeves[27]

The courageous struggle for self-respect amid adversity is an ancient story, the stuff of myth and high drama. Deconstructing the Cuban missile crisis sets us among the columns of ancient Greece. There, in stony amphitheaters, playwrights such as Sophocles scripted narratives that would echo through the centuries. The plot is ancient yet familiar. The protagonist—the aspiring hero—no longer enjoys the charmed life of his youth. Fate casts him into the final crisis of his life, an ultimate tribulation in which he is scourged by humiliation and self-doubt; the climactic crisis which is, in Starn's words, "the moment of truth when the significance of men and events is brought to life."[28] During this ultimate test the aspiring hero must risk everything and miraculously emerge alive. Unless a tragic climax is preordained, a magical machine, the deus ex machina, intervenes, enabling the hero to conquer insurmountable odds. Something dear to the Greeks, and the rest of us, was sure to follow—a happy ending.

Kennedy was not confident about his destiny. Unlike the ideologues of the early Reagan administration who anticipated a triumphant nuclear springtime, Kennedy had a sense of the tragic. After discussing Soviet actions with Kennedy during the crisis, historian Isaiah Berlin wondered whether "deep in the president's mind he may not have a presentiment that he may not live a long time . . . and that he must make his mark on history quickly."[29]

Kennedy's infatuation with heroic scripts is no secret. As Jacqueline Kennedy observed: "For Jack, history was full of heroes."[30] Retelling an ancient saga, Kennedy's heroic leaders defy the conventional wisdom and work wonders in history. However, for Kennedy, history is also populated by pragmatists willing to compromise and settle for second best. But, like the president himself, the managers of the legendary Kennedy have concealed his pragmatic sensibilities. His books are read as panegyrics for politicians destined for great things, morality plays that reveal Kennedy's unalloyed heroic ideals and destiny. The narrative is formulaic: a leader unexpectedly confronts his ultimate life crisis. Enduring the calumny of colleagues and countrymen, he acts decisively and heroically in a dangerous, ambiguous situation. If he is destined to be immortalized as a revered statesman he must venture into uncharted territory—the realm of liminality. What makes or breaks the seeker is courage, not the foolhardy bravado of the fanatic but the classic Greek virtue—bravery tempered by intelligence, grace under pressure. However, Kennedy seldom depicts unalloyed heroes.

Consider his first profile in courage, a troubled Massachusetts politician conflicted by bravado and self-doubt. Could it be that Kennedy likened his fate to the tribulations of John Quincy Adams? Was the Cuban missile crisis derivative? Was, it to paraphrase Yogi Berra, deja vu all over again? Was Kennedy thinking of himself when he described the young senator from Massachusetts as the beneficiary of: "a famous name; a brilliant father who labored unceasingly to develop his son's natural talents; and an extraordinary mother"? And whom did Kennedy have in mind when he lamented:

> Adams . . . was born with everything to make for a happy and successful life except for those qualities that bring peace of mind. In spite of a life of extraordinary achievement, he was gnawed constantly by a sense of inadequacy, of frustration, of failure. Though his hard New England conscience and his remarkable talents drove him steadily along a road of unparalleled success, he had from the beginning an almost morbid sense of constant failure.[31]

Did Kennedy also identify with Adams because of their common indiscretions? He cites Adams's diary: "Passions, indolence, weakness and infirmities have sometimes made me swerve from my better knowledge of right and almost constantly paralyzed my effort of good."[32] Like Kennedy, Adams confronted a formidable adversary. Responding to British provocations, Adams vowed to support "any measure, however serious," in response to British aggression. (This oath is reminiscent of Kennedy's Inaugural Address, in which he vowed to "pay any price, [and] bear any burden . . . to assure the survival and the success of liberty.") Adams, we are told, displayed courage in the face of adversity by supporting a blockade of the British fleet. (The British, of course, protested the blockade in Adams's day. Documents obtained from the National Security Arhive indicate that Her Majesty also protested Kennedy's blockade.) Like Adams, Kennedy blockaded his adversary, but with considerable trepidation—his nemesis possessed nuclear weapons. Worse yet, no one ruled out the possibility that, cast into a desperate situation, Khrushchev might use these weapons.

Kennedy was a complicated (or less generously, indecisive) man who cannot be reduced to a caricature. *Why England Slept* can be read as contesting subtexts —a dialectic between the vainglorious ideals of the "reckless youth" and the pragmatic sensibilities of a maturing politician. The privileged text chronicles Churchill's struggle against the calumny of his countrymen and his triumphant defense of the British Empire. The saga left an indelible imprint on the romantic Kennedy persona: only robust military might and national resolve can safeguard the ship of state. Chamberlain's poignant saga was also didactic: negotiation and compromise invariably invite humiliation and defeat. As William Bundy (the brother of Kennedy's national security adviser) explained, "The incandescent image of Chamberlain and his folded umbrella burned with eidetic certainty in the collective memory of American policymakers."[33] (Films of the Kennedy assassination show a protester waving an umbrella in Dealey Plaza. The protester claimed that he was mimicking Chamberlain to taunt Kennedy. This tawdry performance may have been the last thing Kennedy witnessed.)

But Kennedy was also a realist. True, his romantic public persona was repulsed by the humiliation of Chamberlain, the family friend and patron saint of appeasement. And yet, in numerous passages—glosses that portend his own secret deal—he expressed admiration for Chamberlain and his seemingly necessary compromise. Chamberlain, we are assured, did the best he could under the circumstances: the British persistently underestimated Hitler, refused to rearm and project their resolve. In a phrase that portends the secret deal, Kennedy allowed, "Appeasement did have some realism; it was the inevitable result of conditions that permitted no other decision."[34]

But the pragmatic persona is quickly concealed: Kennedy didn't entitle his work, Why Not Second Best? The work is not a celebration of negotiation and compromise. The lesson that emerges in *Profiles in Courage* is that America needs both the arsenal and the will to confront an enemy as intractable and dangerous as the Nazis—the Soviet Union. As a young reporter covering the proceedings of the nascent United Nations in May 1945, he warned:

There is growing discouragement among people concerning our chances of win-
ning any lasting peace from this war. There is talk of fighting the Russians in the
next 10 or 15 years. We have indeed gone a long way since those hopeful days
early in the war. What these disagreements have demonstrated clearly is that there
is a fundamental distrust between the United States and Russia. It is this distrust
—which is becoming deeper—that is causing grave concern and considerable
discouragement. Where then, is the hope? Will there not be years of distrust and
suspicion finally exploding in the awful climax of war?[35]

This distrust and suspicion—the Curse of Hermes—marked the Kennedy
presidency for good reason. Both Kennedy and Khrushchev were tricksters in a
deceitful world. Neither was excessively trusting, let alone naive. Kennedy mis-
represented the threat posed by the Cuban missiles to the American people, and
deceived the Ex Comm about the secret deal, and Khrushchev kept the missiles
secret from Dobrynin. Not surprisingly, Kennedy and Khrushchev did not take
one another at face value. Their conflicts were about impression management—
bluffing and calling bluffs—wars fought with words, not weapons. Their conflicts were staged in a semiotic realm in which appearance was everything. This
is not to suggest that the adversaries did not take the game seriously. Haunted by
indelible memories, Kennedy relived the 1930s. As Lebow concludes:

Kennedy gave every indication of viewing the Soviet Union through the prism of
the 1930s. It is probably not an exaggeration to describe his world view as largely
shaped by the fiasco of appeasement. . . . His father's commitment [to appease-
ment] . . . and the death of his older brother in the war that followed made him
even more committed to the so-called lesson of Munich and its relevance to
Soviet/American relations.[36]

Likewise, haunted by indelible images of Nazi destruction, Khrushchev retreated before the stakes got too high. Such metaphors and memories set the
stage for the ensuing social dramas between Kennedy and Khrushchev.

Crises In Practice: The Dark Night Of The Soul

All thou shalt undertake, that might bring thee joy and consolation, shall come to
nothing, and all that might make thee suffer and be vexations to thee shall suc-
ceed.
                    —Christian mystic Heinrich Suso, on the dark night of the soul[37]

Kennedy's charmed life ended the day he assumed the presidency. He was
not overwrought that his domestic programs languished in Congress. According
to Nixon, just after assuming the presidency, Kennedy confided:

It really is true that foreign affairs is the only important issue for a president to
handle, isn't it? I mean, who gives a shit if the minimum wage is $1.15 or $1.25,
in comparison to this [the planned Bay of Pigs invasion]?[38]

Like other modern presidents, Kennedy's venue was the world stage, not the domestic arena. In order to make a name for himself, he orchestrated daring foreign ventures, bold schemes faithful to the heroic credo of *Profiles in Courage*:

> We must keep our armaments equal to our commitments. Munich should teach us that; we must realize that any bluff will be called. We cannot tell anyone to keep out of our hemisphere unless our armaments *and the people behind these armaments* are prepared to back up the command, even to the ultimate point of going to war. There must be no doubt in anyone's mind, the decision must be automatic: . . . if we hesitate, if we question, it will be too late.[39]

Kennedy could not forget the past. Struggling to avoid the tragic predicament of prewar Britain, the new president: consolidated power in McNamara's Pentagon; rearmed and increased civil defense expenditures; and devised tactical and strategic schemes to project American power and influence, In so doing, the Kennedy administration—perhaps unwittingly—gave Khrushchev incentive to deploy the missiles by publicly taunting him about American nuclear superiority.[40] The president himself cultivated an air of invulnerability, but, as associates such as Undersecretary of State George Ball suggest:

> He [Kennedy] never forgot that the American people were comparing him with Eisenhower, a looming father figure whose established reputation not only for overwhelming military but also for political victories had given him political self-assurance.[41]

Given his venerable reputation, Eisenhower had little need to prove himself; he tended to define challenges as problems, not crises. Kennedy saw crises as the ultimate test of his mettle. Like a variety of other Kennedy biographers, Michael Beschloss notes that

> Kennedy knew that generating a sense of alarm would help him push his defense requests though Congress . . . [and] insulate him against charges that he had not taken the Soviet threat with due seriousness. At some level of Kennedy's thinking there was always the conviction, as he wrote in *Profiles in Courage,* that "great crises make great men."[42]

In the words of historian Garry Wills, "Accounts by New Frontiersmen make it sound as if the Kennedy presidency was just one crisis meeting after another."[43] But his crises at the Bay of Pigs, Vienna, and Berlin were more than he bargained for. His defining crisis—the joust on the abyss with Khrushchev—was an overwhelming liminal experience. Old narratives proved irrelevant and dangerous, and the improvisation of his new crisis script—the gradual escalation strategy—did not compel the Soviets to cease and desist, or so it appeared on "Black Saturday." Desperate, unable to devise new metaphors, he grasped at straws and regressed to old metaphors that were tried but untrue in an age of assured destruction. As William James lamented: "The same old story . . . concepts first employed to make things intelligible, are clung to often when they make them unintelligible."[44] The Churchill and Chamberlain scripts that gave the 1930s retrospective intelligibility were irrelevant and dangerous for a man who courted neither destruction nor humiliation.

By all accounts the Cuban missile crisis was the culminating episode of the Kennedy presidency. His actions were not merely an irresolute response to Khrushchev's challenge; they were a bewildered attempt to atone for the shame of the past. His crisis promotion cannot be understood apart from the series of cruel and unexpected humiliations that preceded it. It provided Kennedy's final opportunity for atonement and redemption, his last chance to prove that he was a Churchill, not a Chamberlain. He revealed he was both.

Prelude To The Cuban Missile Crisis

It is too simple to explain the missile crisis primarily in terms of miscalculation, for that oversimplifies. . . . Amid deep-rooted . . . antagonisms, the missile crisis must be understood substantially in the context of the events of 1961–1962, in which two powerful men—President Kennedy and Premier Khrushchev—made some crucial decisions that other men, if occupying the same office, might have handled differently.

—Barton J. Bernstein[45]

Kennedy tried to make a name for himself. He and his associates took charge of a project inherited from the Eisenhower administration—the Bay of Pigs invasion, designed to overthrow the Castro regime. (Apparently, he feared he would be seen as a coward if he abandoned the venture.) A witness to the decision-making, Roger Hilsman, explains that Kennedy realized that Nixon knew of the planned invasion, "and that if he turned it down out of hand, Nixon would use this against him on everything else he tried to do."[46] Another witness suggests that personal vulnerabilities influenced Kennedy:

President Kennedy looked around the table—it must have seemed to him that everybody who made him feel insecure was sitting there: all the admirals and generals, all the CIA people, none of whom liked him, and he knew that . . . and he went around the table to each of them, and they all said, "Yes. Go!" I'm sure he was worried about . . . the charge that he was going to be a liberal, peacenik type.[47]

As Theodore Draper writes, "The ill-fated invasion of Cuba in April, 1961, was one of those rare politico-military events—a perfect failure."[48] The predicted uprising against Castro never occurred. The Cuban leader and his forces crushed the invasion in a matter of days. Kennedy's advisers were not sanguine about the disaster. Walt Rostow seemed prescient when he warned the president that the Cubans and their Soviet ally might respond to the invasion by setting up offensive missile bases in Cuba.[49]

Adding proverbial insult to injury, hapless prisoners were paraded through the streets of Havana and held for ransom. Kennedy approved plans to meet Castro's ransom demands. Predictably, Kennedy's actions were denounced as appeasement—surrendering to Communist demands. In not entirely original phrasing, columnist William Safire intoned: "Millions for defense, but not one damn penny for tribute."[50] Eventually pharmaceuticals and tractors were quietly traded for prisoners. This "profile in appeasement" was no source of pride, but neither was it a source of guilt, when guilt is understood as remorse about perpe-trating immoral acts. (As Niebuhr urged long ago, it is doubtful that politics is informed by a strong sense of personal morality.) However, the Bay of Pigs fias-co was a source of shame, an irredeemable embarrassment and disgrace, a defamation of character that destroyed self-esteem.[51] Worse yet, Kennedy's ad-venturism in Cuba may have had dire consequences for the rest of us: Soviet officials (such as Khrushchev's son and speech-writer) have suggested that American actions against Cuba gave the Soviet leader additional incentive to de-ploy the missiles to deter future invasions.

According to these accounts, the Soviets and Cubans were aware of plans for covert attacks against Cuba such as Operation Mongoose, which recommended schemes to cripple the Cuban economy along with psychological warfare to undermine the Castro regime. The operation would culminate with the assas-sination of Castro in October 1962. (Ironically, it was also a goal of the opera-tion to condemn U. N. concern about a possible American invasion of Cuba!) In retrospect, even Kennedy's associates are less than enthusiastic about such James Bond approaches to politics. George Ball indicts these schemes as "either absurd or just plain childish. Some were recklessly dangerous."[52]

A clue to Kennedy's refusal to meet with Khrushchev during the crisis may be found in the unnerving Vienna conference held in June 1961. For three years the Soviet leader had insisted that Berlin (a city entirely within East Germany) must de facto become part of the Soviet block, thereby curtailing Western access to Berlin. (In retrospect, it appears that the Soviets and East Germans needed a pretext to close the border: they were exercised by the defection of thousands of skilled workers and professionals from East Germany.) Confronted with the same demand from Khrushchev, Eisenhower displayed considerable finesse by suggesting that the issue could be negotiated at a future conference. (There is much to be said for crisis deferral.) Of course, the hero of D-Day enjoyed a considerable advantage—he was beyond reproach. Unlike Kennedy, Eisenhower had no need to demonstrate his heroism by alarming the American people with frequent crisis moves.

For Kennedy, the international challenges provided a pretext to overcome his shame by proving himself. He was confident that the Kennedy charisma would prevail in face-to-face diplomacy. In Bundy's recently declassified "Memoran-dum of Conversation" we learn that Khrushchev reminded Kennedy of American nuclear bases in Iran and Turkey, and that it might be appropriate for the Soviets to reciprocate in Cuba.[53] Evidently, Kennedy thought Khrushchev was bluffing. (In a world of tricksters, skillful deceivers sometimes employ a measure of truth.)

The focal point of discussion, however, was Berlin. Like Hermes, Kennedy relied upon his reputation and his charm. He thought he could entice his adversary to abandon his demand to place all of Berlin under Soviet dominion. Applying the "lesson of the Thirties," Kennedy insisted there could be no compromise. The premier's performance was vintage Khrushchev. He issued an ultimatum: he threatened to sign a treaty in December that would de facto put all of Berlin under Soviet hegemony. Pounding the table, he bellowed: "*I want peace. But if you want war, that is your problem.*" He insisted that he would sign a treaty with East Germany effectively denying the West access to Berlin. Kennedy responded, "If that is true, it's going to be a cold winter."[54]

The recollections of those who saw Kennedy immediately afterward are telling. Rusk suggests that Kennedy took the confrontation personally:

> Kennedy was disturbed by Khrushchev's manner—his obvious feeling that he could somehow bluff or intimidate this young new president of the United States. That disturbed Kennedy as much as the substance of the ultimatum on Berlin.[55]

Harold Macmillan confided in his diary that for the first time in his life, Kennedy, "met a man wholly impervious to his charm." The prime minister added that Kennedy seemed out of his league: "He seemed stunned . . . like somebody meeting Napoleon (at the height of his power) for the first time."[56]

Others feared (to twist the historical analogy) that Kennedy had met his Waterloo. Rusk lamented that in response to Khrushchev's bullying, "Kennedy was very upset. . . . He wasn't prepared for the brutality of Khrushchev's presentation."[57] And, in what may be grist for the Freudian mill, Robert Kennedy allowed that the president: "had never really come across somebody with whom he couldn't exchange ideas in a meaningful way. [Dealing with Khrushchev] was like dealing with Dad. All give and no take."[58] The president himself confided that the encounter was the

> roughest thing in my life. . . . I think he thought that anyone who was so young and inexperienced as to get into the mess [the Bay of Pigs fiasco] could be taken; he just beat the hell out of me. . . . I've got a terrible problem. If he thinks I'm inexperienced and have no guts, until we remove those ideas we won't get anywhere with him. So we have to act.[59]

The bumptious Russian peasant threw down the gauntlet to the scion of charm and privilege. Talking with columnist Joseph Alsop, the president resolved, "I won't give in to the Russians no matter what happens."[60] And some time later he told reporter James Wechsler, "If Khrushchev wants to rub my nose in the dirt, it's all over."[61] Shortly thereafter, Kennedy met with his confidant Kenny O'Donnell. After excoriating Khrushchev, the president reflected upon a troubling irony; he was expected to be ready to risk everything in a dubious venture:

> It seems silly for us to be facing an atomic war over a treaty preserving Berlin as the future capital of a reunited Germany when all of us know that Germany will probably never be reunited.[62]

Kennedy's humiliation in Berlin led to a fateful decision that would become a key factor during the Cuban missile crisis: the deployment of American missiles in Turkey.[63] Once again the decision was governed by impression management, not military exigencies. A study ordered by Bundy concluded that the missiles should be installed as planned. The conclusion was based "primarily on the view that, in the aftermath of Khrushchev's hard posture at Vienna, cancellation . . . might seem a sign of weakness."[64]

Kennedy's speech to the American public (the desk behind which he spoke was cleared of all but his own two books) made no mention of the Turkish missiles or of Khrushchev's ultimatum. However, a few days later Khrushchev infuriated the president by publishing his ultimatum in *Pravda*. Kennedy confided to his advisers that the United States was drawing close to war with the Soviet Union.[65]

During the Berlin crisis Kennedy confronted a paradox that would become *the* intractable dilemma of the Cuban missile crisis: not only were his cherished metaphors contradictory, they were irrelevant and dangerous. Neither the Churchill nor the Chamblerlain script had a happy ending—both portended disaster. In the nuclear age the Churchill narrative climaxed in national suicide. And the Chamberlain script was a morality play about the dangers of appeasement and the tragedy of personal humiliation.

Understandably, Kennedy responded to Khrushchev's provocation with words, not weapons. His words echoed Churchill's wartime call to heroism and sacrifice. He vowed to fight to save Berlin and urged preparation for a nuclear attack: "The lives of those families which are not hit in a nuclear blast and fire can still be saved—*if* they can be warned to take shelter, and *if* that shelter is *available.*"[66] Such fighting words are not innocuous. The possibility exists that such belligerency may be misinterpreted and taken seriously.

August 1961 witnessed the construction of the infamous Berlin Wall. When there was no American response to stringing a barbed wire barrier, the East Germans quickly constructed a stone and cement wall. Campaigning for chancellor, Willy Brandt excoriated the Western generals on the scene: "You let Ulbricht kick you in the rear. . . . The entire East is going to laugh from Pankow to Vladivostok." Brandt understandably construed the wall as a major repudiation of American power and prestige. Commenting on Kennedy's role on the world stage, he remarked, "The curtain went up, and the stage was empty."[67] Stressing that the wall violated the Potsdam Agreement, to say nothing of the courage and resolve of the New Frontiersmen, allies accused the president of perpetrating a second Munich. Later, after the Cuban missile crisis, Kennedy appeared in Berlin to demonstrate resolve. He chose the phrase *Ich bin ein Berliner*; some thought *Ich bin ein Munchener* would have been more appropriate.

The president made little mention of the wall in public, but in private he allowed that a wall was preferable to a war. Khrushchev, however, was not averse to escalating the situation through symbolic acts: he ordered resumption of nuclear testing. Apparently, the president's reputation, along with Soviet bravado, made an impression on the president's domestic enemies. At a White

House luncheon Ted Dealey (publisher of the *Dallas Morning News*) outraged the president by exclaiming:

> We can annihilate Russia and should make that clear to the Soviet government. You and your administration are weak sisters. . . . We need a man on horseback. . . . many people . . . think that you are riding Caroline's tricycle.[68]

Somehow, Kennedy took such comments personally. Like Eisenhower, his intelligence reports concluded that the United States did indeed possess strategic superiority. Ignoring Khrushchev's braggadocio, Eisenhower decided it would be unwise to remind the Soviets of American advantage: such a move would antagonize the Soviets and encourage them to escalate the arms race. For a time, Kennedy shared this prudence. (Indeed, the alleged "missile gap" was part and parcel of the 1960 campaign.) However, in the face of strident criticism such as Dealey's, to say nothing of Soviet belligerence, the political became personal: Kennedy publicly confronted the Soviets with their strategic inferiority. In a speech written by Daniel Ellsberg, Roswell Gilpatric detailed the overwhelming American advantage in nuclear weaponry, and he couldn't resist the temptation to taunt Khrushchev about his difficulties with China. Gilpatric himself revealed that the speech was intended "to convince the Soviet Union that we were ready to take on any threat in the Berlin area."[69]

The speech had the intended short-term effect: Khrushchev was humiliated during the Party Congress. As historian Ronald Steel observes:

> For the Russians, the implications [of the speech] were, in Hilsman's [a Kennedy confidant and adviser] words "horrendous." What frightened them was not that we had military superiority, for they knew that all along—but that *we* knew it.[70]

In a dramatically symbolic gesture, Khrushchev ordered the detonation of the most formidable hydrogen bomb ever tested, a thirty-megaton device. The symbolic performances escalated, yet Kennedy could not escape the charge of appeasement, even from subordinates. In response to Soviet tanks, the United States massed its tanks on the East Berlin border. The American commander, General Lucius Clay, informed the president that the Soviet tanks were probably just for show. Kennedy reassured the general that he was confident that the military hadn't lost its nerve. Clay's rejoinder was insulting: "Mr. President, we're not worried about our nerves. We're worrying about those of you people in Washington."[71]

In what may have been a template for the resolution of the Cuban missile crisis, the president secretly instructed his brother to inform the Soviets that he could show flexibility if the tanks were removed within twenty-four hours. The Soviets blinked first. And, in what may have presaged the Trollope ploy, Kennedy ignored a belligerent letter from Khrushchev and responded to a more tractable message. Columnist James Reston seemed to anticipate Kennedy's resolution of the Cuban missile crisis when he opined, "Kennedy talked like Churchill and acted like Chamberlain."[72]

In any case, the war of words abated as the adversaries settled for second best—the Berlin Wall. The Soviets sealed the border while the Americans gained a considerable propaganda advantage. The bad news was that the Gilpatric speech pressured Khrushchev "to do something spectacular to change the widespread perception of the nuclear imbalance between the Soviet Union and the United States."[73] The ensuing spectacle would become known as the Cuban missile crisis.

Kennedy's Ultimate Test

The Kennedy I found did not know what he was doing at the beginning, and in some ways never changed at all, particularly in a certain love for chaos, the kind that keeps other men off-balance.

—Richard Reeves[74]

Kennedy's associates claim that he took Khrushchev's actions personally. Ray Cline, deputy CIA director and Ex Comm adviser, was the first to alert Bundy to the Cuban missiles. In a recent oral history he revealed that "Bundy's reaction was to support the president. He felt Kennedy was going to get mad and get even."[75]

Ben Bradlee suggests that dealing with disrespectful military advisers exacerbated Kennedy's agony: "I'm just thinking about the president sitting around the table, having to stare at Arleigh Burke, who probably thought he was a pipsqueak; to stare at Curtis LeMay . . . who thought it was a goddamn disaster that Kennedy had been elected."[76]

Press Secretary Pierre Salinger recounts his conversation with Kennedy when the president hastily returned to Washington to be briefed on Soviet actions. In order to keep the missiles secret, the public was told that Kennedy had the flu. Salinger remarked to the president, "You know you don't have the flu, you look perfectly well." He said, "That's true, you'll find out why I'm going back to Washington when we get there, and when you do, grab your balls!"[77]

Why did the missiles hit below the belt? Why did Kennedy take Khrushchev's actions personally? What was the threat? The president did not interpret Soviet actions as an increased threat to the survival of the United States. Many of Kennedy's advisers shared this perspective. In a recently declassified document, Sorensen summarizes the consensus that emerged among the majority of the Ex Comm members:

It is generally agreed that these missiles, even when fully operational, do not significantly alter the balance of power—i.e., they do not increase the potential megatonnage capable of being unleashed on American soil. . . .[78]

Kennedy attached surplus meaning to the surreptitious Soviet actions. He interpreted the missiles of October as a dire threat to his integrity. He was not merely concerned about keeping promises to others. Like the protagonists in his crisis narratives, he faced the existential moment of truth: Could he keep his covenant with himself? On two occasions in September 1962 he vowed that offensive Soviet weapons would not be tolerated in Cuba. "Were it otherwise," he warned, "the gravest issues would arise."[79] Kennedy's warning was too much too late. Khrushchev had ordered the installation of Soviet missiles in May 1962.

According to a variety of analysts, Kennedy made the vow primarily for domestic political purposes—it was simply inconceivable that the Soviets would deploy nuclear weapons beyond their borders. The transcripts of the October 16 Ex Comm meetings suggest that Kennedy deeply regretted the vow: "Last month I should have said that we don't care. But when we said we're going to and then they go ahead and do it [deploy missiles], and then we do nothing. . . ."[80]

The missiles of October represented the climax of a great morality play. Against the backdrop of indecisiveness and appeasement at the Bay of Pigs, Vienna, and Berlin, Kennedy vowed that no offensive weapons would be tolerated in Cuba. Like a chorus in a Greek drama, the Soviet missiles drowned out courageous vows and shamed Kennedy with taunts of frailty and appeasement. Khrushchev's challenge became the ultimate personal test: Could he be true to his heroic vision? Such authenticity was decidedly unproblematic for the man Kennedy called "The Field Marshal." LeMay was single-minded; his recommendation was very much in character—obliterate Cuba and the Soviet Union. Indeed, his sensibilities were uncomplicated: kill as many of the enemy as possible until the enemy stops fighting![81] Kennedy's struggle for authenticity, however, was overwrought and irresolvable: he labored under an ironic hubris: he was not a single-minded ideologue. Or, put less generously, he was not of one mind. As Michael Beschloss observed in his study of Kennedy/Khrushchev crises: "Kennedy was a realist disguised as a romantic."[82] The Cuban missile crisis was, perhaps, an irresolvable clash between these personas. His romantic persona wanted to be Churchill; but his realist persona needed to be Chamberlain.

CRISIS MANAGEMENT

> The white knights sitting around the Executive Committee roundtable seem now more complicated and human figures than they once appeared, capable of duplicity, indecision, inconsistency, and even—especially in the president's case—incoherence. The confidence-inspiring certitudes of *Thirteen Days* have begun to dissolve into interpretive complexities and doubts.
>
> —Michael H. Hunt[83]

Kennedy's crisis management must be evaluated before it can be interpreted: the former governs the latter. Those who laud Kennedy are obligated to account for what they construe as his adroit, carefully calibrated strategizing amid daunting adversity. And, not surprisingly, those who indict his management ruminate about why an ordinarily pragmatic politician hazarded such extraordinary risks.

I find myself immersed in such ruminations. In order to account for actions I construe as confused, contradictory, and reckless, I argue that Kennedy lapsed in and out of liminality. His a priori metaphors were unacceptable. Thinking "five or six moves ahead" he foresaw that the Churchill script ended in holocaust, and a *public* enactment of the Chamberlain script climaxed in humiliation. This initial liminality was generative: it produced a new metaphor that would become the schemata for the Indochina War and subsequent nuclear strategy: gradual escalation doctrine. When it appeared that this new doctrine—with its reliance on symbolic performances rather than concrete military objectives—failed to compel Khrushchev to remove the missiles, Kennedy desperately grasped at metaphors indelibly inscribed in his consciousness: despite (or perhaps because of) the risks, he simultaneously improvised Churchill and Chamberlain scripts.

Evaluating Kennedy's Performance

[Kennedy's resolution of the crisis] was a victory not only over the Soviets, but over many of Kennedy's own advisers who favored a more militant course from the start.

—Ronald Steel[84]

The quality of Kennedy's crisis management is, to understate the case, contested. And it is improbable that crisis analysts will embrace a "final analysis": no authoritative tribunal will bestow its imprimatur upon *the* definitive interpretation. But given my present understanding, I construe his struggle as an attempt to establish concord, not only with his enemies (both foreign and domestic) but with the enemy within—the contesting narratives that bedeviled his decision-making. Schlesinger, however, found Kennedy's performance less problematic. He rhapsodized that the crisis represents:

The ripening of an American leadership unsurpassed in the responsible management of power . . . [Kennedy's] combination of toughness . . . nerve and wisdom, so brilliantly controlled, so matchlessly calibrated that [it] dazzled the world.[85]

However Ex Comm member Dean Acheson disagrees.[86] In his essay, "Homage to Plain Dumb Luck," he disputes the commonplace that the Ex Comm was an egalitarian group that democratically framed a carefully calibrated policy for the president:

One cannot escape the conclusion . . . that the chief advice reaching the president during this critical period came to him through his brother . . . out of a leaderless, uninhibited group, many of whom had little knowledge in either the military or diplomatic field. This is not the way the National Security Council operated at any time during which I was officially connected with it.[87]

Based upon this conclusion, Acheson indicts Kennedy's key decisions, and argues that the survival of the United States, if not the western hemisphere, was fortuitous. (Acheson urged immediate military action.) Sorensen agrees that Kennedy was lucky—for different reasons. "Dean Acheson is right in crediting

Kennedy with considerable good luck on this awesome occasion. . . . Among the ways in which JFK was lucky was in not taking Dean Acheson's advice!"[88]

He claims that by rejecting Acheson's reckless advice, "Kennedy . . . relied not on force and threat alone but on a carefully balanced and precisely measured combination of defense, diplomacy and dialogue."[89] Other influential advisers, however, disagree. In his 1992 foreword to the Chang and Kornbluh anthology, McNamara admonishes:

> The record of the missile crisis is replete with examples of misinformation, misjudgment, miscalculation. Such errors are costly in conventional war. When they affect decisions in relation to nuclear forces, they can result in the destruction of nations.[90]

Those who observed Kennedy during this ordeal do not agree even upon his mood. Dean Rusk extols the president's calm, cool deliberations, and declares, "During the Cuban missile crisis, president Kennedy had ice water in his veins." However, Eugene McCarthy observes that "The only time I ever saw Jack [Kennedy] really kind of scared was the time of the missile crisis."[91]

Not surprisingly, influential analysts posit contradictory views. Graham Allison, former Dean of the Kennedy School of Government at Harvard, claims that Kennedy's resolution of the crisis was Kennedy's finest hour.[92] However, across town at MIT, Noam Chomsky alludes to Kennedy's resolution of the crisis as "the lowest point of human history."[93]

No doubt these contradictory perspectives are self-confessional—they reflect authorial biases. However, understood dialectically, these perspectives also reflect the contradictory nature of Kennedy's crisis management—a gambit at once conciliatory and provocative. Put more colloquially, there is good news and bad news. The good news is that Kennedy demonstrated commendable pragmatism and restraint. The bad news is that he simultaneously risked a nuclear holocaust.

Initially, he rejected the advice of his most experienced advisers and his brother, and refused to attack Cuba. Understandably, he feared that such action might precipitate thermonuclear war with the Soviet Union. Recently declassified tapes also indicate that, despite charges of appeasement, he also rejected Senator Russell's plea for an immediate invasion. (There was considerable support among Congressional leaders for such action; even Senator Fulbright urged an invasion.)[94]

It also appears that the president was mindful of the subtext of *Why England Slept*. An epigram from the work is worth reiterating: "Appeasement did have some realism; it was the inevitable result of conditions that permitted no other decision."[95] (Evidently, such realism was not a source of pride. The eventual sub rosa exchange of American missiles in Turkey for Soviet missiles in Cuba was kept secret from most of Kennedy's advisers, to say nothing of Congress, the military, allies, and the American public. Indeed, the Kennedy brothers and their most trusted advisers went to extraordinary lengths to safeguard the secret. The ultimatum, however, was enshrined as the cornerstone of Kennedy's legendary courage.)

Robert Kennedy's role in the secret negotiations is revealing: the president's messenger was type-cast as Hermes. He kept secrets, deceived colleagues and generations of scholars, and delivered cryptic, dissembling messages. Dobrynin claims that he and Robert Kennedy frequently met secretly just after midnight.[96] Garthoff (who assumed partial responsibility for assembling documents for the Kennedy Presidential Library) corroborates this claim: Robert Kennedy's calendar indicates that he met with Dobrynin almost every evening during the crisis. Most significantly, on Friday, October 26, 1962, Robert Kennedy told Dobrynin that his brother might well agree to a quid pro quo. Garthoff suggests that Robert Kennedy's meeting with Dobrynin prompted Khrushchev to send a second letter demanding such a trade. In any case, it appears that this meeting was kept secret from other advisers. Moreover, according to Garthoff, Robert Kennedy's calendar somehow disappeared from the Kennedy Presidential Library's archives.[97]

In *Thirteen Days*, a memoir used by generations of scholars to understand the crisis, Robert Kennedy claims that during the first Ex Comm deliberations he resisted the impetuous recommendations of the hawks; he represents himself as a moderating influence. However, after reading the transcript of this meeting, scholars such as Bernstein draw a different conclusion:

> Attorney General Robert Kennedy, contrary to the later claims in *Thirteen Days*, endorsed a military attack on Cuba—even if it meant war. . . . Better now than later, he said. The attorney general even suggested creating a pretext for attacking Cuba; "Sink the *Maine* again or something," he said.[98]

Immediately after his attempt to provoke the Ex Comm to take military action the Attorney General met with the organizers of Operation Mongoose—the secret cadre planning to overthrow the Castro regime. According to an official CIA document drafted by Richard Helms:

> At 2:30 this afternoon [October 16, 1962], the Attorney General convened in his office a meeting of Operation MONGOOSE. . . . [He] opened the meeting by expressing the "general dissatisfaction of the president" with Operation MONGOOSE. He pointed out that the Operation had been under way for a year, that the results were discouraging, that there had been no acts of sabotage, and that even the one which had been attempted had failed twice.[99]

As documents obtained from the National Security Archive indicate, Operation Mongoose attempted to orchestrate the overthrow of the Castro regime—by assassination if necessary. At recent conferences and in recent publications, Soviet officials claim they were aware of this covert operation. In any case, the provocations planned by the Mongoose cadre and the secret deal were concealed from most Ex Comm members. The official summary of the 4 P.M. Ex Comm meeting on October 27 indicates that Bundy urged that "there would be a serious reaction in NATO countries if we appeared to be trading . . . missiles in Turkey for . . . missiles from Cuba."[100] Following the belated revelations of Schlesinger and Sorensen, Bundy discussed the secret deal in 1988 in his *Danger and Survival*. According to Bundy, the deal was formulated by the president and eight of his most trusted advisers following the 4 P.M. Ex Comm meeting. It was agreed that Robert Kennedy would give Dobrynin an ultimatum—remove the missiles within twenty-four hours or face an American attack—and reiterate the secret deal.

According to Dobrynin, Robert Kennedy was nervous, even tearful, as he simultaneously issued an ultimatum and gave in to Khrushchev's demands. As the attorney general explains in his *Thirteen Days*, "While there could be no [public] deal over the Turkish missiles, the president was determined to get them out and would do so once the Cuban crisis was resolved."[101] Neither the ultimatum nor the secret deal was called by its right name. Robert Kennedy told the ambassador that he was merely presenting a fact, and the secret deal to remove the missiles was not a deal. According to Bundy, the trade was kept secret lest the Turks feel betrayed.[102] (Surely the Turks did not regard the dismantling of the Jupiter bases in April 1963 as sheer coincidence.) Even the official CIA chronology of the Cuban missile crisis reveals nothing about Robert Kennedy's nocturnal diplomacy, the meeting of the "mini-Ex Comm" or—of course—the secret deal.[103] Could it be that sensitivity to the Turk's sensibilities was a very good reason for such extraordinary secrecy, but the real reason was avoiding the appearance of appeasement? In any case, Kennedy's trusted advisers were sworn to secrecy. Given these clandestine intrigues, it is not surprising that Rusk and McNamara lied to Congress. In 1963, for example, McNamara testified:

> Without any qualification whatsoever there was absolutely no deal . . . between the Soviet Union and the United States regarding the removal of the Jupiter weapons from either Italy or Turkey.[104]

Again, Bundy insists that such duplicity was necessary to avoid offending the Turks. It appears, however, that other motives were operative. Bundy cannot explain why the clandestine arrangement was kept secret *after* the Jupiters were removed from Turkey in April 1963. Indeed, only after Dobrynin insisted that the Kennedy administration acceded to Khrushchev's demands did Sorensen confess that in the process of editing Robert Kennedy's *Thirteen Days*:

> I took it upon myself to edit that [the secret deal] out of his [RFK's] diaries, and that is why the Ambassador [Dobrynin] is somewhat justified in saying that the diaries are not as explicit as his conversation.[105]

The Soviet ambassador was sworn to secrecy. When he tried to formalize the agreement in writing, Robert Kennedy warned that publishing the letter would void the settlement of the crisis.[106] Dobrynin reports that on October 30,

> RFK informed me that the president confirmed the accord on closing American missile bases in Turkey . . . no connection was to be drawn in public between his decision and the events surrounding Cuba. . . . Very privately, RFK added that some day—who knows?—he might run for president, and his prospects would be damaged if this secret deal about the missiles in Turkey were to come out.[107]

Sixteen years later, Schlesinger offered the following gloss on the incident:

> So concluded a singular exercise in secret diplomacy—secret not only in process
> . . . but in result, which is generally inadmissible. Macmillan and NATO were
> told nothing, nor was the American Congress, nor even the Executive Committee
> [Ex Comm].[108]

It is noteworthy that Adlai Stevenson recommended what was to become the essence of the secret deal during the first day of the crisis. By and large, his recommendation elicited contempt and ridicule. Perhaps he should have been Kennedy's tenth "profile in courage."

The bad news in evaluating Kennedy's crisis management is that he knowingly hazarded unprecedented risks, gambits that brought the world close to nuclear war. The deliberate risks are well known, and include: publicly demanding that the Soviets withdraw the missiles; blockading Cuba; going to an unprecedented state of nuclear alert; and mobilizing the armed forces for an attack on Cuba.

According to Sorensen, Robert Kennedy intended to examine the morality of such risk-taking, but his tragic death intervened. In a gloss that concludes *Thirteen Days*, Sorensen explains:

> It was Senator Kennedy's intention to add a discussion of the basic ethical question involved: what, if any circumstances or justification gives this government or any government the moral right to bring its people and possibly all people under the shadow of nuclear destruction?[109]

One would hope that there is an eloquently simple answer—none! That such a question can be broached and discussed reveals the most disturbing aspect of the crisis: as far as I know, no one on the Ex Comm has developed a systematic, thoroughgoing justification for risking what Bernstein calls "annihilation without representation." However, at the Hawk's Cay conference, Schelling offered a brief justification.

> The Cuban missile crisis was the best thing to happen to us since the Second World War. . . . Sometimes the gambles you take pay off. If I took the risks of nuclear war to be McNamara's one in fifty, I'd conclude that the risks were worth taking if the risks were greater than one in fifty of things going on as they were in Berlin and elsewhere. . . . I worry enough about nuclear war that I am willing to take a one-shot risk to reduce the risks over the long run.[110]

Schelling somehow calculates the risks hazarded in October 1962 and in crises that never occurred—a dubious enterprise. His retrospective risk assessment of the Cuban missile crisis also suffers from a liability—it is counterfactual. He claims that if the palpable risk of nuclear war had not occurred during the Cuban missile crisis, even more daunting risks would have vexed decision-makers later. His claim is difficult to disconfirm: it would involve accomplishing what God cannot do—rewriting history. History would have to be rerun without the Cuban missile crisis. Only then could we determine whether more daunting crises would have occurred. In any case, I am not persuaded that such speculation about what never happened justifies bringing the world under the shadow of nuclear destruction.

The risks of catastrophe cannot be represented with precision; however, most analysts and members of the Ex Comm agree with Khrushchev: "The smell of burning was in the air."[111] Dean Rusk found it rather remarkable that he awoke alive after the president publicly confronted the Soviets in his speech on October 22, 1962.[112] McNamara reveals the depth of his despair when he laments that he paused to watch a particularly beautiful sunset after the last Saturday Ex Comm meeting; he thought it might be his last.[113] Shortly thereafter, Robert Kennedy issued the ultimatum: dismantle their missiles within twenty-four hours or face an American attack. Like Disraeli, the Kennedy brothers hoped for the best but expected the worst; (in the nuclear age there is no way to *prepare* for the worst). Robert Kennedy writes: "The president was not optimistic, nor was I. . . . The expectation was a military confrontation by Tuesday and possibly tomorrow."[114] Dining with the brothers amid such ruminations, the person often regarded as the president's best friend, Dave Powers, thought it might be his last supper.[115]

The deliberate risks hazarded by the "best and the brightest" were daunting and unprecedented. Surely Kennedy realized that unforeseen insubordination and mishaps might be even more horrific. (Indeed, various analysts suggest that Kennedy and Khrushchev ended the showdown because, to say the least, things were not unfolding as planned.) In any case, Kennedy's apprehension about the fog of crises was justified: instances of insubordination and mishaps are plentiful. An evaluation of Kennedy's crisis management must attend to these risks.

McNamara continually insists that he was trying to send the Soviets a message, not start a war. He placed the Strategic Air Command on an unprecedented state of alert—Defcon 2; but, to avoid provoking the Soviets, he ordered the alert broadcast in secret code. However, the SAC commander, General Thomas Powers, refused; he broadcast the order in plain English.[116] (Apparently, he wanted to convey his resolve to the Soviets.) Garthoff (who revealed this insubordination to surviving Ex Comm members years later) regards himself as a hawk. Nevertheless, he empathizes with the Soviets:

> Soviet communications interception personnel must have been shocked suddenly to hear all the alert orders from Omaha and a steady stream of responses from bomber units reporting their . . . nuclear armed flights poised for attack on the Soviet Union.

If Soviet officials were shocked by such bravado, so were surviving members of Ex Comm; Garthoff continues:

> When I mentioned this incident to a recent conference [1987] of former Ex-Comm members . . . [including Bundy and McNamara] I discovered none had been aware until now of this happening.[117]

In a recent study, Scott Sagan chronicles other instances that almost turned the crisis into an unparalleled disaster. For example:

> At the start of the crisis, the Strategic Air Command secretly deployed nuclear warheads on nine of the ten test ICBMs in place at Vandenberg Air Force Base and then launched the tenth missile, on a . . . test over the Pacific.[118]

Obviously, Soviet reconnaissance might misinterpret the objective of such a launch. Other incidents include jerry-rigging Minuteman missiles to permit launch without proper authorization; accidentally running a program that indicated a missile launched from Cuba was about to hit Tampa; and misinterpreting a bear's intrusion into a SAC base as a launch of enemy missiles. (According to Sagan, this final mishap was due to technical malfunctions in the SAC alarm system.)[119]

American authorities claim that a U-2 on a weather surveillance mission inadvertently strayed over Soviet airspace during the height of the crisis. (This explanation evokes suspicion. The same explanation was given for Francis Gary Powers' ill-fated flight over the Soviet Union during the Eisenhower administration.) In any case, the Soviets understandably construed the incident as a provocation, if not a prelude to an American first strike. (Soviet and American fighters were scrambled, but somehow, no confrontation occurred.)

Finally, in an incident worthy of the best black comedy, an American double agent, Oleg Penkovsky, was captured by Soviet authorities on October 22, 1962, the day of Kennedy's public promotion of the crisis. Garthoff reveals that: "One of the key CIA clandestine service officers responsible for directly managing the Penkovsky case, whom I had come to know well as a reliable person, is my source for this information." Garthoff explains that, in the event of an imminent apocalypse, Penkovsky was authorized to send a secret telephone signal to the CIA indicating the Soviets were about to launch a nuclear attack on the North American continent. This is precisely what he did prior to Kennedy's speech. Garthoff reveals:

> So when he was about to go down, he evidently decided to play Samson and bring the temple down on everyone else as well. . . . Fortunately, his Western intelligence handlers, at the operational level, after weighing a dilemma of great responsibility, decided not to credit Penkovksy's final signal and suppressed it.[120]

Perhaps these handlers should be the eleventh profile in courage.

Interpretation

However detailed may have been our study of his life, each man remains something of an enigma. However clear the effect of his courage, the cause is shadowed by a veil which cannot be torn away. We may confidently state the reasons why—yet something always eludes us. . . . Motivation, as any psychiatrist will tell us, is always difficult to assess . . . in the murky sea of politics.

—John F. Kennedy[121]

How shall we interpret the good news and the bad news regarding the crisis: Kennedy was at once prudent and reckless. This defining feature of the crisis will continue to be subject to multiple interpretations. These explications will, of course, have a profoundly self-confessional element: those who champion Kennedy's actions will interpret his prudence and daring ("recklessness" would be deemed pejorative) as further confirmation of Schlesinger's encomium; the secret deal and the ultimatum were part and parcel of a brilliantly conceived grand strategy that balanced a credible fear of punishment with a sub rosa promise of reward. (To invoke a nautical metaphor that Kennedy might have found congenial, the ship of state was reeling in a tempest. Kennedy's tacking may have appeared fitful to the uninitiated; indeed, it may have seemed that he was pulling in opposite directions, but he knew what he was doing.)

As we have seen, most of the surviving Ex Comm members reject such encomiums to Kennedy that praise his crisis management as an adroit, carefully calibrated grand strategy. The consensus that emerged during the Hawks Cay conference depicts the crisis as a sudden and cruel turn of events that threw Kennedy and the others off balance. Khrushchev's motives were opaque; all they knew was that they wanted the missiles removed. No carefully conceived, precisely formulated tactics and strategy were implemented. Indeed, there is rare consensus among actors and analysts that no "off-the-shelf" strategy existed for dealing with Soviet nuclear weapons in Cuba. The situation was deemed a crisis precisely because Kennedy and his advisers did not know how to respond. According to most inside accounts, they spent the first week of the crisis debating, in fits and starts, possible tactics and strategy.[122] No wonder Michael Hunt concludes:

> The . . . unexpected impression conveyed by the ExComm transcripts is one of confusion. Faced by a host of unknowns, the participants wrestled with the consequences of their actions. . . . Kennedy himself is the most conspicuous. . . . At times he struggled to put a clear, complete sentence together.[123]

Of course, Kennedy critics who side with Acheson will interpret the latest news of mishaps, insubordination, and confusion as further confirmation of Kennedy's "plain dumb luck." But ironically, Kennedy's incoherent responses may have inadvertently prompted Khrushchev to resolve the crisis. It is not wildly implausible to suggest that Khrushchev ended the crisis when he began to suspect that events were veering out of control in the United States and Cuba.[124]

Whatever the case, Kennedy responded to Soviet actions by authoring texts and by improvising symbolic performances. These actions require interpretation. My take is indebted to Turner's and Geertz's studies of crises at other times and places. These studies, as we've seen, explicate the crisis narratives that actors improvise to render harrowing experiences understandable, and resolvable. Liminality is a key factor in understanding the interplay of fecundity and desperation typical of these episodes.

Crisis Management As Impression Management

For twelve days I lived in the Pentagon . . . because I feared that they [the military] might not understand that this was a communication exercise, not a military operation. . . . [I was] trying to send a message, not start a war. This was not a blockade, but a means of communication between Kennedy and Khrushchev.
—Robert McNamara[125]

McNamara once declared, "There is no such thing as strategy, only crisis management."[126] Given the symbolic turn in international relations, perhaps this oft-quoted aphorism needs updating. His remark about his duty as chief Pentagon semiotician reflects a crucial but neglected transition: there is no more crisis management, only impression management. Kennedy's impression management of the crisis evolved in five phases.

Again, there is little controversy that the initial phase, the first week of secret deliberations, was marked by indecision. Kennedy knew what he didn't want: Soviet missiles in Cuba were intolerable due to his personal and political vulnerabilities; however, the thought of immediately risking nuclear war with the Soviets was also repulsive. Given this novel predicament, his limited stock of crisis narratives seemed dangerous or unacceptable. In an age of assured destruction, the Churchill script portended a tragic climax; at the same time he was haunted by visions of Chamberlain slouching toward Munich.

Thrown into a liminal predicament, Kennedy assembled his Ex Comm advisers to discuss alternatives. (It is possible, of course, that the Ex Comm served other functions. Perhaps it occurred to Kennedy that the Ex Comm would legitimize his course of action, or—in the event of disaster—would share the blame. Or, if all went well, the Ex Comm would immortalize his performance as a profile in courage.) In any case, during this interlude betwixt and between metaphors, he should be commended for resisting the impetuousness of the hawks, but, lamentably, he did not have the courage to heed the advice of the doves.

Nevertheless, this initial phase of liminality proved productive; it engendered the strategic improvisations that marked the second phase. For public consumption Kennedy scripted a social drama that he hoped would compel his adversary to retreat, thereby vindicating his preconceived destiny. However, there was a marked difference between his public promotion of himself and his private life: he would be Churchill on the world stage while cleverly implementing a new strategy in camera. (Thanks to his talents and those of his advisers, and a generally sympathetic press, Kennedy was unusually successful at managing the contradictions between his public and private lives. Suffering from serious infirmities, he portrayed himself as a robust outdoorsman exuding vitality and health. A notorious womanizer, he was also the devoted family man who won the hearts of Middle America. And I suspect that despite the secret deal, JFK will be remembered as a jaunty young hero/statesman—the Kennedy magic still works.)

Kennedy's October 22 speech, the first scene in his public performance, was classic Churchill. His plea for forbearance, heroism, and ultimate sacrifice virtually paraphrased a legendary Churchill oath. The redoubtable prime minister vowed that he would not flag or fail whatever the cost; the British would fight on the beaches, they would fight in the fields and streets, and surely they would never surrender.

But Churchill's pledge of total war was a tough act to follow in the radically transformed world of the 1960s. It was far easier to be Churchill in the prime minister's situation. Had Kennedy faced an unmistakable threat from conventional weapons, he could have courageously emulated the stalwart Englishman by matching word and deed. He hesitated because, unlike Churchill, he confronted a novel dialectic between uncertainty and certainty.

1. Unlike Churchill, Kennedy faced an ill-defined challenge. He inhabited a symbolic milieu of ambiguous texts and performances. He was not required to accomplish something as tangible as mobilizing the Royal Air Force against a blitzkrieg or invasion. His difficulties were more literary: he had to find the right words and improvise the most compelling script. (The Trollope ploy is a different genre than the Normandy invasion.)

2. Also unlike Churchill, Kennedy faced the all-too-tangible threat of assured nuclear destruction. True, his public bravado may have been an act—he may have been bluffing. However, he staged a bravura performance to impress the public and to intimidate a volatile adversary with his finger on the nuclear button. Put more technically, the Churchill improvisation created crisis instability: his act gave Khrushchev every reason to strike first. (According to this prevailing strategic model, a weaker power threatened by a superior force could minimize its losses by striking first in a decisive, surprise attack.) This was not the only peril. What would the president have done if Khrushchev called his bluff by running the blockade, threatening Germany or Turkey; or refusing to remove the missiles from Cuba? "Fighting them in the fields and the streets" (or in Europe and the Caribbean) with nuclear weapons was suicidal. For the redoubtable Englishman the unconditional surrender of the Nazis was a real, historical possibility. The troubled American president knew that war meant the end of American civilization, if not history.

Fortunately, in the third phase, while Kennedy was acting out the part of a latter-day Churchill in public, another Kennedy persona emerged in camera—a man under the sway of a new strategic metaphor. He resisted considerable pressure to match his oratory with deeds. Just as wars enable the generals to test their new weapons, crises enable actors to test their new strategies. The initial liminality that beset Kennedy and his associates was generative: it produced a resonant metaphor that would influence generations of crisis managers and warplanners—the gradual escalation strategy.

The strategy—an avowedly symbolic performance—responded to the exigencies of the nuclear age. It eschewed two terribly tangible alternatives: massive retaliation or surrender. As numerous defense intellectuals had warned, the prevailing strategy of massive retaliation (a full-scale nuclear attack on the Soviet Union in response to Soviet aggression) was suicidal—the Soviets could respond in kind. And, given the arresting metaphors of Munich, compromise was construed as surrender and humiliation. As McNamara urged, a "flexible re-sponse" was needed. Gradual escalation was the answer.

The strategy was designed to give adversaries the time and incentive to back down. Obviously, the Eisenhower/Dulles policy of massive retaliation was inimi-cal to this goal—or any other rational objective, for that matter. Mutually assured destruction could not be threatened credibly. Somehow, the New Fron-tier impression manager had to persuade an adversary that he had much to lose if he continued to defy American demands. As McNamara realized, such unfriend-ly persuasion depended upon sending the proper message: namely, that Ameri-can actors had the will and the weapons to continue turning up the heat on an ad-versary by escalating the conflict. The message was conveyed by verbal threats backed up by symbolic performances to make the threats credible.

The escalation, of course, had to be calibrated carefully to send the right message. Too strident a message might provoke needless belligerence, or—worse yet—military reprisals. On the other hand, a weak message might convey timidity. In any case, after initiating the communications at a level suitable to the occasion, an adversary was given time to reconsider and to back down. If he remained intransigent, the threats and performances were escalated to give him the incentive to back down. The impression manager hoped to enjoy "escalation dominance"—the ability to communicate credible threats at virtually every level of escalation.

An Ex Comm member, former CIA Director John McCone, summarized the new strategic thinking in his correspondence with Raymond Garthoff:

> In the Ex Comm deliberations we pursued many alternative courses of action, ranging from presenting the issue to the UN . . . as advocated by Adlai Steven-son, or striking militarily . . . as advocated by Dean Acheson. The committee reasoned that the UN could (and would) do little . . . and that military action would prompt an array of Soviet responses such as taking over Berlin, and acting violently elsewhere. Also it was noted that military action would spill quantities of Soviet blood, thus causing a most serious confrontation that probably would escalate into war. It was decided . . . [by the president] that we should move positively, and always providing Kruschev [sic] with an opportunity to retreat. For that reason, military actions including a blockade (in itself an act of war) were temporarily set aside, and a program of a "quaranteen" [sic] of Cuba was adopted. This was the first step, but if it was ineffective then military action would follow, and Krushcev [sic] was so informed through channels that we knew he respected.[127]

This strategy was operationalized during the Cuban missile crisis, but the escalation was far from gradual. Rapid escalation accomplished its tactical goal: each increment of escalation made the Soviets more fearful. However, in an iron-ic dialectic, the Ex Comm became ever more fearful as they approached the threshold of nuclear war. Evidently, they empathized with Khrushchev. What would they have done if, in response to the U.S. deployment of the Jupiter mis-siles, the Soviets had publicly demanded a withdrawal; blockaded American shipping; and ordered an unprecedented alert and mobilization? Nevertheless, they persisted.

The escalation began when Kennedy threw down the gauntlet during his speech to the nation on October 22: Khrushchev had to remove the missiles. The pressure was turned up through a massive mobilization and an unprecedented state of alert. However, the "quarantine" (a quintessential clinical crisis metaphor) became the very embodiment of the gradual escalation strategy. Indeed, the choice of the term "quarantine" rather than "blockade" reflects the new strategic thinking. A blockade—an embargo against all shipping—is considered a highly provocative act of war. A quarantine—a selective restriction on shipping—was deemed less provocative, at least by its Ex Comm proponents. (Like many analysts, I choose to use the less tendentious term "blockade.") Kennedy and his colleagues realized that the blockade per se could not remove the missiles or prevent them from becoming operational. (The CIA reported that some of the missiles were operational prior to the blockade.) But it was fervently hoped that the blockade would send the right message. A Department of State memorandum issued on October 20, 1962, summarized the situation:

> Imposition of the blockade itself does not of course dispose of the problem of offensive weapons already in Cuba. It only embarks us on what is likely to be a long course of action and counteraction. . . . It is impossible to foresee with any certainty what some of the more likely sequences of events may be and how they may be used to accomplish our ultimate aim of eliminating these offensive weapons from Cuba.[128]

The blockade, of course, was provocative, but unlike the proposed air strike, it was reversible; moreover, it did not necessarily involve killing Soviet personnel. It was hoped that the blockade would "send a message" to Khrushchev; it would convey American resolve. In Lebow's words, the blockade was "a tradeoff between the imperatives for action, which pushed him up the ladder of escalation, and the risks of a confrontation, which pulled him down."[129]

However, recent revelations by those close to Khrushchev suggest that the message may have lost something in the translation. The fine distinction between a belligerent blockade and a more conciliatory quarantine eluded the premier; he didn't get the message.[130] Exercised, reacting angrily, he ordered work speeded up on the missile installations, and vowed that American "pirates" would not stop Soviet ships. Vessels bound for Cuba were accompanied by Soviet attack submarines. Despite McNamara's claim that he got word to the Navy that the blockade was designed to send a message, not start a war, it appears that the Navy didn't get the message. Following routine procedures, Navy aircraft tracked the submarines by dropping depth charges to force them to surface.

In order to give Khrushchev time to reconsider, Kennedy ordered the blockade line retracted (although there is controversy as to when the Navy carried out the order). The anxiety became almost unbearable. As the Soviet armada approached the blockade line, Robert Kennedy allowed that "I felt we were on a precipice with no way off. . . . President Kennedy had initiated a course of events, but he no longer had control over them."[131]

Again, there was good news and bad news. The Soviets did not challenge the blockade, or at least they did not provoke a military confrontation. (Unlike most American officials, many Soviet officials claim that blockade enforcement was lax; see Dobrynin's discussion in *In Confidence*).[132] The bad news was that—as the hawks had warned—the blockade was merely a symbolic gesture that did not resolve Kennedy's problem. Responding to Khrushchev's orders, work speeded up on the installations as more missiles became operational.

Unfortunately, the new strategic metaphor—gradual escalation strategy— appeared to fail. Indeed, throughout the crisis, good news was almost invariably followed by unexpected bad news. As we've seen, on the last Friday of the crisis, the Ex Comm celebrated a seemingly conciliatory letter from Khrushchev. It appeared that the crisis could be resolved if the Americans merely agreed not to invade Cuba. However, the next day a more belligerent missive was received: the Soviets insisted that the Americans must remove their Jupiter missiles quid pro quo. To make matters worse, during that "Black Saturday," a U-2 was shot down over Cuba and another U-2 violated Soviet airspace. In sum, not only did the new strategy of carefully calibrated impression management fail to compel Khrushchev to remove the missiles, it seemed to make matters worse.

The Kennedy brothers entered the fourth phase of the crisis—desperate liminality. It was as if they were lost and abandoned in a darkness with no horizon and no omens to light the dark night of the soul. If such prose seems overwrought, consider Robert Kennedy's lamentations. While questions have been raised about the veracity of RFK's account of the crisis,[133] given the predicament he and his brother faced that final Saturday, his account of their anguish seems credible:

> The president was not optimistic, nor was I. He ordered twenty-four . . . squadrons of the Air Force Reserve to active duty. They would be necessary for an invasion. He had not abandoned hope, but what hope there was now rested with Khrushchev's revising his course within a few hours. It was a hope, not an expectation. The expectation was a military confrontation by Tuesday and possibly tomorrow.[134]

He reports that he and the president found the situation depressing:

> The thought that disturbed him [JFK] the most, and that made the prospect of war much more fearful than it would otherwise have been, was the specter of the death of the children of this country, and all the world—the young people who had no say . . . but whose lives would be snuffed out like everyone else's.[135]

Others close to the president relate the nuclear angst experienced during the last, fateful day of the crisis. Ball refers to the last Ex Comm meeting as "a time of great depression,"[136] and Gilpatric allows that "At times the president would appear distracted or depressed. He was visibly shaken on Saturday morning when the news came in that Major Anderson had been shot down."[137]

It appears that Kennedy lost his faith in the Ex Comm during this critical phase. Evidently, what advice they offered was not seriously entertained. In a speech to the National Press Club early in his administration, Kennedy approvingly cited Lincoln's address to his wartime cabinet. Had he been as forthright as Lincoln, he might have chastened the Ex Comm with his predecessor's remarks: "I have gathered you together to hear what I have written down. I do not wish your advice about the main matter—that I have determined myself."[138]

Indeed, recent evidence suggests that Ex Comm deliberations were not as significant as once believed. Robert Kennedy's nocturnal meetings with Dobrynin in which the secret deal was discussed were not mentioned. And—after the final Ex Comm meeting—Kennedy met secretly with his most trusted cabal of confidants. (Hawks and doves were excluded from the determinative, eleventh hour decision-making regarding tactics and strategy.) As Allyn and his associates suggest, in the final analysis, the Ex Comm was reduced to a ceremonial role:

> The Ex Comm had become largely irrelevant to the president's decision-making at the height of the crisis. Crucial decisions were being made by the president and a few close advisers, well away from—and unknown to—the Ex Comm as a whole.[139]

In any case, the Ex Comm offered no new suggestions for resolving the crisis. Evidently, like the president, Ex Comm had begun to abandon hope. It appeared that the newfound gradual escalation strategy was ineffective at the present level, and hideously dangerous at a higher stage of escalation. Desperate, bereft of new metaphors, Kennedy grasped at straws and regressed to the only metaphors he knew. Not knowing which metaphor to choose, he clung to both by simultaneously playing the parts of Churchill and of Chamberlain: the president's messenger gave the Soviet ambassador a cryptic ultimatum while acceding to Soviet demands. Khrushchev kept quiet about the quid pro quo as agreed.[140]

Just as Kennedy and his associates feared that Khrushchev had lost control because he sent conflicting messages, perhaps Khrushchev reached the same disturbing conclusion about the best and the brightest. He may have retreated because Kennedy's indecisiveness and mixed messages indicated he was losing control of the situation. (Indeed, during his last meeting with Dobrynin, RFK warned of the almost irresistible pressures that were being brought to bear by the military.) Khrushchev may have been empathetic: he was unsure about how to respond to Kennedy's unexpected life crisis; worse yet, it seemed that events were getting out of control in Cuba. Whatever the case, he unexpectedly backed down—"better red than dead!" As Nathan concludes:

> John F. Kennedy was thus salvaged for 25 years from the ignominy of having to make his eagerness to initiate a public swap known to most of his advisers. Kennedy had stood firm. He was tough, and he prevailed.[141]

REMEMBERING THE CUBAN MISSILE CRISIS

> Ever since the successful resolution of that crisis, I have noted among many
> political and military figures a Cuban-missile-crisis syndrome, which calls for a
> repetition in some other conflict of "Jack Kennedy's tough stand of October 1962
> when he told the Russians with their missiles either to pull out or look out!"
>
> —Theodore Sorensen[142]

The posthumous management of the president's image was a stunning success. Decades have passed, new generations have flourished, yet Kennedy's
legendary daring remains an icon of popular culture. Everyone from George
Wallace to James Meredith is enamored with JFK. In Wallace's words, "John F.
Kennedy had guts enough to back Khrushchev down."[143] And Meredith credits
the Kennedy era with "the egalitarian ideal that makes me believe that race is no
longer a factor in America."[144] While adroit impression management nurtured
the legend, the Kennedy administration was not above humiliating and silencing
heretics. As Thompson observes, Canadian Prime Minister John Diefenbaker
stridently criticized Kennedy's handling of the crisis; his unwelcome comments
apparently contributed to his downfall:

> Diefenbaker publicly questioned JFK's veracity, and *then* said, as was leaked to
> the press, that he thought Kennedy "perfectly capable of taking the world to the
> brink of thermonuclear destruction to prove himself the man for our times." Two
> months later, Diefenbaker fell from office. In his memoirs, he charged that the
> Kennedy administration had conspired . . . to throw him out—as if Canada were a
> "banana republic."[145]

However, perhaps the Kennedy legend prevails primarily because people
need heroes. A charismatic, fallen leader is a likely candidate. His bravura crisis
is indelibly etched upon popular consciousness as a template for heroic confrontations. For example, Roseanne Barr is profiled in courage—perhaps rather sar-
donically—because, during her acrimonious contract negotiations, "Once they
couldn't bluff, they lost their ability to intimidate her. It was kind of like the
Cuban missile crisis, when Dean Rusk said, 'The other guy blinked.'"[146]

And CNN characterized a new singing sensation, Alvita Rodriguez, as "the
hottest thing to come out of Cuba since the Missile crisis."[147] Of course, Holly-
wood gets into the act. The latest James Bond film (this genre was a Kennedy
favorite) *Golden Eye* depicts a fictional confrontation as "the worst standoff
since the Cuban Missile crisis." Naturally, the drama climaxes in the discovery
and destruction of a secret Russian base in Cuba.

Columnist Christopher Matthews writes of a preliterate tribesman who
"never saw JFK on television, much less in person." Nevertheless, his most cherished talisman was a Kennedy half-dollar. Matthews wonders:

> What magical powers did he believe were contained in this daunting adornment?
> What blessing did he hope would come from wearing this badge of distinction?
> . . . The answer . . . was on garish display [at the auction of Jacqueline Kennedy's

estate] last week. . . . Why would a person pay $450,000 for a rocking chair, $2.6 million for a ring? For much the same reasons, I suppose, that a rural tribesman might wear a foreign 50-cent piece as a talisman: partly to show wealth; partly to partake of the object's magic.[148]

Did Dostoevky's Grand Inquisitor understand such enchantment? As the haggard Inquisitor chided the radiant Christ on the hot streets of Seville, humans are not content with simple truths; they crave miracles, mystery and magic. How well the Kennedy legend satisfies these desires! The Kennedy of popular consciousness jousted with the Russian ogre on the abyss, risked everything, and miraculously emerged alive—his heroic quest consummated. The Kennedy assassination remains shrouded in mystery and terrible secrets. And time has not dimmed the magic of Camelot. As Tim Carroll concludes: "This event [the Cuban missile crisis] has become a cultural metaphor applied to seemingly intractable problems, potentially explosive dangers, firm resolve, and cleverly creative solutions."[149]

The evolution of the Cuban missile crisis into a latter-day legend merits further study. The transformation of the beleaguered Kennedy bedeviled by indecision into a distillate of Prince Valiant and Winston Churchill is no mean accomplishment. This study, however, is concerned with the impact of the remembered crisis on strategic doctrine and foreign policy.

The Crisis As A Condensation Symbol

Condensation symbols evoke the emotions associated with the situation. They condense into one symbolic event . . . patriotic pride, anxieties, remembrances of past glories or humiliations, promises of future greatness.

—Murray Edelman[150]

The most resonant symbols unify opposites by somehow integrating and concealing contradictions. For example, fundamentalists view God as a benevolent, loving deity considerate enough to condemn their enemies to eternal torment. Likewise—as an absolution from past fiascoes—the crisis is represented as a salutary learning experience that reduced the danger of nuclear holocaust, and a celebration of thermonuclear bravado.

Surely some good emerged from the waning days of October 1962. As Sorensen suggests, the crisis was cathartic:

The effect [of the crisis] was to purge their [those of Soviet and American officials'] minds at least temporarily, of cold-war clichés. . . . Surely there had to be a more sensible way of competing against each other than building still more exorbitantly expensive nuclear weapons. The chief lesson learned from the first nuclear crisis was not how to conduct the next one—but how to avoid it.[151]

In this passage, Sorensen overstates the salutary impact of the crisis; as he warned, the "Cuban missile crisis syndrome" became a misleading and dangerous metaphor. To be sure, the immediate aftermath of those harrowing thirteen days encouraged more amicable relations between the adversaries—or at least better communications through a "hot line" between Washington and Moscow. More significantly, it seems reasonable to argue that the crisis also encouraged the ratification of the Atmospheric Test Ban Treaty of 1963. (Of course, it might be noted that Linus Pauling—not Kennedy or Khrushchev—was awarded the Nobel Peace Prize for his advocacy of the treaty.)

Unfortunately, the salutary effects were temporary. The remembered crisis encouraged nuclear revivalism, folly in Indochina, and unsuccessful attempts to replicate Kennedy's legendary crisis management.

Nuclear Revivalism

In the wake of Russia's forced withdrawal from the Caribbean, a new leadership emerged in the Kremlin whose overriding thought was never again. Never again would the Soviet Union be allowed to suffer such a humiliation at the hands of the Americans.

—David Horowitz[152]

Horowitz's analysis is shared by a variety of Soviet and American analysts. At the time, Soviet analysts and apparatchiks interpreted Khrushchev's capitulation as the inevitable outcome of an inferior Soviet arsenal.[153] He was deposed as the Soviets raced to attain strategic parity. (By the time of the 1970 Cienfuegos crisis, the Soviets enjoyed strategic parity; but strangely, most American actors were rather blasé about this more ominous Soviet challenge.) As Fred Kaplan concludes, prompted by their apparent humiliation during the crisis,

The Soviets . . . completed their crash missile program over the next decade[;] they ended up with 1400 ICBMs. They also built a fleet of nuclear missile submarines, emulating the American Polaris program, and they began to bury their land based missiles in . . . silos similar to those of the American Minuteman.[154]

Nuclear revivalism was not limited to the Soviets. The crisis became a morality play about the virtue of daring gambles and superior weapons. Just as Chamberlain is chastised for appeasement, Kennedy is lionized for his heroics. As James Nathan observes:

The successful and determinedly civilian orchestration of the great panoply of persuasion that was brought to bear on the Soviets . . . seemed to herald an era wherein vastly expanded power, blessedly, had become a relevant, useful, and rational instrument of American policy.[155]

Defense intellectuals concluded that the American nuclear arsenal could be more than an emblem of the Cold War stalemate known as deterrence. Nuclear weapons could be used for "compellence": while deterrence supposedly *prevents* an adversary from acting upon his intentions, compellence forces an adversary to act in a manner inimical to his interests. Consider the case of Michael Mandelbaum (currently a member of the Council on Foreign Relations). Throughout his

The Nuclear Question he argues that the American and Soviet nuclear arsenals deter risk-taking: a correct "nuclear etiquette" has evolved that according to the author, creates the best of all possible worlds. In a vision worthy of any eighteenth century drawing room, he argues:

> I believe that technology and politics have combined to create what has been called a nuclear weapons "regime" . . . that . . . govern[s] the role of nuclear weapons in war, peace and diplomacy, and that this regime constitutes the . . . doctrines most likely to keep the nuclear peace. In this sense *The Nuclear Question* is the story of the evolution of the best of all possible worlds.[156]

His response to Khrushchev's and Kennedy's nuclear faux pas reveals the nuclear revivalism sparked by Kennedy's legendary achievement. Mandelbaum implies that Kennedy's incommensurate response to the Soviet move violated the deterrence doctrine that has given us the best of all possible worlds. As he allows, Soviet moves in Cuba were not an attack or even a substantial threat to American strategic interests:

> It [the Soviet move] was not a nuclear attack upon the United States or an American ally. It was not the kind of step that historically triggered war. . . . Neither was it a clear violation of international law.[157]

And Mandelbaum acknowledges that Kennedy responded to the Soviet move with "gunboat diplomacy" rather than the more genteel etiquette that he insists informs—or should inform—superpower relations: "It was to be sure a rather unusual diplomatic settlement. It was arranged literally at gunpoint."[158] He also acknowledges that such disregard for well-established protocol profanes *the* canon of nuclear theology—deterrence doctrine:

> The Cuban missile crisis clarified the workings of deterrence in the nuclear age. It began . . . with the failure of deterrence. . . . And the outcome of the crisis cannot properly be termed "deterrence," either. It belongs to a different category of relations among states—"compellence."[159]

Nevertheless, like Allison and other mainstream analysts, Mandelbaum breathlessly celebrates Kennedy's joust on the abyss. The lesson he culls is "that a large, invulnerable nuclear arsenal would discourage a great deal of political mischief by the Soviet Union."[160] Of course, nuclear diplomacy must be used with care. Like many others, Mandelbaum believes that the crisis demonstrates the virtue of gradual escalation strategy. By gradually turning up the heat one sends the message that continued defiance will result in more punishment. In the interim, by adroitly calibrating diplomacy with measured—but credible—threats, one offers an adversary the time and incentive to back down. Recalling the crisis, McCone explains: "When our determination became known to him [Khrushchev], the withdrawal of missiles took place almost immediately."[161]

As former Secretary of Defense James Schlesinger's congressional testimony suggests, Kennedy's impromptu reliance upon gradual escalation strategy evolved into the credo of American nuclear war-fighting plans:

> If we were to maintain continued communication with the Soviet leaders during the war, and if we were to describe precisely and meticulously the limited nature of our actions . . . political leaders on both sides will be under powerful pressure to continue to be sensible. . . . I believe that leaders will be rational and prudent. I hope I am not being too optimistic.[162]

In order to operationalize his arguably optimistic faith, Schlesinger recommended the development and deployment of weapons sufficiently accurate to destroy Soviet silos. He claimed that this technology would be indispensable in the event of a limited nuclear war; in the interim, it would send the right message to the Kremlin.[163]

In an article co-authored with George Kennan and Gerard Smith, Ex Comm veterans Bundy and McNamara suggest that they learned a different lesson from the crisis:

> Given the appalling consequences of even the most limited use of nuclear weapons and the total impossibility for both sides of any guarantee against unlimited escalation, there must be the gravest doubt about the wisdom of a policy which asserts the effectiveness of any first use of nuclear weapons by either side.[164]

It appears, however, that Schlesinger's thinking prevails. Despite a substantial reduction in strategic and tactical weapons, and a moratorium on weapons testing, the gradual escalation doctrine seems to guide current war-fighting scenarios. Based upon their critical oral history of the crisis, Blight and Welch suggest that such facile application of gradual escalation strategy to war-gaming scenarios ignores the nuclear angst of an actual confrontation between nuclear powers. "Those who strongly felt the burden of responsibility were inclined to understand power and risk in a radically different way from those who did not."[165] Indeed, as Kaplan concludes, despite their pretensions of realism, nuclear strategists suffer a loss of reality: "[T]he strategists in power treated the theory [of gradual escalation] as if it *were* reality. For those . . . in the corridors of officialdom, nuclear strategy had become the stuff of a living dream-world."[166]

The continued faith in gradual escalation strategy is surprising in light of its less than successful application in Indochina. Perhaps Hegel was right: we learn one thing from history—namely, that people learn nothing from history.

Folly In Indochina

Prompted by Khrushchev's challenge of wars of liberation, a by-product of the limited-war [gradual escalation] strategy emerged: counterinsurgency, which blossomed into the great cult of the Kennedy years with the president himself as its prophet.

—Barbara Tuchman[167]

The efficacy of gradual escalation strategy is arguable: fortunately, it has not been tested in a nuclear war, limited or otherwise. A priori arguments about the advantages and dangers of a gradually escalated nuclear war are speculative. However, there can be little doubt of the efficacy of the strategy in Indochina. As Kaplan's inquiry reveals, in May 1964, Bundy assembled a "small, tightly knit group" (apparently something akin to Kennedy's "mini-Ex Comm") to fashion American policy. Bundy reported:

> The theory of this plan is that we should strike to hurt but not to destroy, and strike for the purpose of changing the North Vietnamese decision on intervention in the south. . . . [The U.S. should] use selected and carefully graduated military force against North Vietnam.[168]

Once again, the recommendations, if not the existence, of this cabal were kept secret. Indeed, Bundy's concern with "credible deniability" during the mercifully brief Cuban missile crisis became a veritable obsession during the seemingly interminable Indochina War. Discussions frequently invoked fashionable "nukespeak" that emerged from the celebrated gradual escalation doctrine. To communicate American resolve, the Vietnamese would be subject increasingly to "counterforce" assaults (that is, attacks on military targets). If this spectacle failed to communicate the power of American weapons and resolve, "countervalue" attacks would begin (put less euphemistically, civilians would be killed.)

According to McNamara, Bundy's plan for a graduated and sustained bombing of North Vietnam had two symbolic objectives: it would diminish the opposition's will, and promote optimism among America's Vietnamese allies. However, McNamara claims that just as he and Bundy were pessimistic about the efficacy of gradual escalation during the crisis, they also were pessimistic about its persuasive power in Vietnam. Nevertheless, Bundy urged that his recommendation would correct "the widespread belief that we do not have the will and force and determination to take the necessary action and stay the course."[169] America's Vietnamese adversaries didn't get the message. Rather belatedly, McNamara laments that "we were wrong, terribly wrong."[170]

The Demise Of Gradual Escalation?

> The model [for Desert Shield] is the Cuban missile crisis of 1962. In that crisis, as in this one, the United States sought to restore the status quo ante—no Soviet missiles capable of reaching the United States in Cuba. Then, as now, there was no backing down on the basic demand. The missiles had to go then, and Iraq has to leave Kuwait now.
> —Les Aspin, chair of the House Armed Services Committee[171]

In response to the Iraqi invasion of Kuwait, Bush sent Hussein a "message" by going public, sending strident communiqués, blockading Iraq and gradually increasing American military presence in the area. And just as Kennedy's strategy appeared to fail in October 1962, Bush's strategy also appeared to fail in

October 1990: Hussein didn't get the message; Iraqi troops remained in Kuwait. Of course, unlike Khrushchev, the Iraqi leader did not back down.

Bush, of course, had the luxury of wholeheartedly resorting to an older metaphor—massive retaliation. (Had the Iraqis possessed nuclear weapons or been allied with a nuclear power such as the former Soviet Union, Bush would have faced Kennedy's dilemma.) In any case, in order to make Kuwait safe for feudalism, the Iraqi infrastructure was devastated by massive bombardment, and the Iraqi army was routed in what can best be described as a massacre.[172]

Bush's triumph overcame the "Vietnam syndrome" (the reluctance of American actors to intervene militarily lest they suffer another humiliation like Vietnam). The application and the success of massive retaliation suggest that the gradual escalation doctrine is no longer embraced enthusiastically and uncritically. Future conventional conflicts may be guided by military sensibilities rather than semiotic strategies of impression management such as gradual escalation. Perhaps some updated, "high-tech" version of massive retaliation doctrine will attain canonical status. In any case, the millenarian search for weapons and strategies that will usher in an epoch of uncontested American power and prosperity continues.

Dostoevksy was right: humans are animals that walk on two legs and feel ungrateful. The occasional pleasures of terrestrial existence do not satisfy more grandiose desires. The relentless search for new weapons and strategies is a variation on a familiar theme: the quest for heroics. This quest is personalized in popular culture's great man theory of history. Among defense intellectuals, the quest becomes a search for heroic weapons and marvelous strategies that will overcome the vagaries of international life by working wonders in history. Dialogue in Brecht's *Galileo* comes to mind:

> Unhappy is the land that breeds no hero.
> No. . . . Unhappy is the land that needs a hero.[173]

NOTES

1. Graham Allison, *The Essence of Decision: Explaining the Cuban Missile Crisis* (Boston: Little, Brown, 1971), frontispiece.

2. John F. Kennedy, *Profiles in Courage* (New York: Harper & Brothers, 1956), frontispiece.

3. Quoted by James A. Nathan in "The Heyday of the New Strategy" in The *Cuban Missile Crisis Revisited*, James A. Nathan, ed., (New York: St. Martin's Press, 1992), 26.

4. Anticipating other contingencies, Sorensen wrote a similar speech for JFK justifying an immediate air attack on Cuba. Many of the paragraphs were invoked in the speech presented. It is chilling to read the word that were almost spoken:

My fellow Americans: With a heavy heart, and in necessary fulfillment of my oath of office, I have ordered—and the United States Air Force has now carried out—military operations, with conventional weapons only, to remove a major nuclear weapons build-up from the soil of Cuba. . . . Further military action has been authorized to ensure that this threat is fully removed and not restored. [The public was urged not to panic.]. . . . I ask that the American people remain calm and self-confident and go about their business. There will be no major war; the strength and determination of your defenses are answer against that. [This document was declassified 2/10/88, and obtained from the National Security Archive, hereafter NSA.]

5. Quoted by Robert Divine in *The Cuban Missile Crisis*, Robert Divine, ed., (Chicago: Quadrangle Books, 1971), 32.

6. Ibid., 34. One cannot help but wonder: If a nuclear war is a war without winners, why risk such a conflagration under any circumstances? Ray Cline, the CIA adviser to the Ex Comm, claims that he inserted the nuclear threat in the president's speech because he felt emboldened by overwhelming U.S. strategic superiority.

7. Quoted in Ibid., 113.

8. Transcript of the 6:30 p.m. Ex Comm meeting of October 16, 1962, 33; obtained from the Kennedy Library.

9. The Kennedy/McNamara dialogue is excerpted from the tape of the October 16 Ex Comm meeting, obtained from the Kennedy Library.

10. Quoted by James G. Blight and David A. Welch in *On The Brink*, Blight and Welch, eds., (New York: Hill and Wang, 1989), 23.

11. Quoted ibid., 54–55.

12. Barton J. Bernstein, "Reconsidering the Missile Crisis," in *The Cuban Missile Crisis Revisited*, James Nathan, ed., (New York: St. Martin's Press, 1992), 102.

13. Pierre Salinger, "Gaps in the Cuban Missile Crisis," *New York Times*, February 5, 1989, 2.

14. The Soviets rejected the charge that the Cuban missiles were "offensive." They argued that the missiles were deployed to deter another American invasion. Many analysts now agree that this was an objective, but they also agree with Dobrynin that defending Cuba was not the only objective. Dobrynin claims that Khrushchev hoped to redress the strategic imbalance and ultimately achieve nuclear parity with the United States. He also thought the missiles might be a useful bargaining chip in controversies such as Berlin. [See his discussion in *In Confidence* (New York: Times Books, 1995), 73.] Other analysts suggest that Khrushchev was responding as well to domestic political pressure and to pressure from the Chinese to project Soviet power more forcefully.

15. See Richard Ned Lebow's discussion of the role of domestic politics in his "The Traditional and Revisionist Interpretations," in *The Cuban Missile Crisis Revisited*, James Nathan, ed., (New York: St. Martin's Press, 1992), 166.

16 Robert F. Kennedy, *Thirteen Days: A Memoir of the Cuban Missile Crisis* (New York: W.W. Norton, 1969), 67.

17. Richard E. Neustadt, *Presidential Power* (New York: John Wiley, 1980), 158.

18. Quoted in Bernstein, 81.

19. See, for example, George Ball, "JFK's Big Moment," in *The New York Review*, February 13, 1992, 16–20.

20. Quoted by Lebow, 175.

21. Quoted by Richard Rhodes in "The General and World War III," in *The New Yorker*, June 19, 1995, 58.

22. John F. Kennedy, Presidential Papers, Washington, D. C.: U.S. Government Printing Office, 1962, 635; obtained from the Kennedy Library.

23. Certain historians, such as Garry Wills, argue that while Kennedy *authorized* these books by presiding over the writing and editing, he did not *author* them. Specifically, Wills contends that while Theodore Sorensen and Jules Davids authored *Profiles in Courage*, JFK supervised and approved the writing. [See Wills's discussion in *The Kennedy Imprisonment* (Boston: Little Brown, 1981), 134–135].

24. *Profiles in Courage*, 4–5.

25. Ibid., 19.

26. Ibid., 238–239.

27. Richard Reeves, *President Kennedy: Profile of Power* (New York: Simon and Schuster, 1993), 41.

28. Randolph Starn, "Historians and Crisis," in *Past and Present*, 52 (Fall 1971), 2.

29. Quoted by Michael Beschloss in his *The Crisis Years* (New York: HarperCollins, 1991), 9.

30. Quoted in Ibid., 472.

31. John F. Kennedy, *Profiles in Courage*, 34.

32. Ibid., 35.

33. Nathan, 5.

34. John F. Kennedy, *Why England Slept*, 192.

35. Quoted in the *San Francisco Chronicle*, June 13, 1995, C–13.

36. Lebow, 170.

37. Quoted by Evelyn Underhill in her *Mysticism* (New York: Meridian Books, 1955), 406; my account of the "dark night of the soul" is indebted to her study.

38. Quoted by Richard M. Nixon in his *RN: The Memoirs of Richard Nixon* (New York: Grosset & Dunlap, 1978), 235.

39. John F. Kennedy, *Profiles in Courage*, 239–240.

40. Beschloss is among the numerous historians who discuss the pivotal incident, 328–330.

41. Quoted in Ibid., 503.

42. Ibid., 330.

43. Wills, 218.

44. Quoted by James G. Blight, in his *The Shattered Crystal Ball* (Lanham: Rowman & Littlefield, 1992), 38.

45. Bernstein, 106.

46. Gerald S. Strober and Deborah H. Strober, *"Let Us Begin Anew": An Oral History of the Kennedy Presidency* (New York: HarperCollins, 1993), 334.

47. Ibid., 334–335.

48. Quoted by Nancy Clinch in her *The Kennedy Neurosis* (New York: Grosset & Dunlap, 1973), 160.

49. Memo from Rostow to Kennedy, 4/24/61; obtained from the Kennedy Library.

50. Quoted in Beschloss, 427.

51. I would feel both guilty and ashamed if I did not acknowledge that this distinction between guilt and shame is indebted to a conversation with Tom Reed.

52. Quoted in Beschloss, 502; these plans are detailed in the declassified Operation Mongoose documents obtained from the National Security Archive.

53. Laurence Chang and Peter Kornbluh, eds., *The Cuban Missile Crisis, 1962* (New York: New Press, 1992), 11–12; this volume contains recently declassified documents collected by the authors' organization, the NSA, Washington, D.C.

54. Quoted in Beschloss, 223–224.

55. Strober and Strober, 357.

56. Beschloss, 226.

57. Quoted by Ibid., 224.

58. Quoted by Ibid., 234.

59. Quoted by Ibid., 224–225.

60. Quoted by Ibid., 228.

61. Quoted by Ibid., 311.

62. Quoted by Ibid., 225.

63. Whether Kennedy ordered the missiles removed prior to the crisis is an ongoing debate. Allison accepts at face value RFK's claim that the president ordered the missiles removed. Not surprisingly, he uses his bureaucratic model to explain why the order was not implemented. Bernstein, however, is more attuned to the daunting problem of interpreting executive documents and deeds. Referring to the study JFK requested regarding removing the missiles, he writes:

A more subtle approach [than Allison's] would acknowledge that a chief executive may often express preferences (not orders) for policies, and that he may sincerely reinterpret them as orders when his own inaction leaves him woefully unprepared for a crisis. (Bernstein in Nathan, 111.)

64. Chang and Kornbluh, 15.

65. See Beschloss' discussion of these events, 230–235.

66. Quoted in Ibid., 230.

67. Ibid., 273– 274.

68. Ibid., 327.

69. Ibid., 329.

70. Ronald Steel, "Lessons of the Cuban Missile Crisis" in *The Cuban Missile Crisis*, Robert Divine, ed., (Chicago: Quadrangle Books, 1971), 229–230.

71. Quoted by Beschloss, 334.

72. Cited by Patrick Glynn in his *Closing Pandora's Box* (New York: Basic Books, 1992), 179.

73. Beschloss, 332.

74. Reeves, 18.

75. Strober and Strober, 375.

76. Ibid., 382.

77. Ibid., 386.

78. Chang and Kornbluh, 114. The hawks, of course, disagreed. Indeed, as various analysts observe, the Ex Comm members with the most extensive foreign policy and military experience were hawks advocating immediate military action.

79. Cited in Chang and Kornbluh, 355; see their chronology of events 347–399.

80. Ibid., 103.

81. Blight and Welch, 91–92.

82. Beschloss, 405.

83. Michael H. Hunt, *Crises In U.S. Foreign Policy* (New Haven: Yale University Press, 1996), 418.

84. Ronald Steel, 214.

85. Arthur Schlesinger, Jr., *A Thousand Days* (Boston: Houghton Mifflin, 1965), 840–841.

86. Even Acheson's seemingly obvious criticism is subject to interpretation. His disparaging comments were published in influential anthologies such as Divine's. However, just after the crisis, Acheson wrote the president a personal letter (obtained from the Kennedy Library) thanking him for sending a memento of the crisis:

I am deeply grateful for [the memento], and grateful, too—as I wrote to you earlier—for the opportunity you opened to me to take part in the campaign so wisely conceived and vigorously executed. . . . You confounded de Tocquville's opinion that a democracy "cannot continue if it measures with secrecy or awaits their consequences with politics." [Given my understanding of etiquette, and Acheson's sensibilities, I give credence to his published comments, rather than to what I regard as an obligatory thank you note.]

87. Dean Acheson, "Homage to Plain Dumb Luck," in *The Cuban Missile Crisis*, Robert Divine, ed., (Chicago: Quadrangle Books, 1971), 207. It is noteworthy that the "hawks" were the most experienced Ex Comm advisors, such as Acheson.

88. Theodore C. Sorensen, "Kennedy Vindicated," in *The Cuban Missile Crisis*, Robert Divine, ed., (Chicago: Quadrangle Books, 1971), 209.

89. Ibid., 211.

90. Chang and Kornbluh, xiiii.

91. Strober and Strober, 393.

92. Allison, 39.

93. Noam Chomsky, "Interventionism & Nuclear War" in *Beyond Survival*, Michael Albert and David Dellinger eds., (Boston: South End Press, 1983), 271.

94. This information is contained on an audiotape declassified by the John F. Kennedy Presidential Library in December 1994; the tape is #33.2 from the Presidential Office File, "Meeting with Congressional Leaders, 10/22/62." The meeting occurred just before the president's public address.

95. John F. Kennedy, *Why England Slept*, 192.

96. Dobrynin, 82.

97. Interview with Raymond Garthoff, at the Brookings Institution, Washington, D.C., May 1990.

98. Bernstein, 69.

99. Richard Helms, "Memorandum for the Record, 'MONGOOSE Meeting with the Attorney General,' 16 October, 1962," in, *CIA Documents on the Cuban Missile Crisis 1962;* obtained from the NSA.

100. "Summary of Record of NSC Executive Committee Meeting no. 8; October 27, 1962, 4:00 p.m."; declassified 9/87. Obtained from NSA.

101. Robert F. Kennedy, *Thirteen Days*, 106–107.

102. McGeorge Bundy, *Danger and Survival* (New York: Random House, 1988)

103. "CIA Chronology of the Cuban Missile Crisis, October 15–28, 1962"; declassified 6/5/92 and obtained from the NSA.

104. See citations and discussion, Nathan, 23.

105. Quoted by Bernstein, 96; Bernstein indicates that Sorensen's statement comes from their correspondence of August 17, 1990.

106. See Beschloss' discussion, 546–547.

107. Dobrynin, 90.

108. Arthur Schlesinger, Jr., *Robert Kennedy and His Times* (Boston: Houghton Mifflin, 1978), 522; this was one of the earliest revelations of the secret deal. According to Sorensen, a letter sent by Khrushchev articulating and formalizing the arrangement was returned unopened. Officials were fearful that such a document might become part of the archival record.

109. Robert F. Kennedy, *Thirteen* Days, 128.

110. Blight and Welch, 104.

111. Quoted by Steel, "Lessons of the Missile Crisis" in Divine, 213.

112. Rusk expressed his relief in an interview conducted by the Public Broadcasting Corporation for its *Missiles of October* documentary, October 1992.

113. Sloan Foundation videotapes, "1982 Interviews with Surviving Ex Comm Members." I wish to thank Art Singer, vice president of the foundation for these tapes.

114. See Robert Kennedy's recollection of these events in *Thirteen Days*, 106–109.

115. Public Broadcasting Corporation interview, October 1992 .

116. See Rhodes, 57.

117. Raymond L. Garthoff, *Reflections On The Cuban Missile Crisis* (Washington: Brookings Institution, 1987), 38.

118. Scott D. Sagan and Kenneth N. Waltz, *The Spread of Nuclear Weapons* (New York: W.W. Norton, 1995), 78.

119. Ibid., 78–79. Sagan recounted the last incident at the Institute on Global Conflict and Cooperation's Nuclear Proliferation Seminar at the University of California, Berkeley on April 12, 1996.

120. Garthoff, 40–41. In *In Confidence*, Dobrynin reports that he learned of the incident from Garthoff and endorses Garthoff's account. (See Dobrynin's comments, 81.)

121. John F. Kennedy, *Profiles in Courage*, 237.

122. Based upon interviews in Moscow and Havana with many of the surviving American, Soviet, and Cuban actors, Bruce J. Allyn, James G. Blight and David A. Welch offer an account of the crisis from diverse perspective in their "Essence of Revision," *International Security* 14: 3 (Winter 1989/1990).

123. Hunt, 245.

124. This possibility broached by Daniel Ellsberg is discussed by Allyn, et al., 163.

125. Quoted in Blight and Welch, 63–64.

126. Quoted by Nathan, 1.

127. Personal letter from John A. McCone to Raymond L. Garthoff, September 22, 1987. I am grateful to Garthoff for sharing this correspondence.

128. "Cuban Missile Crisis Memorandum," issued 10/20/62 by the United States Department of State, and obtained from the NSA.

129. Lebow, 174.

130. See Dobrynin's discussion, 80–81.

131. Robert F. Kennedy, 70–71.

132. Dobrynin, 78–85.

133. RFK's account of events in *Thirteen Days* differs from accounts in the recordings and transcripts. Moreover, as Bernstein notes, RFK's diary along with drafts of the book, are unavailable to independent scholars. (Bernstein, 95.)

134. Robert F. Kennedy, 109.

135. Ibid., 106.

136. Strober and Strober, 399.

137. Ibid., 394.

138. Theodore Sorensen, *Kennedy*, (New York: Harper & Row, 1965), 112.

139. Allyn et al., 109.

140. Much is made of the so-called Cordier maneuver. In a letter to the Hawk's Cay conference, Rusk claimed that the president instructed him that in the event that the Soviets did not respond to the ultimatum, he was to contact Andrew Cordier, a former diplomat. In turn, Cordier would instruct U Thant (Secretary General of the United Nations) to propose publicly a quid pro quo. (Blight and Welch, 83–84). However, this "Rusk revelation" presents serious hermeneutic problems: Why did JFK assign such momentous responsibility to one who was often treated with derision? (Indeed, Rusk is chastised for missing many Ex Comm meetings.) More significantly, Rusk himself urges that his so-called revelation "was not all that much of a big deal. . . . No one can possibly know what president Kennedy's decision would have been; I think we've made a mountain out of a molehill." Bundy concurs that the Cordier maneuver was a contingency, not a decision. (Blight & Welch, 114.)

141. Nathan, 22.

142. Theodore Sorensen, *The Kennedy Legacy* (New York: Macmillan, 1969), 187.

143. Strober and Strober, 495.

144. Ibid., 501.

145. Robert Smith Thompson, *The Missiles of October* (New York: Simon and Schuster, 1992), 351.

146. John Lahr, "Dealing with Roseanne," *The New Yorker*, July 17, 1995, 50–51.

147. CNN News, produced by Brian Calboney, November 16, 1995.

148. Christopher Matthews, "Kennedy Talismans: Magic for Sale," *San Francisco Chronicle*, April 28, 1996, B–9.

149. Tim Carroll, "The Cuban Missile Crisis: Representations and Misrepresentations" presented at the American Association for Popular Culture Conference, Las Vegas, NV, March 26, 1996.

150. Murray Edelman, *The Symbolic Uses of Politics* (Urbana: University of Illinois Press, 1985), 6.

151. Sorensen, *The Kennedy Legacy*, 192.

152. David Horowitz, "The 1980 Guide to Both Cold Wars," *Mother Jones*, May 1980, 252.

153. See, for example, P.N. Fedoseyev, "Technology, Peace and Contemporary Marxism," *Soviet Marxism And Nuclear War*, John Somerville, ed., (Westport: Greenwood Press, 1981).

154. Fred Kaplan, *The Wizard of Armageddon* (New York: Simon and Schuster, 1983), 306.

155. Nathan, 1.

156. Michael Mandelbaum, *The Nuclear Question*, (New York: Cambridge University Press, 1979), vii.

157. Ibid., 134.

158. Ibid., 145.

159. Ibid., 141.

160. Ibid., 155.

161. McCone to Garthoff, September 22, 1987.

162. Quoted by Peter Pringle and William Arkin in *S.I.O.P.* (New York: W.W. Norton, 1983), 178–179.

163. See Kaplan's discussion of NSDM–242, 382–391.

164. McGeorge Bundy, George Kennan, Robert McNamara, and Gerard Smith, "Nuclear Weapons and the Atlantic Alliance" in *Foreign Affairs*, Spring, 1982: 757.

165. Blight and Welch, 319.

166. Kaplan, 390.

167. Barbara Tuchman, *The March of Folly* (New York: Alfred Knopf, 1984), 288.

168. Kaplan, 333.

169. McNamara, *In Retrospect*, 171–172.

170. Ibid., xvi.

171. Quoted by Thompson, 356.

172. A study by the Harvard School of Public Health estimated that approximately 75,000 Iraqi children died as a result of the destruction of the infrastructure. And the mainstream press estimates that over 100,000 Iraqi troops were killed during the 100 hours of ground combat. See Ron Hirschbein, "Support Our Tropes: A Critique Of Persian Gulf Discourse," in *From the Eye of the Storm*, Laurence F. Bove and Laura Duhan Kaplan, eds., (Amsterdam: Rodopi, 1994), 179–186.

173. Quoted by Clinch, 368.

Nixon likely to go head to head — wouldn't
guess forward
afraid
Soviet leadership my agan
w/ new American leader

CHAPTER 4

WHAT IF THEY GAVE A CRISIS AND NOBODY CAME?

On Friday, September 18, 1970, while I was waiting for Golda Meir to arrive, I received an urgent memo from Kissinger. It was headed, "TOP SECRET/SENSI-TIVE/EYES ONLY." Its first sentence stated: "analysis of reconnaissance flight photography over Cuba this morning confirmed the construction of a probable submarine base in Cienfuegos Bay."

—Richard Nixon[1]

By secretly constructing a nuclear submarine base in Cuba, it seemed that the Soviets were inviting Nixon to the most momentous crisis of the nuclear age—a potential Götterdämmerung. As Ambrose observes, Nixon declined: "[Nixon] rejected one obvious option, to play up the crisis as Kennedy had done almost exactly eight years earlier, on the eve of the '62 elections."[2] Quite conceivably, he could have interpreted the memo as a disaster, a crisis, or a problem. While he briefly acknowledges the threat in several of his voluminous works, he down-played—if not ignored—the submarine base during his presidency. His indiffer-ence is puzzling. It appears that he had political, strategic, and personal reasons for promoting this episode as *the* defining crisis of his presidency.

Nixon, it can be maintained with some confidence, was not averse to playing politics. Strident anticommunism was the hallmark of his career. As Ambrose concludes: "Nixon, for all his political convolutions over his long career, had [been consistently] the most prominent and persistent advocate of taking the offensive against Communism."[3] (Ambrose avers that Nixon's anticommunism was a deeply felt commitment. I suggest that it was more opportunistic than ideological or visceral.) In any case, the surreptitious construction of a nuclear submarine base in Cuba presented a near-perfect opportunity for Nixon to vin-dicate himself politically by castigating his predecessors, and by settling scores with the Soviets and Cubans. He ceaselessly maligned Kennedy for appeasing the Castro regime. Even before the Kennedy administration discovered the missiles, Nixon excoriated his predecessor for being "soft on Communism," and demanded an immediate naval blockade of Cuba. Shortly after the crisis, he indicted Kennedy for "pulling defeat from the jaws of victory." And he maligned Kennedy for endorsing the "informal understanding": pledging not to invade Cuba in return for a Soviet pledge not to deploy offensive weapons. Nixon claimed: "As a result of this weak-kneed foreign policy . . . shiploads of Soviet arms have continued to pour into Cuba."[4] He assured the public that—given the opportunity—he would depose Castro. His April 1963 speech before the American Society of Newspaper Editors—a strident, partisan attack on his rival—was vintage Nixon:

> If only I were the partisan type, what a field day I could have. . . . In Cuba we have goofed an invasion, paid tribute to Castro for the prisoners, then given the Soviets squatters' rights in our backyard. . . . [As a result of Kennedy's policies] the Atlantic alliance is in disarray, Cuba is western Russia, and the rest of Latin America is in deadly peril.[5]

Curiously, however, during his presidency, Nixon did not blame his predecessor for setting the stage for the submarine base by failing to depose Castro, thereby allowing a Soviet military buildup in Cuba. Not only did Nixon fail to make a crisis move, he quickly endorsed and formalized Kennedy's "informal understanding." Even a scholar as conversant with Nixon as Ambrose is perplexed that Nixon did not respond to the understanding with a "thunderous no!"

> Instead, for reasons he never explained, Nixon decided to "reaffirm" the understanding in writing, thereby giving it virtually the force of a treaty. In effect, Nixon bestowed the imprimatur of two administrations and both political parties on concessions he maligned throughout his career.[6]

His indifference to the threat posed by the submarine base confounds a host of Nixon legends. It is widely believed that Nixon had an abiding interest in foreign policy. For example, it is a commonplace that he was preoccupied with managing strategic challenges to the fragile balance of power he and Kissinger were struggling to construct. However, according to one of Kissinger's aides:

> Kissinger liked to tell the story of meeting Mrs. Nixon at a reception and making a special point of telling [her] how much he was impressed with . . . her [husband's] grasp of issues. . . . The First Lady frowned and said, "Haven't you seen through him yet?"[7]

Due perhaps to Nixon's successful post-Watergate impression management, many have not seen through him.[8] He was preoccupied with managing Nixon, not foreign affairs. His impression management, of course, began well before Watergate. In a recently declassified letter to Haldeman, Nixon instructs his assistant on "the best way to get across to Henry [Kissinger] some of the points that you think he might make in his backgrounders [press conferences, interviews and broadcasts]. . . ." Specifically, in order to strengthen Nixon's image in foreign affairs, Kissinger was to stress that the president:

1. Is better prepared for negotiations than any of his predecessors;
2. Given his background, has exceptional knowledge of foreign affairs;
3. Treats foreign dignitaries with respect;
4. Never gives an inch on principle;
5. Never quibbles over trivial points;
6. Possesses subtlety and humor;
7. Is thoroughly acquainted with his counterparts;
8. Possesses remarkable candor;
9. Possesses remarkable stamina.[9]

This was a tough sell, even for Kissinger. While he was part of the administration, he attempted to represent Nixon as an adroit statesman. However, his memoirs depict the president as a rank amateur, or—worse yet—someone strangely indifferent to international events. As we shall see, Kissinger is particularly critical about the Cienfuegos incident. He faults Nixon because he refused to act—let alone postpone his vacation—despite their shared perception that the submarine base presented an unmistakable strategic threat. This was neither the first nor the last time that personal indulgences would take priority over momentous events.

To be sure, Nixon recognized the gravity of the threat. Unlike the confrontation of 1962, in which Kennedy and his closest advisers concluded that the land-based missiles did not bestow any strategic advantage upon the Soviets, Nixon and Kissinger determined that the nuclear submarine base confirmed their worst fears. As Nixon explains in his brief retrospective on the episode:

U-2 flights confirmed our worst fears. The construction was proceeding at a rapid pace, and unless we acted quickly and decisively, we would wake up one morning to find a fully functioning nuclear equipped submarine base ninety miles from our shores.[10]

Nixon and Kissinger agreed that such a base would present a "quantum leap" in Soviet strategic capability for two reasons:

1. Unlike the more primitive, immobile, land-based missiles the Soviets attempted to deploy earlier, this new generation of mobile, undetectable weapons was capable of venturing into American territorial waters with impunity; they posed an immediate threat to the North American continent.

2. According to the Department of Defense assessment (which Nixon and Kissinger endorsed), the Cienfuegos base gave the Soviets additional advantages: it enabled their submarines to increase their patrol time within range of the United States by approximately one-third, and it reduced the necessity of passages between the United Kingdom, Greenland and Iceland—a zone where the United States could monitor submarine activity more readily.[11]

Given this situation, surely Nixon could have convinced himself that Soviet actions undermined both his presidency and national security; the case was strong indeed. It could have been argued that just as Khrushchev was testing Kennedy in 1962, so Brezhnev was testing Nixon's courage and credibility in 1970—a bold, decisive response was essential. And, placing the challenge in broader perspective, it could have been maintained that if Nixon could not uphold the Monroe Doctrine and the informal understanding that resolved the 1962 episode, no friend or foe would take American leadership seriously.

Kissinger made this case, and Nixon recognized the threat. But his recognition was purely academic: much to Kissinger's chagrin, Nixon did not want to act. He was adamant—there would be no crisis. Such disregard for Soviet deception and strategic threats was surprising because, according to most of Nixon's biographers, Cuba was a deeply personal concern: Nixon was obsessed with proving that he was a more courageous man and more adroit statesman than Kennedy—Cuba was the litmus test. It would seem that the Cienfuegos incident provided an ideal opportunity for Nixon to act out a social drama: a morality play that would prove beyond a doubt that Nixon detractors were wrong—he was a better man than his charming predecessor. In a phrase, the Cienfuegos incident presented a pretext to settle scores.

Cienfuegos also provided an ideal opportunity for atonement. As Kissinger quips, "Cuba was a neuralgic problem for Nixon." Cuba, to press the metaphor, struck a raw nerve in Nixon's debate with Kennedy during the 1960 presidential campaign. (Surely this insignificant island posed no threat to the United States; however, a socialist regime ninety miles from American shores was a potent symbol then, as it is today.) Indeed, the Cuban issue became the centerpiece of the debate: Who knew how to deal with Castro? Kissinger explains that Nixon was well aware of plans he and Eisenhower had devised for what would become the abortive Bay of Pigs invasion. Nixon had bristled when Kennedy charged that Nixon, the hard-line anticommunist, was soft on Cuba. But when Kennedy urged American intervention to overthrow Castro, Nixon had a brush with morality. In order to safeguard the secret invasion plans he felt obligated to disavow Kennedy's exhortation. According to Kissinger, Nixon—in his usual self-pitying manner—convinced himself that his noble deed contributed to his defeat. Stressing Nixon's bitterness, Kissinger concludes: *"Nixon was determined that no one would ever be able to make this charge again* [italics mine]."[12]

And no doubt, Nixon was exercised when he learned Kennedy's popularity soared after the ill-fated Bay of Pigs invasion. He was so consumed by Kennedy and Cuba that he took the Cuban missile crisis personally; he thought it accounted for his defeat in the 1962 California gubernatorial campaign. Nixon seldom forgave slights, real or imagined. Years later he would claim:

> After falling behind the incumbent . . . we closed the gap, and three weeks before the election we thought we had a good shot. Then came the Cuban missile crisis. This galvanizing drama brought our momentum to a halt. California's voters were far more interested in what was happening in Washington than in deciding whether to replace the governor.[13]

Kissinger goes even further when he maintains that Nixon "never ceased believing that Kennedy had timed the showdown to enhance Democratic prospects in the midterm elections."[14] And Nixon was not indifferent to the fact that the press—ever mocking and critical of him—gave favorable treatment to Kennedy despite his failures. As Ambrose observes:

> The way the press had fawned on Kennedy made Nixon furious and jealous; all the money and things Kennedy had gotten away with had made Nixon resentful: Kennedy's policies—backing down on the Bay of Pigs, allowing Soviet troops to remain on Cuban soil, wiretapping his opponents, refusing to tear down the Berlin Wall. Nixon could hardly avoid feelings of envy about Kennedy's good looks and charm and wit and bearing and money—every politician felt some envy for the man.[15]

Advisers such as Patrick Buchanan were painfully aware Nixon would never be a Kennedy. He advised Nixon to cancel a televised appearance before the Detroit Economic Club (a favorite forum for presidents, aspiring and incumbent) because the usual, overly long Nixon speech would not captivate the public. Worse yet, Nixon would have nothing new to say. Moreover, it was essential for Nixon to create a mystique by appearing inaccessible and aloof. But perhaps most important—he lacked the Kennedy charisma. Buchanan did not mince words when he advised the president:

> I have never been convinced that Richard Nixon, Good Guy, is our long suit. . . . We are simply not going to charm the American people; we are not going to win it on "style" and we ought to forget playing ball in the Kennedys' Court.[16]

In sum, Cienfuegos presented an opportunity for personal vindication: bold, decisive action could prove Buchanan wrong by showing that Nixon, not Kennedy, was a profile in courage. And he could come to the aid of his party by playing the anticommunist card for political advantage. Finally, in the process, he could resolve what he and Kissinger believed was a serious threat to national security. Not only was Kissinger frustrated and chagrined by Nixon's disregard of the situation, he was puzzled:

> For anyone who knew him it was out of the question that he would tolerate the establishment of a Soviet naval base in Cuba. . . . Too much of his political life had been tied up with taking a tough stance on this issue; his friendship with Charles (Bebe) Rebozo, who hated Castro with a fierce Latin passion, guaranteed that he would be constantly exposed to arguments to take a hard line; he would never want to appear weak before his old friend.[17]

Kissinger responds to his puzzlement with a series of plausible conjectures. He suggests that Nixon was preoccupied with a crisis in Jordan, and that another October crisis would generate massive pre-election cynicism among an already suspicious press and public. Finally, we learn that Nixon "had his heart set" on vacationing in the Mediterranean—he did not want to miss the long-awaited spectacle of the Sixth Fleet's firepower.[18]

Kissinger's sardonic remark about Nixon's vacation is telling. In the process of creating new Nixons, Nixon penned reflections on public issues—particularly foreign affairs; but his heart was set on gratifying his private desires. (As we shall see, his unwillingness to cancel his vacation during the "Pumpkin Papers crisis" nearly lead to a personal disaster—the vindication of Alger Hiss.) In order to understand why Nixon did not promote a crisis in response to the Cienfuegos incident, it is essential to emphasize what Kissinger could only intimate: Nixon's concerns were personal. The European excursion indulged his desire to be entertained by naval firepower. As Ambrose suggests, Nixon preferred playing the part of a world statesman in Europe to staying in Washington and actually being one during the Cienfuegos incident.[19] In a phrase, Cienfuegos was simply not a Nixon-style crisis. Nixon's crises were precipitated by attacks on his credibility and reputation, not by the vagaries of international relations.

In order to understand why Nixon construed certain personal embarrassments as crises while ignoring international provocations, we must ask: What manner of man was Richard Nixon? Apparently, being Richard Nixon was crisis enough for the thirty-seventh president; he suffered the Curse of Hermes as only "Tricky Dick" could. True, he represented himself as a statesman who profoundly altered history—a Wilson or a Churchill. But his deeds, especially his crisis narratives, suggest that he was more like Willy Loman, the feckless salesman who wanted to be well-liked in the here and now. Indeed, his biographers could be depicting the low tragedy of Willy Loman when they portray Nixon as a man shaped by early misfortune and humiliation, an insecure individual who felt cheated by life. Not only did Hermes curse him with intractable vulnerabilities and an indelible recollection of slights, real and imagined, but Hermes exacerbated these vulnerabilities and bitter memories as Nixon attained power. Due to his hypervigilance about his credibility and reputation, and his relentless craving for recognition, he became embroiled in a series of embarrassments and petty confrontations he construed as crises. Hermes constantly put him to the test: every encounter that called his credibility into question—be it in his father's grocery store, in a model kitchen in Moscow, or in the White House—was yet another crisis, a battle (to invoke Nixon's favorite metaphor) to vindicate his reputation and avenge his enemies.

This chapter tales a closer look at Nixon's defining crises. There is little difficulty understanding why Nixon virtually ignored a Soviet nuclear submarine base. His liminal crises of meaning and identity were venal and personal: they were sparked by rejection and humiliation—situations that rubbed his face in the realization that he was not "well-liked." Just before his "Great Debate" with JFK, Walter Cronkite reminded Nixon that he was not an object of affection:

> Nixon was asked a deflating question by CBS's Walter Cronkite. "I know you must be aware . . . that there are some . . . who would say, 'I don't know what it is, but I just don't like the man; I can't put my finger on it; I just don't like him.'"[20]

Even Nixon's successes eventually became a curse. His cunning sometimes extricated him from embarrassing situations. But ironically, perhaps his defeated opponent, Helen Gahagan Douglas, ultimately triumphed when she attached the indelible "Tricky Dick" label to Nixon. But even Tricky Dick was no match for Hermes. His reputation as the consummate trickster plagued and ultimately defeated him in a highly suspicious world. Given his reputation, he was usually abandoned and betrayed during his crises. Understandably, this desertion by those he regarded as friends and allies left a lasting impression: it exaggerated his propensity to misinterpret every future threat—real or imagined—as a grave, unmistakable attack upon his presidency. The stage was set for a variation on this familiar Nixon theme—Watergate. During this ultimate test of his credibility and reputation, he mimicked the unforgettable ploys he used to escape the embarrassment he endured during episodes such as the Hiss case, the campaign fund scandal, and the Kitchen Debate. But his tried-and-true methods of dissembling were his undoing.

Likewise, in order to enhance our understanding of why Kissinger construed Cienfuegos as a crisis, we must ask, "What manner of man is the Harvard don who craved recognition and adulation in high places?" His peculiar kinship with Nixon suggests that, he too, was profoundly shaped by his past. (As Freud would have it, the child is the father of the man.) Many of his biographers conclude that, despite their obvious differences, both Nixon and his national security adviser craved recognition: they chose different paths that eventually brought them together.

A closer look at vintage Kissinger crises, will reveal that the academic-turned-media celebrity tried to make a name for himself by becoming the "Doctor of Diplomacy," the premier physician/statesman of his day who was not merely knowledgeable, but wise. He could not forget the nineteenth century diplomats, such as Metternich, whom he had lionized in his dissertation.[21] Unlike Nixon's sagas of personal embarrassments, Kissinger crises go beyond the subjective to abstract concerns about "equilibrium." In his view, the nuclear submarine base would undermine, if not destroy, the delicate homeostasis in East/West relations he was struggling to construct and maintain. Cienfuegos presented a classic challenge. However, Kissinger's secret, quiet diplomacy differed markedly from Kennedy's bravado.

I suggest that given Kissinger's preoccupation with titrating the balance of power in the international body politic, Cienfuegos was a Kissinger-style crisis: unlike Kennedy, he was guided by the medical crisis model in which the physician/statesman excludes amateurs and intervenes at the decisive moment to restore homeostasis. If Nixon was a victim of his own failure, Kissinger was a victim of his success. The arrogant celebrity/specialist prescribed the wrong protocol for victory in places such as Indochina and Iran as detente fell into disrepute.

And could it be that those of us who interpret the Nixon/Kissinger years are also enchanted by Hermes? Our historical memory is highly selective. Nixon was the man we loved to hate for reasons that are not entirely clear: his infractions were no worse than those of his predecessors and successors. Spying on the opposition party and intimidating opponents are not unknown inside the Beltway. Worse yet, Nixon is maligned for his complicity in breaking into Democratic Headquarters, but not for the illegal U.S. entry into Laos and Cambodia. Ironically, both Nixon and Kissinger are responsible for the fact that what is arguably their finest hour is all but forgotten. These men were not reluctant to celebrate their accomplishments. Yet, Nixon spent only five pages on the episode that he immodestly and inaccurately claims was resolved through his strong, quiet diplomacy. According to Nixon, his adroit management averted a "Cuban Nuclear Submarine Crisis . . . that might have taken us to the brink of nuclear confrontation with the Soviet Union."[22] The loquacious Kissinger is critical of Nixon, and unhesitantly credits himself with averting what could have been the most horrific episode of the Cold War. Yet, he spends but twenty pages discussing Cienfuegos in his massive memoir. Cienfuegos seldom merits an annotation in subsequent writings. Heroic crisis narratives are celebrated; clinical crisis narratives are marginalized and soon forgotten, even among their most adroit practitioners. What is remembered, and what is forgotten, reveals a great deal about the characters of Nixon and Kissinger, and their defining crises.

RICHARD NIXON—EVERYMAN

There is no doubt that if a character is shown on stage who goes through the most ordinary actions, and is suddenly revealed to be the president of the United States, his actions immediately assume a much greater magnitude, and pose the possibilities of much greater meaning than if he is the corner grocer.
                                        —Arthur Miller's gloss on Willy Loman[23]

You may be interested to know that my father owned a small [grocery] store . . . and all the Nixon boys worked there while going to school.
                                        —Nixon to Khrushchev during the Kitchen Debate crisis[24]

What manner of man was the son of the corner grocer who became president? This question must be confronted in order to understand why Nixon interpreted certain issues as crises, and downplayed or disregarded others. The question is daunting; Nixon was not transparent, even to himself. The thirty-seventh president remains enigmatic. New Nixons and old Nixons emerge from his cryptic life script—the saga of an anticommunist ideologue and sojourner in China. Most Nixon associates and biographers concur with Kennedy's observation that: "Nixon is a nice fellow in private. . . . I worked with him on the Hill for a long time, but it seems he has a split personality and he is very bad in public, and nobody likes him."[25]

Apparently, Kennedy had compassion—or at least understanding—for his old friend. According to John Kenneth Galbraith, "Kennedy felt sorry for Nixon because he does not know who he is, and at each [campaign] stop he has to decide which Nixon he is at the moment, which must be very exhausting."[26]

Even Nixon's confidants and speech writers view Nixon's representation of himself with suspicion. William Safire quipped that "to the real Nixon, the real

Nixon is not the real Nixon."[27] And Garry Wills's barb about the 1972 presidential inauguration is not completely in jest: like the protesters who bedeviled the president with Nixon masks, the president himself donned a Nixon mask—"he was the least authentic man alive."[28] Nixon biographers speculate as to what, if anything, was beneath the evanescent Nixon personas. John Dean, his personal counsel, observes:

> There are many Richard Nixons. There is somebody who is caring—who worries about when your wife has the flu . . . and there is somebody who is mean-spirited at the other extreme; who will do anything he has to do to accomplish what he wants to accomplish; he was all those people—a very complex person.[29]

The "real" Nixon is variously condemned as a fraud, pitied as a flawed idealist, and celebrated as the consummate realist. Or, to paraphrase Gertrude Stein, perhaps there is no "there" there. Since Nixon sold himself for political success, no authentic self remained—only masks clumsily worn to suit the occasion. As Wills writes, "There is one Nixon only, though there seem to be new ones all the time—he will try to be what people want. He lacks the stamp of place or personality because the Market is death to style, and he is the Market's servant."[30]

Indeed, perhaps there was only one Nixon: a chameleon clumsily changing his persona to suit the occasion. These obviously contrived attempts at sincerity, let alone transformation, provoked embarrassment, if not derision, among Nixon observers. Arthur Miller's comment about the fictive Willy Loman resonates when we recall the real grocer's son: "His emotions were displayed at the wrong times always and he never knew quite when to laugh."[31] Likewise, Wicker *could* easily be talking about the hapless salesman when he suggests:

> Could it be that many detested Nixon, or [he] at least made them uncomfortable, because he was transparent. It was obvious that he had no authentic self. The vacuum and anguish of a vapid and insecure inner life somehow registered.[32]

Perhaps we search for the "real Nixon" in vain. And yet, it appears that Nixon had a discernible character—a disposition to act predictably. His mother, Hannah, claimed that "Richard never changed."[33] There may be no authentic Nixon, but it might be possible to understand the Nixon routine by examining the repertoire of personae he donned to suit the occasion. Perhaps we can come to appreciate the relentless tempo and rhythm—the utter predictability—of the Nixon charade. Nixon was more like Willy Loman than the heroes celebrated in his writing. Like the tragic salesman, Nixon was the product of the American lower middle class. William Popkin seems to describe Richard Nixon when he recounts Willy Loman as:

> Drab and average, the surest guarantee of his drabness is in his commitment to standard ideals, the standard commercial products, and even standard language. His fidelity to the great American dream of success is at the very heart of the play. He believes that success is the reward for making friends and influencing people—being impressive, being persuasive, being well-liked.[34]

Like his later years, Nixon's early life was marked by unforgettable rejection and humiliation. His biography is explored in detail in numerous sources.[35] These sources narrate his escalating battle against these demons; indeed, humiliations—real and imagined—are milestones in Nixon's life. Few biographers, for example, fail to mention Eisenhower's rebuffs. When asked to list major ideas his vice president contributed to his administration, the general replied: "If you give me a week, I might think of one. I don't remember."[36]

Nixon's associates share the perspective of his biographers. For example, Richard Kleindienst (attorney general during the Nixon Administration) observes, "One of the problems he had—and it might have been his great, limiting factor—was that he carried around within him grudges; he permitted himself to develop thoughts of retribution and revenge."[37] His Pyrrhic victories climaxed in his devastating defeat during the Watergate scandal.

The more psychologically attuned biographers suggest that, as a child, Nixon endured a harsh father he could never please, and a kindly mother too distracted by sick children to provide much nurture. Many of Nixon's associates agree. Howard Phillips (Nixon's director of the Office of Economic Opportunity) observes:

> To understand Nixon, you have to understand his relationship to his father, Frank: the dominant factor in his psyche was rejection by his father, and his love-hate relationship with his father was mostly hate, with exaggerated exaltation of his mother, Hannah.

Phillips goes on to suggest that, denied his father's approval, Nixon spent the rest of his life "trying to win the approval of the American establishment through his activities in foreign policy."[38]

Most biographers note that Nixon was considered as an unpopular "loner" in college. Lacking wealth and popularity, he was rejected by the prestige fraternity. We can almost hear Willy Loman baring his soul to his wife, and crying out for understanding, when Nixon laments:

> What starts the process [of character formation] really are the laughs, and slights and snubs when you are a kid. . . . But if you are reasonably intelligent and if your anger is deep enough and strong enough, you learn that you can change those attitudes by excellence, personal gut performance, while those who have everything are sitting on their fat butts.[39]

Regardless of their slant, no biographer depicts the mature Nixon as Zorba the Greek: friendship, let alone joie de vivre, did not come easily to this troubled, insecure man. Driven by resentment against the rejection and ridicule he endured from "those who have everything," Nixon played the game, redoubled his efforts, and became a diligent law student. However, despite his considerable efforts he was rebuffed by prestigious New York firms and even rejected by the FBI. He found himself relegated to obscurity in his native Southern California where his ill-conceived orange juice business failed.

In a somewhat psychoanalytic vein, Wicker concludes that:

> A sense of emotional deprivation deep in Nixon's . . . personality might go far to explain his fear . . . that people didn't like him, perhaps subconsciously that he was not worthy of their liking—a fear causing him . . . to try too hard and too obviously, sometimes too clumsily to appear as an ordinary . . . God-fearing sports-loving . . . American humbled by prominence and responsibility.[40]

George Schultz (Nixon's secretary of labor) is puzzled that Nixon went to great lengths to ingratiate himself when he was interviewed for his cabinet position:

> He talked about how, as a university professor, I could be comfortable in his Cabinet. I couldn't get a word in edgewise. I thought to myself: this man has just been elected president, and he is selling himself to me; it was his insecurity in talking to a university person.[41]

Not only do Nixon's associates note his insecurity, they are taken aback by his vindictiveness. Trespasses against Nixon—real or imagined—precipitated fire-in-the-belly crises, not abstract concerns about Soviet strategic advantages. As Alexander Butterfield (Nixon's special assistant) recalls:

> He heard the president of Harvard [Derek Bok] was on the White House grounds: [Nixon phoned to inquire] "What is that son-of-a-bitch, Bok doing here?" . . . So I said, "He is meeting with Mrs. Nixon; he's a member of her committee, and she is entertaining those people in the East Room." [Nixon replied] "Never again! How did he get in, in the first place?" He asked me once—in very profane language—"Did one of those dirty bastards ever invite me to his f-ing men's club or his goddamn country club? Not once." He was shaking. He was a guy from Whittier; he didn't have the social graces, the education. The hatred was very deep-seated. . . . He hated them.[42]

Freud's observation regarding his depressed, insecure patients is worth recounting. He determined that much of their despair was engendered by the belief that they were failed human beings no one liked, let alone appreciated. The Father of Psychoanalysis mordantly suggested that these sufferers simply had more realistic beliefs than better defended "normal" people. In any event, most Nixon biographers chronicle his life as a saga of ridicule and humiliation: he had few friends, and significant individuals in his life such as Eisenhower spurned him—and he knew it. Nevertheless, as Ambrose remarks, "Nixon tried to be a 'nice guy.' However, as Ann Whitman, Ike's secretary [once remarked] . . . Nixon spent too much time trying to act like a nice guy instead of just being one."[43]

Wicker's take on Eisenhower's relations with Nixon is shared by many biographers. Ambrose, for instance, suggests that:

> In addition to his doubts about Nixon's qualifications, Eisenhower . . . apparently did not much *like* his vice president. Nixon's inner fear came true. The vice

president's obvious ambition and opportunism, his lack of real bonhomie . . . his sheepish humility contrasted with flashes of political savagery . . . none of this made Richard Nixon easy for *anyone* to like. . . .[44]

And despite the fact that Vice President Nixon was much younger than Eisenhower and other Republican luminaries, he was unpopular with the younger generation. Speculating about the youth culture, the *New York Times* concluded that "the rock-and-roll set went strongly for Eisenhower, but simply did not go for Nixon."[45] And, while Nixon dutifully came to the aid of his party in countless campaigns, most Republicans distanced themselves from Nixon or abandoned him during Watergate. Nevertheless, he attained the highest office in the land. Yet, he suffered from emotional impoverishment. Even though Haldeman and Kissinger were in contact with him virtually every day of his presidency, they never became friends.[46] Just after Nixon's resignation, Kissinger made an un-characteristically maudlin, but perhaps accurate, remark. He tried to imagine what the man everyone loved to hate could have been had someone loved him: "I don't think anybody ever did, not his parents, not his peers. . . . He would have been a great, great man had somebody loved him."[47]

Of course, it is also possible that Nixon's quest for the approval and recognition he never got as a child or adult compulsively drove him to the highest office in the land. Whatever the case, given Nixon's vulnerabilities, his crises were triggered by slights and affronts, real or imagined. As Barber recognizes, Nixon's defining life crises were sparked by personal traumas such as exposure of personal inadequacy, ridicule and humiliation; indictments of character, and serious risk of losing power.[48] As Ambrose remarks, Lyndon Johnson was not above taunting Nixon about Eisenhower's rebuffs. The Texan struck a raw nerve when he told reporters:

> He [Nixon] never did really recognize and realize what was going on when he had an official position. . . . You remember what President Eisenhower said, "that if you give him a week or so he'd figure out what he [Nixon] was doing."

According to Ambrose, Pat Buchanan was exercised by this pronouncement. He told Nixon, "He *hit* us. Jesus, did he hit us. You'll never believe how he hit us."[49]

Nixon's ambitions were transparent; he gave opportunism a bad name. Indeed, his attempts at sincerity evoked contempt and ridicule. Like the hapless Willy Loman, Nixon had an unquenchable appetite for recognition, respect, and popularity. As Barber concludes, "Far from being a President preoccupied with great and high affairs of state, Nixon regularly involved himself in the most picayune details of political calculation."[50] The durable Dobrynin, who re-mained Soviet ambassador to the United States during the Nixon administration, shares Barber's perspective about Nixon's calculating nature. Based upon his encounters with the president, he concludes that the legendary anticommunist ideologue was not really preoccupied with the communist threat; it was just a convenient means to climb the political ladder.[51]

The higher he climbed, the farther he fell. Willy Loman's "low tragedy" resonates throughout the Nixon drama. In the words of critic John Gassner; "It
[*Death of a Salesman*] is the tragedy of modern, urban middle class drama; venal
conflicts that lack the profundity and expressiveness of Shakespearean High
Tragedy."[52] Indeed, Richard Nixon is more akin to Willy Loman than to Richard
III. Miller's synopsis of *Death of a Salesman* might well serve as Nixon's epi-
taph:

> It is the tragedy of a man who did believe that he alone was not meeting the
> qualifications laid down for mankind by those clean-shaven [new] frontiersmen
> who inhabit the peaks of broadcasting and advertising office. From those forests
> . . . he heard the thundering command to succeed as it ricochets down the news-
> paper-lined canyons of his city, heard not a human voice, but a wind of a voice to
> which no human can reply in kind, except to stare into the mirror of failure.[53]

As diverse Nixon biographers suggest, his meteoric rise to success intensified
his chronic vulnerabilities. His hubris was plain to those who cared to look: personal affronts enraged Nixon. The presidency did not heal his vulnerabilities; it
opened old wounds. *The Haldeman Diaries* are revealing. Nixon once again experienced rejection and humiliation when *Time* did not name him "Man of the
Year" during the first year of his presidency. As Haldeman confided to his diary:
"They *did* pick FDR, HST, JFK and LBJ in their first years. Interesting!"[54]
Naturally, he experienced dismay and envy when *Time* pictured Nixon *and* Kissinger as men of the year.

Nixon was not above envy. He was not pleased when Kissinger received an
accolade he had long hoped to attain, the Nobel Peace Prize. Apparently, in
order to save face, he had an assistant send a letter to the Nobel Committee indicating that, as president, he could not accept an honor and award for merely
doing his duty. Accordingly, the committee should resist any future temptation to
consider him for a prize.[55]

Recognition eluded Nixon, but as president he was empowered to exact revenge. His venality was hardly worthy of Shakespearean tragedy. *The Haldeman
Diaries* chronicle his vindictiveness—a representative sample should suffice. In
early 1970 a sector of the Jewish community protested French Middle Eastern
policies by organizing a boycott of various events scheduled for French President Pompidou during his visit to Washington. Nixon thought the boycott tarn-
ished his lustrous presidency—he took it very personally. According to Haldeman, Nixon "raged again today against United States Jews because of their behavior toward Pompidou." In addition to postponing delivery of arms to Israel,
Nixon also declared—in Kissinger's presence—that no Jews should be allowed
to talk to him about the Middle East. Haldeman notes that Nixon was "as mad as
he's been since we got here."[56]

There was nothing out of character about Nixon's behavior. As Ambrose
contends upon reading *The Haldeman Diaries*:

The old Nixon is here, on every page—the hatred and jealousy of the Kennedy family, the contempt for bureaucrats, liberals, professors, the educated . . . the obsession with Alger Hiss, the amazing memory.[57]

During his presidency Nixon visited retribution upon "the people who had everything," whose claim to fame was charm and wealth. He retaliated against the intellectual elite who derided his ability and integrity—men like Daniel Ellsberg, who released the Pentagon Papers. The liberal press got its due from FBI agents and tax auditors. And, just as his opponents had no qualms about smearing his reputation with gossip and innuendo, his "plumbers" tried to dredge up sensational scandals during their nocturnal visits to Chappaquiddick, Ellsberg's psychiatrist's office, and, of course, the Watergate complex.

There was something predictable, if not inevitable, in all this. Given the rigidity of Loman's character, Miller explains that he wanted his audience to react to the Loman script as follows: "They would not wonder about 'What happens next and why?' They would be thinking, 'Oh, God, of course!'"[58] Nixon biographies elicit the same response. In Barber's biography, for example, Nixon's career is an open book. His take on Nixon also begins with an "Oh, God, of course!"

> All of us should have known how Richard M. Nixon would approach his work as President. He came to office after 22 years as a politician and public figure. In speeches, interviews, and especially in his book *Six Crises*, Nixon had described and analyzed and defended in extraordinary detail his feelings, his reactions to events and personalities, his life history, and his special techniques for coping with life.[59]

Like Barber—or Aristotle, for that matter—Nixon agrees that leaders reveal their character when they are forced to choose—crises reveal what a person is made of. Throughout his checkered career Nixon celebrated crises as the defining events of his life; indeed, he often expressed a veritable hunger for crises lest his talents starve: a crisis "engages all a man's talents. When he looks back on life, he has to answer the question: did he live up to his capabilities as fully as he could?"[60]

However, he overlooks a more subtle and fundamental possibility: Could it be that what individuals construe as crises—and what they ignore or downplay—reveal more about their character than their style of crisis management? What individuals define as crises discloses the hierarchical structure of their value systems; crises reveal what individuals deem supremely significant—their summum bonum. But what individuals ignore is more revealing. It is essential, of course, to distinguish between Nixon rhetoric and reality. Nixon seldom personified his ideals.

Like Kennedy, the thirty-seventh president wrote extensively about great men and their crises. He lauded leaders such as Wilson, Churchill, de Gaulle and MacArthur for their courage and tenacity at critical junctures.[61] He was, of course, particularly impressed by the resilience of figures such as Churchill and de Gaulle. And naturally he paid obligatory homage to the courage and sacrifice of leaders who somehow prevailed against overwhelming odds. However, Nixon shows considerably more talent and passion when he is absorbed in himself. His tales of the tribulations of great men seem shallow and platitudinous. His analysis of leadership relies upon tired nostrums such as "The successful leader does not talk down to people. He lifts them up." Or, to cite other clichés more akin to small town boosterism than sociological insight: "The successful leader must know when to fight and when to retreat." And Nixon—himself a prolific reader and writer—is less than profound when he urges that "Reading not only enlarges and challenges the mind; it also engages and exercises the brain."[62]

Nixon does not conceal his own character and sensibilities in his account of great men and their crises. His panegyrics to the famous and the powerful are ultimately about Nixon. Barber agrees: "Nixon was forever taken up with himself, testing and checking the condition of his power and virtue."[63] *Leaders* impresses an overarching fact upon the reader: he, Richard Nixon, was personally acquainted with great men. He was received by these men, and he entertained and advised them. More impressive yet, he forcefully expressed his views to leaders as diverse as Churchill and Chou En-lai. (He fails to note that during his vice presidency Churchill usually ignored him.)

Leaders, of course, is also a vehicle for disparaging Kennedy. His predecessor is not mentioned by name, let alone lionized as a great leader. In classic Nixon style, his former friend is alluded to obliquely as a naive, if not cowardly, victim of a commanding, sinister presence—the brash and cunning Khrushchev:

> He [Khrushchev] was the man who put nuclear missiles on Cuba . . . [and] extracted American pledges to pull U.S. missiles out of . . . Turkey and to refrain from supporting those who might threaten Fidel Castro's sanctuary in Cuba.[64]

By and large, *Leaders* reveals more about Nixon than the leaders it purportedly analyzes. It provides yet another pretext for recounting his personal crises in Venezuela and the model home exhibit in Moscow in pictures and prose. Of course, he cannot resist the temptation to retell the saga of the mother of all Nixon crises, the campaign fund episode. What is particularly noteworthy, is that his chapter on the critical junctures in foreign policy confronted during his presidency is entitled "Decisions," not "Crises." The Indochina War presents no crisis for Nixon; it merely invokes lonely decisions: "My loneliest decision was on December 13, 1972. After agreeing before the election to peace terms that we and Saigon considered acceptable, the North Vietnamese backed off."[65]

Haldeman succinctly captures Nixon's sensibility when he quips: "History, to him, is what has happened to Nixon—and what might happen later."[66] One would be hard pressed to find a biographer who likens Nixon to those he idealized. Nixon's heroes triumphantly resolve crises engendered by world-historical events such as world wars. But what are defining Nixon crises? It is difficult to imagine Churchill, de Gaulle or MacArthur boasting—as Nixon did in *Six Crises*—that he got revenge against a heckler by "kicking . . . [the] weird-looking character in the shin; nothing I did all day made me feel better."[67] Like Willy

Loman's travails, Nixon's crises at best evoke domesticity, at worst, mean-spirited banality: pumpkin papers, cocker spaniels, and model kitchens are the icons in the Nixon crisis pantheon. He and Willy Loman are kindred spirits: they work hard, play the game—sometimes honestly, always diligently—and yet they are betrayed and humiliated; despite—or because of—their desperate efforts to gain acceptance and recognition, they simply are not "well-liked." Loman's agonizing crises were not ushered in by changes in the balance of power or the looming threat of war—neither were Nixon's. As Barber observes, Nixon was exquisitely sensitive to public exposure of inadequacy and duplicity, and he was —to say the least—preoccupied with the threat of losing power. However, as his crisis moves illustrate, he was exquisitely vulnerable to ridicule and mockery.[68]

Vintage Nixon Crises

Despite his rhetorical exaggerations, it is hard to see in his six crises (except per-haps the 1960 campaign) issues of world-shattering significance. In his confron-tation with Khrushchev [the "kitchen crisis"] Nixon sees his action as "a small part in the gigantic struggle" in which "at stake was world peace and the survival of freedom," but it is doubtful that Dick and Nikita's colloquy about the relative merits of appliances in a model kitchen would do much to alter the East-West balance of power. Rather, this was a crisis in the personal life of Richard Nixon, a critical moment for him in that it required . . . a nearly total mobilization of his mental and emotional apparatus.

—James Barber[69]

There is little difficulty determining why Nixon regarded certain personal embarrassments as momentous crises, and why he treated the Cienfuegos in-cident with profound indifference. His account of the crises he endured prior to the incident—early in his career as a congressman, senator and vice president—reveals that he virtually ignored episodes that most actors and analysts consider momentous crises. These episodes listed below receive negligible attention in the volume he regarded as his best book, *Six Crises:*

· The Berlin Blockade, 1948
· The victory of Chinese communism, 1949
· The detonation of a Soviet atomic bomb, 1949
· The Korean War, 1950–1953
· The detonation of a Soviet hydrogen bomb, 1954
· The defeat of the French in Indochina, 1954
· The Soviet invasion of Hungary, 1956
· The British, French, and Israeli invasion of Egypt, 1956
· The Soviet Sputnik, 1957
· The Berlin crisis, 1958
· The advent of the Castro regime, 1959
· The U-2 incident, 1960.

Likewise, during his presidency, Nixon seemed indifferent to events such as the Cambodia invasion; the mining of the Haiphong harbor; and the Christmas bombing of Hanoi. Paraphrasing the reports of Nixon aide Winston Lord, Isaacson writes that rather than attending to these events, Nixon "went to Camp David with his drinking buddy Bebe Rebozo." He concludes that "Nixon was out of touch."[70]

What, then, were Nixon crises? Like the fictive Willy Loman, the real Richard Nixon endured crises when he felt cheated by life because—despite his diligence and willingness to play the game—he realized that he was not "well-liked" by the powers that be. As Willy confessed to his wife, "You know, the trouble is, Linda, people don't seem to take to me."[71] Nixon had a similar apprehension: "It is true that of all the Presidents in this century, it is probably true, that I have less . . . supporters in the press than any other President. I'm one of the most hated."[72]

No wonder Wills quipped that Nixon, ". . . called his life a series of crises. He might have said a series of disasters. Even the victories hurt."[73] (Indeed, Nixon must have noticed that Eisenhower left the 1968 Republican convention before his acceptance speech.) In any case, just as Willy Loman's crises were precipitated by personal affronts, vintage Nixon crises were sparked by a spectrum of affronts, from slights (incurred during goodwill missions to South America and the Soviet Union) to orchestrated assaults on his character (such as the campaign fund episode and Watergate scandal). Nixon did not make a crisis move at Cienfuegos because this impersonal event simply had no semblance to the embarrassments narrated in *Six Crises.*

Nixon allows that his crises were personal, but he insists that "each also involved far broader consequences which overshadowed my personal fortune."[74] He intimates that given the nature of the communist conspiracy, the vindication of Alger Hiss, the demise of his candidacy, or unopposed boasting and bullying by Nikita Khrushchev would adversely affect the security of free men everywhere. This claim is, at best, dubious. But these incidents undoubtedly affected Richard Nixon. And surely the critical Cold War junctures that Nixon ignored were more consequential. Nixon crises are self-confessional: they reveal more about Nixon than about the fate of "free people everywhere." Joan Hoff-Wilson's synopsis of *Six Crises* is apt: "With embarrassing candor Nixon detailed . . . how he politicized certain personal events in his career."[75] Perhaps the reader suffers embarrassment because Nixon's preoccupations and responses seem childish. As his biographers suggest, Nixon tended to interpret events in terms of childhood metaphors.

His crisis narratives are highly stylized. As we recount these tales of personal embarrassment we shall find that Nixon invariably portrays himself as a fair-minded ultra-moderate not taken in by ideologues. His liberal adversaries are depicted as dupes seduced by un-American ideologies such as "positivism, pragmatism and ethical neutrality."[76] With a tone that verges on self-pity, he represents himself as the victimized, misunderstood seeker of truth and justice, selflessly crusading against communism only to suffer the calumny of the liberal establishment.

The Pumpkin Papers Crisis

> Fearing that they [the secret documents] might be found in his house by Hiss'
> investigators [Communist secret agents] . . . he [Whittaker Chambers, Nixon's
> informant] stashed the rolls of microfilm away in a hollowed-out pumpkin and
> replaced the pumpkin in its original place in the patch. . . . Where Communist
> espionage was concerned, we had to become accustomed to actions that stretched
> our credibility.
>
> —Richard Nixon's gloss on the Alger Hiss case[77]

As a freshman congressman, Nixon made a name for himself as a member of
the House Committee on Un-American Activities. By recounting this episode, I
do not intend to pass judgment on Alger Hiss. Rather, I discuss the incident to
illustrate the highly personal nature of the first of the vintage Nixon crises.
Whittaker Chambers, a contrite former communist, testified that Alger Hiss—a
respected State Department official—was a communist. Chambers claimed that
he and Hiss were close friends—comrades working closely to infiltrate and undermine the federal government. Nixon believed him or so he claims. Hiss eloquently denied the charge, and claimed that he had never met Chambers. Depicting himself as a willing martyr in the crusade against communism, Nixon
urged that he wanted to convict Hiss in order to fight the dangerous, international communist conspiracy. Nixon biographers and associates suggest other motives. Wicker concludes:

> Nixon had another reason . . . to pursue Hiss, one that he may not have fully
> realized and would not have wished to talk about. . . . Alger Hiss was tall, hand-
> some, elegantly mannered and impeccably dressed. He was everything the "have-
> not" and proudly "self-made" Richard Nixon could not . . . claim for himself—
> everything he tended to envy and disdain.[78]

And Robert Stripling, the committee's chief investigator, goes so far as to
suggest that Nixon's prosecution of Hiss was personal, not ideological:

> Stripling told historian Allen Weinstein that Nixon's investigation of Hiss was a
> personal thing. He was no more concerned about whether or not Hiss was [a
> communist] than a billy goat. Stripling later cited a . . . remark by Hiss to Nixon:
> "I graduated from Harvard. I heard your school was Whittier."[79]

According to Nixon, Hiss was convincing, at least initially. Indeed, Truman
and a host of distinguished officials—even Republican colleagues on the committee—believed him. Nixon stood alone and endured liminality. He thought he
had dug himself into a hole, and there was no escape. Prominent officials accused him of red-baiting and ruining yet another reputation. He felt abandoned
and lost; his credibility was on the line. Would it be "fight or flight"? He confessed that he was tempted to retreat. He claims that, after considerable soul-
searching, he decided to respond with "fight" rather than "flight." (However,

those closest to him suggest that he did not want his vacation ruined: he succumbed to temptation and fled to Panama.) [80]

But even his detractors agree—Nixon was tenacious. He favors the reader with a suspenseful narrative, a triumphant account of his protracted efforts to discredit Hiss. A cocker spaniel was destined to play a part in this episode: (Checkers was not the first of his breed to play a cameo role in these Nixon dramas.) His faith was vindicated when Chambers testified that he knew Hiss so well that he recalled that "Hiss and his wife had a cocker spaniel . . . which they had boarded at a kennel on Wisconsin Avenue in Washington when they went on vacations to Maryland's eastern shore." [81]

Further investigation revealed that Hiss *indeed* had a brown cocker spaniel he boarded in a kennel near Rock Creek Park. [82] This episode, however, would not come to be known as the first cocker spaniel crisis—the spaniel remained unnamed. The Pumpkin Papers entered the scene like a deus ex machina.

Nixon complains that despite the considerable evidence he and his associates gathered, Justice Department officials refused to investigate, let alone indict, Hiss. (He concludes that the department succumbed to political pressures from the Truman administration.) As the crisis narrative unfolds, we learn that Hiss and Chambers sued each other for libel. Nixon explains that there was nothing more he could do: the courts would resolve the case. He allows that his "mind turned to some purely personal matters": he and Pat would, at last, enjoy a long-postponed vacation. His associate tells a different story:

> Despite his obsession with Hiss, Nixon didn't want his vacation spoiled. When Stripling tried to persuade him to interview Chambers again . . . Nixon refused: "I'm so goddamned sick and tired of this case, I don't want to hear any more about it and I'm going to Panama. And the hell with it and you and the whole damned business!" [83]

(Stripling speculates that Nixon was angry with Chambers for giving the "bombshell"—the Pumpkin Papers—to the FBI, not to Nixon. Wicker claims that somehow Pat Nixon persuaded Stripling to allow her husband to take credit for the case because "Dick was going to run for the Senate.") [84]

In any event, in 1948 and in 1970 Nixon refused to allow anything to spoil his vacation plans. However, while Nixon was cruising toward Panama, Stripling discovered the Pumpkin Papers. (Nixon's right; the story *is* incredible!) Chambers claimed that while he and Hiss were communist agents during the 1930s, Hiss stole secret State Department documents. Chambers maintained that he microfilmed the documents and hid his copies. Years later, during the Hiss controversy, he decided to reveal these documents allegedly penned and typed by Hiss himself. However, during the controversy he hid the films in a pumpkin lest they be recaptured by Hiss and other communist agents.

Nixon breathlessly recounts being spirited off the ship and flown to the east coast to peruse the documents and to interview Chambers. However, euphoria quickly turned to despair. Nixon depicts a classic liminal experience. The tenacious Nixon did his homework. Chambers claimed the documents were copied on Kodak film during the 1930s. Nixon contacted Kodak to check the veracity of the claim. A technician indicated that the film in question was manufactured *after* 1945. Nixon confessed that he was at a loss for words—virtually in shock. He thought he had been deceived by a diabolical maniac who made a fatal mistake.[85]

Confronted with the technician's analysis, Chambers saw himself as a latter-day Job: "God is against me." He attempted suicide. And Nixon determined that he had just committed political suicide—there was nowhere to turn. He planned a press conference that "would be the biggest crow-eating performance in the history of Capitol Hill."[86] However—to continue Nixon's narrative—the technician called at the last moment and apologized for his mistake: the film was manufactured in 1938. To compress the story, Nixon and Chambers were vindicated, and Hiss was eventually imprisoned for perjury. Nixon laments that despite his triumph, he still was not well-liked; the crisis—"left a residue of hatred and hostility toward me—not only among the communists but also among substantial segments of the press and the intellectual community." In a more humorous vein, Nixon notes that he learned that during one of his campaign speeches an elderly woman remarked, "I like Eisenhower, but I don't like Nixon. . . . He was mixed up with that awful Alger Hiss!"[87]

Nixon concludes that he came to realize that the danger of communism cannot be overestimated. The Pumpkin Papers crisis proved beyond a reasonable doubt that Communists will stop at nothing to achieve their goals: deception, intimidation, and treachery are routine tactics. He emphasizes that he responded vigorously to the communist threat, although critics suggest the real crisis was about Hiss's insolence. In any case, it is doubtful that the aging Pumpkin Papers were more threatening than Soviet nuclear submarines ninety miles from the United States. However, Nixon did not take the Soviet challenge personally. There was no crisis.

The Checkers Speech

> Tuesday night the nation saw a little man, squirming his way out of a dilemma, and laying bare his most private hopes, fears and liabilities. This time the common man was a Republican for a change. . . . Dick Nixon.
> —Columnist Robert Ruark on the Checkers Speech[88]

The Campaign Fund crisis—the template of all Nixon crises—was precipitated by the unjust charge that Nixon appropriated benefactors' contributions for his personal use. It was resolved by a maudlin televised performance known as the "Checkers Speech"—an allusion to Nixon's confession about his cocker spaniel. He recounts this "most scarring crisis" by recalling "the most exciting day of his life": the day he was nominated for vice president. Perhaps his euphoria was not unalloyed: he fails to mention a fact widely known to Nixon biographers and insiders. According to Eisenhower confidants such as Arthur Larson, the general allowed the party to select his vice president; Eisenhower was not enthusiastic about their choice.[89] Indeed, Eisenhower apparently never befriended Nixon, and the vice president became increasingly sensitive to the venerable Ike's rebuffs. As Barber explains, "After an outdoor ceremony at Gettysburg, Ike jovially escorted some pals into his farmhouse, leaving Nixon on the lawn. 'Do you know,' Nixon said, 'he's never asked me into that house yet.'"[90]

Unlike the other Nixon crisis sagas, the fund episode invites empathy, even compassion, for the man. During the 1952 campaign he worked hard and did nothing illegal, yet, he endured calumny and betrayal. Despite Eisenhower's attitude, Nixon—ever the good soldier—fought hard. Despite (or perhaps because of) his realization that he was not in the general's good graces, he campaigned vigorously for the ticket, sometimes beyond the point of exhaustion. Typically, he made ten whistle-stop speeches a day in addition to other appearances.

Admittedly, he misinterpreted the significance of the *New York Post* banner headline—"SECRET NIXON FUND." He concluded that the story was a typical smear crafted by "the most partisan Democratic paper in the country." Moreover, he believed that there was nothing unethical, let alone illegal, about the fund. There was solid precedent for supporters donating money for campaign expenses; Eisenhower and Stevenson had similar funds.[91] (Perhaps they remained mute on the controversy and let Nixon take the criticism for this reason.) In any case, unlike future Nixon escapades, the fund withstood the test of probity. Audits and legal opinions determined that it was not used for personal extravagances, and—as Nixon claimed—it was legal and properly managed.

Nevertheless, Nixon would soon endure a liminal experience only surpassed by Watergate. His initial response to the controversy was predictable. He boasts about pointing the finger and red-baiting. (Of course he realized that the attack was orchestrated by his Democratic opponents, operatives not averse to using tactics perfected by Nixon himself, and not by the minuscule Communist Party USA.) Seldom accused of complete candor, Nixon represented the smear as part and parcel of communist subversion. He explains that his response was guided by a tried-and-true Nixon tactic: don't be defensive—counterattack! With some pride, he recounts responding to hecklers by literally pointing his finger and proclaiming: "When I received the nomination for the vice presidency I was warned that if I continued to attack the communists . . . they would continue to smear me."[92]

As usual, Nixon was trying to sell himself, but even his old allies and constituencies were not buying. His efforts at salesmanship were embarrassing, even transparent. No wonder literary critic Jeremy Hawthorn mentions Nixon and Loman in the same breath:

> When American voters were asked whether or not they would buy a used car from Nixon, they were being encouraged to recognize precisely the same sort of untrustworthiness in the politician as they knew had to be guarded against in the salesman [Willy Loman].[93]

Nixon could not understand why he was abandoned by Eisenhower and the Republican leadership. As he explains: "when Republicans as well as Democrats began to demand my scalp, the roof caved in."[94] The general quickly distanced himself from Nixon; he refused to contact his running mate or to issue a statement of support. Leading Republican newspapers demanded his resignation. Nixon laments: "The handwriting on the wall seemed to say: 'Dick Nixon is through.'"[95] He had no metaphors to account for his predicament, just a daunting, unforeseen reality. Eisenhower's closest associates began the first "Dump Nixon" campaign; Nixon was at a loss. A rare close friend, Murray Chotiner, recalls:

> Dick was sitting in a huge leather chair, his arms stretched out, his hands dangling in that characteristic way of his. His brooding face and his posture reminded me of the statue in the Lincoln Memorial. . . . I knew I was in the presence of total despair. The scene is so deeply etched in my memory that I will never forget it.[96]

Liminal episodes, to reiterate, can also be periods of fecundity and daring. Nixon planned to resolve the crisis by pleading directly to the American public through a new and largely untried medium—television. And, with unusual bravado, he de facto presented Eisenhower with an ultimatum. When the general equivocated about supporting him, and insisted that Nixon himself must decide whether to resign, candidate Nixon's response violated the usual protocol. With considerable relish he claims that he pulled rank and told the general, "Fish or cut bait." He insisted that Eisenhower must watch his televised apologia and decide for himself immediately.[97]

Eisenhower remained evasive. He told his running mate that no decision could be made until four or five days after the speech. Nixon focused his efforts on writing the speech and practicing his delivery.

> The speech was to be the most important of my life. I felt that it was my battle alone. I had been deserted by so many I thought were friends but who had panicked in the battle when the first shots were fired. I realized I had to . . . convince . . . [the public] of my honesty and integrity.[98]

However, just before he was scheduled to deliver the speech, Thomas Dewey, an Eisenhower confidant, called and told Nixon that Eisenhower's advisers had reached a consensus: he should resign at the close of the speech. Nixon was devastated. He admits that he was at a loss for words; he simply didn't know what to do. Dewey's news was unbearable. Nixon's rejoinder did not endear him to Eisenhower and his associates. Nixon offers a dramatic eleventh-hour rendition of the climax of the crisis. In *Six Crises* we read that Dewey's call was so disconcerting that Nixon had no time to prepare the final draft of his speech. At this critical juncture during this mother of all Nixon crises, we learn that candidate Nixon berated Dewey: "'Just tell them I haven't the slightest idea as to what I am going to do and if they want to find out they'd better listen to the broadcast.' . . . I slammed down the receiver."[99] The stage was set for a classic Nixon performance, an improvisation he would invoke time and again to attempt to extricate himself from liminality.

As he walked down the corridor to the studio, Nixon feared it was his "last mile." Beardstick was applied to his telltale five-o'clock shadow. There was no time to test the lighting or the moves he would make on stage. He confesses that since he could not attend the television rehearsals, the producers of what would become the "Checker's Speech" relied upon a used car salesman as a stand-in.[100] (From that day on, Democratic opponents would taunt, "Would you buy a used car from Nixon?")

The Nixon campaign spent $75,000 to buy air time to explain the $18,000 fund. Nixon's performance followed the popular Milton Berle Show. To this day the speech is subject to diverse interpretations. Critics see the speech as a shamelessly self-serving spectacle, a base appeal that ranged from the maudlin to the sanctimonious. Supporters interpret the speech as the courageous expiation of a tenacious fighter wronged by adversaries and betrayed by friends. The speech's effectiveness, however, is beyond dispute. After enumerating his meager assets, Nixon cited the considered opinion of auditors and lawyers—the fund was legal and ethical. Following his allusion to his wife's "Republican cloth coat," he favored viewers with a sure-fire anecdote that would forever dog his career. Candidate Nixon determined that if FDR could use his dog, Fala, to advantage, surely he could use dogs—and kids—to *his* advantage. Solemnly, he detailed receiving an unreported gift, a child's pet he vowed not to return regardless of the consequences:

> A man down in Texas heard . . . that our two youngsters would like to have a dog and, believe it or not . . . we got a message from Union Station . . . saying they had a package. . . . It was a little cocker spaniel dog . . . the six-year-old named it Checkers. . . . Regardless of what they say about it, we are going to keep it.[101]

And yet, Nixon's harrowing ordeal was not at an end. In an audacious move, he disregarded Eisenhower's advisers, pulled rank on the general, and urged viewers to contact the Republican National Committee to indicate whether he should remain on the ticket. But, as fate would have it, he omitted the address. He thought the performance was a flop, and—worse yet—there was no word from Eisenhower. He collapsed into tearful despair. Several days passed before he learned that viewers such as Mamie Eisenhower wept during the oration that would put the family pet in the history books. But Nixon had the last laugh. Somehow the National Committee and a host of Republican luminaries were besieged by telegrams supporting Nixon. Reintegrated into the Republican establishment, he was summoned by the general. When Nixon answered the call Eisenhower unexpectedly turned out to greet him. Another liminal interlude passed; Nixon's rite of passage put him back in the race. Once again, he was properly awed and obsequious: "General, you didn't need to come out to the airport," was all I could think to say. "Why not?" he said with a broad grin, "you're my boy."[102]

In a footnote to history, Christopher Matthews reveals:

Last week, word arrived of the late cocker spaniel's reward. Checkers will be shipped westward to the Nixon Library . . . where he will rest not far from the man who made him famous and whose young political career he saved.[103]

The Kitchen Debate

"This resolution stinks. It stinks like fresh horse shit, and nothing smells worse than that!" [Khrushchev's tirade against Nixon concerning the Captive Nation's Resolution of 1959.] I recalled from my briefing materials that Khrushchev had worked as a pig herder in his youth. . . . I replied in a conversational tone: "I am afraid that the Chairman is mistaken. There is something that smells worse . . . pig shit." [Nixon's resolution of a "mini-crisis" that preceded the Kitchen Crisis.]
—Richard Nixon [104]

The crises Nixon endured during his visit to Moscow in the summer of 1959 have a distinctly domestic air. The admittedly ceremonial trip marked by unpleasant encounters with Khrushchev precipitated personal crises. Yet, Nixon insists, "Every move in this crisis-laden struggle was important. At stake was world peace and the survival of freedom."[105] Given the stakes, Nixon dilates at great length about his exchange of insults and his "one-upmanship." He narrates a series of small crises that cascaded in the American model city exhibit set up in Moscow: the exchange of insults, accusations, and threats began in Khrushchev's office, escalated in the model TV studio, continued at the model grocery store, and culminated in a defining moment in the model kitchen.

The ceremonial visit began unceremoniously. Not one to forget slights, real or imagined, years later Nixon would rail about the cool reception that was merely correct, nothing more. He took offense when ceremonial welcomes failed to provide sufficient narcissistic nutrients. Much to his dismay, there were no bands, no anthems, and no crowds.[106] (As Haldeman discloses, Nixon "really ate up" pomp and circumstance.[107] Indeed, the new Nixon installed trumpeters at the White House and cloaked the guards in uniforms that would embarrass the Vatcan's Swiss Guard.) However, returning to the "old Nixon," we learn that, adding insult to the proverbial injury, his visit was not featured in Soviet papers.

As we have already seen, Nixon—according to his lights—successfully managed the Captive Nations Resolution controversy; he made ready for loftier feats. A social drama was about to unfold at the American model television studio. Khrushchev insulted the vice president and boasted that "When we catch up with you, in passing you by, we will wave to you. Then if you wish, we can stop and say: Please follow us."[108] Such was the level of discourse; Nixon cites other examples. He stridently reminded Khrushchev that "You don't know everything!" To which the chairman replied, "If I don't know everything, you don't know anything about communism—except fear of it."[109] Nixon claims that he comported himself well during these insulting exchanges. He did not lapse into liminality despite Khrushchev's goading. Recognizing that he was Khrushchev's host, and conscious of their difference in rank, Nixon did what was expected—"it was not the time to take him on." But the time would come for a dramatic showdown—in the kitchen.

On the way to the kitchen, the pair passed the model grocery store prompting Nixon to try to charm Khrushchev with a remark about his father's grocery. But charm, as Nixon's advisers warned, was not the vice president's strongest suit. Khrushchev was unmoved. Still exercised by the Captive Nations Resolution, he retorted, "all shopkeepers are thieves." After further dialogue more typical of homespun acrimony than the Congress of Vienna, Nixon confesses that he couldn't let the incident pass. He reminded Khrushchev that he saw people weighing food "after they had bought it from the State [store]."[110]

According to Nixon, the discussion in the model kitchen began innocently enough—a discourse about the relative merits of washing machines. Nixon, however became agitated when Khrushchev charged that American products suffered from planned obsolescence. He detailed the choices available to American consumers, only to be interrupted by yet another bumptious Khrushchev diatribe on washing machines. Attempting to give the clash some redeeming value, Nixon moralized that competition in washing machines was preferable to competition in rockets. Khrushchev went ballistic, so to speak: jabbing his finger in the vice presidential chest, he declared that American generals were warmongers.

A crisis was at hand; decorum unraveled. Nixon had to strike back, lest he leave the impression that "the second-highest official of the United States, and the government I represented were dealing with Khrushchev from a position of weakness."[111] Nixon apparently poked Khrushchev with *his* finger and urged that if war comes, both countries lose. His exhortation did not quell the dispute: a new controversy raged as to whether the Nixon and Khrushchev grandchildren would live under communism or capitalism. Nixon responded to his adversary's accusations and threats in kind. He reports that Khrushchev finally gave in and agreed that he too wanted peace and friendship with all nations, especially America. The crisis ended as Nixon put his hand on the chairman's shoulder and confessed, "I'm afraid I haven't been a good host." Suddenly conciliatory, Chairman Khrushchev turned to the American guide and thanked the "housewife for letting us use her kitchen for our argument."[112]

The wire services quickly picked up the picture of Nixon jabbing Khrushchev with his finger (or so it appeared in the carefully contrived photographs Nixon circulated upon his return). In one of his more successful efforts at impression management, Nixon got extraordinary political mileage out of this pictorial representation of the event—it became a veritable Nixon icon.

The Kitchen Debate was not the last Nixon crisis. Future episodes replayed the script. According to Pulitzer Prize-winning journalist, Seymour Hersh, Nixon's visit to India during 1971 precipitated yet another venal, highly personal crisis. Offended by the lack of a proper welcoming ceremony, and by Indira Gandhi's refusal to serve his customary alcoholic beverages, Nixon once again blurred the personal and political: he sided with Gandhi's rival, Ayub Kahn, in their 1971 border dispute—a conflict that evoked the specter of a superpower confrontation. Hersh observes: "Nixon hated . . . Gandhi and viewed her as a deceitful 'bitch'. . . . Nixon had visited New Delhi . . . and had been treated there with little ceremony, to his everlasting dissatisfaction."[113]

According to Hoff-Wilson, Nixon's closest advisers tried to move him beyond his personal preoccupations by invoking challenges in foreign affairs to cultivate a crisis mentality in the White House.[114] The Cienfuegos incident was not their only failure. Apparently, Nixon treasured vacations and a good night's sleep. Due to his strict instructions not to be awakened, he did not initially participate in a harrowing incident that threatened to escalate into a superpower confrontation—the 1973 Yom Kippur War.

Watergate was the culminating Nixon crisis. Because Barber was conversant with the Nixon's character expressed in his crises—and non-crises—his prediction (hazarded in 1971) seems prescient. He predicted the Watergate disaster:

> [His] character could lead the President on to disaster. . . . The danger is that crisis will be transformed into tragedy—that Nixon will go from a dramatic experiment to a moral commitment, a commitment to follow his private star, to fly off in the face of overwhelming odds.[115]

The details of Watergate have been rehearsed in other places. However, as Matthews notes, Nixon had good reason to feel particularly bitter about the scandal. During his congressional campaign, burglars from Democratic headquarters stole the entire stock of pamphlets Pat Nixon had financed with her own funds.[116] While Nixon was, no doubt, wondering "Why me?" Senator Bob Packwood favored the president with his analysis of his Watergate predicament. He knew whence he spoke. Confronting the president directly, Packwood declared:

> All of us, Mr. President . . . have weaknesses. For some, it's drinking. For others, it's gambling, for still others, it's women. None of these weaknesses applies to you. Your weakness is credibility. This has always been your short suit with the news media and the general public.[117]

As Nixon admitted, unlike his other crises of credibility, Watergate ended in disaster. During what must have seemed like an interminable period of liminality, he even considered doing another Checkers Speech: he would make a last maudlin appeal, and ask the public to determine his fate. Perhaps it occurred to Nixon that his old tactics were no longer viable, or, like the hapless Willy Loman, he was too despondent to try. Barber's account of the last days of the Nixon presidency reads like *Death of a Salesman* just before the curtain falls:

> Near the end, as his political defenses crumbled, so did his psychological defenses. Then Nixon revealed the fragility of his self-esteem, the fear and trembling which lay hidden behind his mask. . . . Often enraged and raging, frequently out of touch with the reality gathering around him . . . he was a weeping, staggering, irrational man.[118]

Perhaps literary critic Raymond William's synopsis of the low tragedy of Willy Loman also applies to a president discarded by the system:

Willy Loman is a man who from selling things has passed to selling himself, he has become, in effect, a commodity which like other commodities will at a certain point be discarded by the laws of the economy. He brings tragedy down on himself, not by opposing the lie, but by living it.[119]

And yet, in Linda Loman's poignant words, "attention must be paid." For Nixon, in Wicker's telling phrase, was one of us:

He was . . . Richard Nixon, American—working and scheming without let-up to achieve his dreams, soured by the inequities of life, perhaps by his own fallibilities, surely by the cynical lesson that "in politics most people are your friends only as long as you can do something for them". . . . Nixon was one of us.[120]

Given the possible outcome of a superpower confrontation, it was preferable to have "Everyman" in the Oval Office during the Cienfuegos incident, rather than a would-be hero like Kennedy: venality is preferable to grandiosity. (One can only speculate as to the disaster that might have occurred had Nixon emulated Kennedy. In light of the public humiliation the Soviets endured in 1962, and the nuclear parity they enjoyed in 1970, would they have felt emboldened to risk nuclear omnicide had Nixon promoted a public confrontation?) To be sure, Nixon's response—or rather, lack of response—was far from ideal; but politics is not noted for ideal solutions. It is, in the words of a colleague, "a choice between the undesirable and the unacceptable."

Fortunately, Cienfuegos was simply not a vintage Nixon crisis: indifferent to that which did not personally concern him, lacking any sense of urgency or passion for risk-taking, he disregarded the Soviet base and vacationed as planned. In retrospect, it is difficult to see how the base would have made a difference in the scheme of things. Perhaps the thirty-seventh president must be credited for being in the right place at the right time, and for doing the right thing for the wrong reasons.

DR. KISSINGER—PHYSICIAN/STATESMAN

It makes no difference whether . . . [a statesman's] subjects be willing or unwilling: they may rule with or without a code of laws. . . . It is the same with doctors. We do not assess the medical qualification of a doctor by the degree of willingness . . . to submit . . . to their painful treatment. Doctors are still doctors whether they work according to fixed prescriptions or without them. . . . So long as they control our health on a scientific basis . . . we must insist that in this disinterested scientific ability we see the distinguishing mark of true authority in medicine—and of true authority everywhere else as well.

—Plato, the *Statesman*[121]

He [the statesman] owes it to his people to strive, to create, and to resist the decay that besets all human institutions.

—Henry Kissinger[122]

Why was Kissinger's response to a Soviet provocation in Cuba remarkably different from those of Nixon and Kennedy? Unlike Nixon, Kissinger was perturbed by the discovery of Soviet activities in Cuba. (In Isaacson's telling phrase, after Kissinger saw the reconnaissance photos, he "did a Paul Revere ride through the West Wing."[123]) But unlike Kennedy, he avoided a public confrontation, minimized risk-taking, and relied upon secret diplomacy. It is tempting, of course, to presuppose an obvious possibility: Kissinger was a different sort of man. This facile response, however, is more problematic than it seems, for it appears that Nixon and Kissinger were vexed by the same demons. However, as we shall see, Kissinger's response to these vulnerabilities differed markedly from Nixon's.

The Odd Couple

Richard Nixon . . . often stressed how different he and Kissinger were. . . . But it was some inner similarities rather than their surface differences that helped forge the murky bond that was to unite them. As each of them acquired the power he had long sought, they retained the personal insecurities they found reflected in each other.

—Walter Isaacson[124]

Biographers such as Isaacson and Mazlish make a compelling case when they draw parallels between the Harvard don and the grocer's son. Some of the similarities are incidental. Cocker spaniels, for example, were the favored pet. Just as Checkers may have been kept in violation of campaign codes, so Kissinger also kept a cocker spaniel in violation of regulations: while a student at Harvard, he illicitly kept the pet in his room.[125]

On a more serious note (as various biographers suggest) both of these highly secretive men seemed to suffer from a narcissistic disorder: due to the humiliation they endured early in life and their unrequited needs for affection and approval, they developed an insatiable craving for adulation. The good news is that they got what they desired—international prominence; the bad news is that they could never attain what they *needed*—unconditional affection and nurturing from their parents. Both of these self-made men came from humble backgrounds and achieved astonishing success. Unfortunately, according to these biographers, they remained insecure and venal because their unmet childhood needs for affection and approval could never be fulfilled. In order to attain the approval they craved, they became emotional chameleons. (Kissinger, however, was more self-reflective than the president: he would sometimes joke about his strategic use of flattery to curry favor with the prominent and powerful.) Their success exacerbated their vulnerability. According to Mazlish, despite their exalted positions, Nixon and Kissinger remained loners prone to mood swings and to increasing suspicion of those around them.[126]

Due, perhaps, to the intensity of their needs, their pursuits were seldom inhibited by moral scruples. Duplicity characterized their personal and professional affairs. For example, Kissinger often ridiculed Nixon among academic colleagues—who loved to hate the president. However, in his fawning personal contact with Nixon, he gave hypocrisy a bad name. (Nixon and his staff returned the favor by mocking Kissinger behind his back.) Kissinger was guided by what Isaacson calls "the courtier's instincts:"

> Even while he was denigrating Nixon behind his back, Kissinger was fawning to his face. . . . "Nixon desperately wanted to be told how well he had done," Kissinger recalled. He obliged. . . . After his first meeting with . . . Dobrynin, Nixon called Kissinger into his office four times to hear him tell him how well he had done.[127]

Likewise, the Watergate tapes are no tribute to Nixon's integrity. In his public pronouncements, Nixon portrayed himself as a martyred innocent, a decent man defamed by accusations of racism, even drunkenness, by his enemies. After listening to the tapes, Seymour Hersh writes:

> The tapes show him to be a racist. Pejorative words and phrases dominated. . . . Jews were "kikes," blacks were "niggers," and reporters were "press pricks." His problem was not that he drank too much but that he had very little capacity for handling liquor.[128]

Nixon and Kissinger penned apologetics to justify their lack of scruples. Nixon's admonition in *Leaders*—a veritable paean to Hermes—is also vintage Kissinger. Both these officials thought they could put certain tricks to good use while public servants—but don't try this legerdemain at home:

> The qualities required for leadership are not necessarily those that we would want our children to emulate—unless we wanted them to be leaders. . . . Guile, vanity, dissembling in other circumstances . . . might be unattractive habits, but to the leader they can be essential.[129]

Nixon and Kissinger cultivated these habits—they took dissembling to new heights, or depths. Of course, neither of these actors wanted to be trapped in blatant lies. Like Hermes, they relied upon guile, half-truth, ambiguity, and "inoperative" statements to finesse difficult situations. (On occasion Nixon even tried charm, but with little success. But Kissinger's carefully cultivated charm was extraordinarily successful—until the magic vanished.) Commenting on an admired practitioner of realpolitik, Kissinger notes:

> It was not that Bismarck lied—this is much too self-conscious an act—but that he was finely attuned to the subtlest currents in any environment and produced measures precisely adjusted to the need to prevail.[130]

As Hersh suggests, Kissinger's tenacity and deviousness did not go unnoticed or unrewarded in high places:

The President also realized that . . . only Kissinger had the intellectual stamina and the deviousness to be successful at conducting simultaneous back-channel negotiations with the Soviets and the Chinese.[131]

Nixon and Kissinger suffered the Curse of Hermes—a special fate awaits those who would play god. For a time the Kissinger magic worked. (Nixon, of course, was not averse to taking credit for his adviser's miraculous deeds.) In addition to resolving the Cienfuegos provocation, Kissinger legitimized détente, improved relations with China, and enjoyed considerable success in his "shuttle diplomacy."

Ironically, it undoubtedly occurred to this unlikely pair that they were not the only practitioners of guile. Indeed, their view of human nature was less than exalted. Lawrence Eagleburger, a long time Kissinger aide and State Department official, claimed that "Kissinger and Nixon both had degrees of paranoia."[132] That Nixon and Kissinger suffered from clinical paranoia is dubious; like Bismarck, they were merely aware of their environment. Given the nature of the international environment, there was nothing delusional about their apprehension that friend and foe alike were duplicitous and plotting against them.

Despite these similarities, Nixon and Kissinger responded to their vulnerabilities differently. The marked contrast in their crisis narratives put these differences in stark relief. As Mazlish suggests:

> In the case of Richard Nixon there was no intellectualization, no conceptual system worthy of the name, that mediated between him and his . . . impulses. He acted directly on the political process, uninspired by almost anything other than opportunism and his inner need.[133]

Unmoved by deeply held convictions, let alone conceptual systems, Nixon's crises, as we have seen, were personal, if not venal. Since these episodes are about his unmet emotional needs, it is difficult for more sophisticated audiences not to read *Six Crises* without discomfort. To be sure, the origins of Kissinger's world view can also be understood psychologically—it may have been a response to many of the vulnerabilities that bedeviled Nixon; but once it was established, Kissinger's conceptual system buffered his vulnerabilities, and took on a life and momentum of its own. Unlike Nixon, Kissinger played to a different audience: he pegged his self-esteem on the intellectual elegance and political efficacy of this system. Unlike Nixon's anecdotes about his emotional life, Kissinger's crisis narratives are carefully crafted explications of realpolitik.

The World According to Dr. Kissinger

> Crisis management, the academic focus of the Sixties, was no longer enough. Crises were symptoms of deeper problems which if allowed to fester would prove increasingly unmanageable. Moral exuberance had inspired both over involvement and isolationism. . . . [The correct] concept of our fundamental national interests would provide a ballast of restraint and assurance of continuity.
>
> —Henry Kissinger[134]

Unlike Nixon, who evidently sought power and acclaim for their own sake, Kissinger represented himself as the premier foreign policy expert of his day—the doctor of diplomacy. Deconstructing this representation takes us beyond the Baroque palaces of nineteenth-century Vienna to the Agora of ancient Athens and the teachings of Plato. Seldom tempered by excessive humility, Kissinger envisaged himself as the Platonic physician/statesman of the *Republic*: a practitioner of statecraft at once knowledgeable and wise. Unlike Kennedy, who tried to represent himself as a hero, Kissinger represented himself as the serene, unperturbed expert who diagnoses and treats the international body politic as it is, not as it should be. And like Plato, he seems to hold that each generation—if it is fortunate—produces one such as he, a premier expert able to harmonize antagonistic forces.

Envisaging himself as *the* physician/statesman of his generation, Kissinger took it upon himself to pass judgment on competitors, past and present. Eisenhower was ridiculed as a general practitioner naively prescribing "peace at any price" despite the consequences. Nixon was considered an "amateur" not to be taken seriously. And Kissinger derided the enduring bureaucracy of presidential advisers and foreign policy analysts: the "businessmen" and "lawyers" who ran the bureaucracy lacked his gifts. (As his critics note, such arrogance has little justification. There was nothing original, let alone seminal, in Kissinger's conceptual framework. He relied upon his ethos and celebrity to bestow stature and profundity on the commonplace political realism that influenced academics in his generation.)

In Kissinger's view, he alone possessed the synoptic grasp of world-historical events, the reflective wisdom essential for establishing and maintaining equilibrium in the international body politic.[135] The doctor of diplomacy diagnosed maladies in past crisis management and prescribed a cure. For the most part, according to Kissinger, political malaise results when amateurs and bureaucrats attempt to manage foreign affairs. And, to repeat a perennial Kissinger theme, this mixture of naive idealism and incompetence often leads to disaster. The fate of the earth must be in the hands of a specialist. He was not above appealing to American popular culture to stress this point. As Mazlish explains:

> He [Kissinger] *is* a solitary actor—or nothing. This is clearly his self-image, as made evident . . . in his fantasy [related to] Oriana Fallaci of being . . . "the cowboy entering a village or city alone on his horse."[136]

Kissinger would regret depicting himself as a Prussian cowboy, especially as he rode into the sunset during the Ford Administration. But his theory and practice retained an enthusiastic, uncritical faith in experts, or rather *his* expertise. (After reading Kissinger's latest work, *Diplomacy*, it appears that most of the debacles of the past occurred because Kissinger himself was unavailable to properly titrate the balance of power.) Kissinger's embrace of expert sagacity is usually traced to his celebration of Metternich and the Congress of Vienna:

> The international system which lasted the longest without a major war was the one following the Congress of Vienna. It combined legitimacy and equilibrium, shared values, and balance-of-power diplomacy.[137]

However, this faith can be traced back to Platonic visions of the physician-statesman: the indisputable expert, who assures the health and survival of the polity through his or her remarkable ability to harmonize contending forces. Such a man (or woman—Plato was remarkably free of sexism on this issue) was accountable to no one. Plato taught that the attainment of harmony in the body—or the body politic—was not possible through referenda or cabals. The blessings of harmony required the wisdom of an extraordinary individual, and each generation, if it were fortunate, might produce such a person. (Like Plato, Kissinger believes that harmony is transitory, at least in this world. However, the physician/statesman is best qualified to establish and preserve harmony as long as possible.)

According to Dr. Kissinger his patient—American foreign policy—suffers from a general malaise. Due to intemperate American idealism, it suffers mood swings between manic excitement over moral crusades, and demoralization induced by the traumas inflicted by these hopeless causes. (In his later writings, he was concerned with the "Vietnam syndrome." He feared that America was withdrawing into isolationism. He would restore the nation to robust health through a wholesome appetite for foreign adventure, a properly balanced diet of capabilities and expectations.)

This diagnosis and prescription inform his case studies. There might well be some truth to Kissinger's claim that Wilson became a broken man because he was obsessed with subjective ideals rather than objective power relations.[138] Kissinger prescribes realism; high-minded altruism is contraindicated. The balance of power can be measured, altruism cannot. In his words, "National interest can be calculated; altruism depends on the definition of its practitioner."[139] (That the balance of power can be measured is arguable. The concept seems more metaphorical than algebraic. What attempt at precise ratiocination, for example, would settle disputes about the balance of power in the Middle East or the Balkans?)

Likewise, laboring on the fringes of Kennedy's Camelot, Kissinger became critical of the youthful bravado of impatient tacticians who eschewed reflective planning and succumbed to quick fixes. Specifically, he found fault with Kennedy's impulsiveness and heroic posturing during crises in Berlin and Cuba. Kissinger saw himself as more than a strategist; like Plato's physician/statesman, he believed that he alone had a synoptic grasp of the forces that produce harmony and disorder.

Other administrations erred by trying to discern or somehow modify an adversary's intentions: they should have determined how to balance antagonist forces in order to produce homeostasis in the international body politic. As Kissinger insists, a nation's self-interest and long-term capabilities are decisive, not transitory or falsely stated, intentions. He was painfully aware of the naiveté and misdiagnosis of those who tried to divine Hitler's intentions:

Great Britain and France were absorbed trying to read Hitler's mind. . . . But foreign policy builds on quicksand when it disregards actual power relationships and relies on prophesies of another's intentions.[140]

And yet, his resolution of the Cienfuegos incident relied upon accurately reading and cleverly manipulating the intentions of foreign and domestic political actors.

CIENFUEGOS

There was no dispute about the facts; all agreed that a base capable of servicing nuclear submarines was being built and that the Soviets were seeking to skirt the Kennedy-Khrushchev understanding.

—Henry Kissinger[141]

Just as Kennedy had established the Ex Comm to manage the Cuban missile crisis, the Nixon/Kissinger administration established the Washington Strategic Action Group (WSAG) to manage crises. Kissinger convened the group in response to Soviet actions. Curiously, although the perceived threat during the 1970 episode was more harrowing than the perceived threat in 1962, the WSAG response was surprisingly conciliatory and understanding of Soviet sensibilities. No hawks demanded an immediate air strike and invasion. And no moderates discussed public confrontations, blockades, ultimatums, and clandestine deals. There were only different varieties of doves in the WSAG aviary.

As Kissinger stresses, his colleagues agreed upon the facts, but the facts did not speak for themselves. (He fails to mention that he drew the right conclusion from a mistaken interpretation of Cuban culture. Reconnaissance photos revealed that the Soviets, among other things, were building a soccer field. Kissinger explains: "In my eyes this stamped it indelibly as a Russian base, since as an old soccer fan I knew Cubans played no soccer."[142] Cubans actually do play soccer.) In any case, Dr. Kissinger evaluates various diagnoses and prescriptions, and concludes that he knew best.

The president, as we have seen, downplayed—if not ignored—the situation; he did not want a crisis. True, Nixon sounded tough when he recommended irritating Castro; boycotting nations dealing with Castro; or putting missiles back in Turkey—or a submarine base in the Black Sea. Kissinger rejected such "amateurish" prescriptions: "these [suggestions] were all a waste of time." However, Nixon soon became indifferent. Even as Soviet fighters harassed American reconnaissance planes and chased them from Cuban airspace, "Nixon," in Kissinger's words, "urged me to play it all down." Indeed, the president seemed to fear bad public relations more than nuclear submarines. Following Nixon's instructions, Kissinger reports that he convened a WSAG meeting in which "The discussion dealt entirely with press guidance should Cienfuegos become public while the President was in Europe."[143]

However, other members of the WSAG construed the submarine base as a chronic problem to be resolved in due course, not an acute crisis. Kissinger's nemesis, Secretary of State William Rogers, suggested a summit meeting or perhaps secret talks at a future date. Kissinger rejected this proposal because the Soviets might go public, thereby fomenting another joust on the abyss. In any case, any delay would provide the opportunity for the Soviets to complete the base, thereby upsetting the fragile balance of power.

As he had done during the 1962 crisis, Sovietologist Llewellyn Thompson urged negotiations. Offering more of a psychodynamic view than a strategic assessment, he argued that the Soviets were responding merely to a "national inferiority complex." Seeking parity with their American counterparts, they wanted to deploy nuclear submarines at foreign bases, as the Americans had done for years.[144] Kissinger, of course, rejected such attempts to divine adversarial intentions.

An official usually regarded as a hawk, Secretary of Defense Melvin Laird, was among the most dovish. Despite the threat posed by the base, and Soviet harassment of American reconnaissance aircraft, he insisted that no crisis existed because the American arsenal could deter any Soviet threat.[145] (If the United States could deter an attack in a situation of nuclear parity in 1970, surely it also could have deterred such an attack in 1962, when it enjoyed overwhelming superiority.)

Kissinger disagreed. Obviously the American arsenal did not deter the Soviets from undermining the balance of power by secretly building a nuclear base in Cuba. He endorsed an assessment that the secretary of defense evidently rejected, the assessment of the secretary's own "shop." Kissinger explains that the Department of Defense (DOD) concluded that the Cienfuegos base would enable Soviet submarines to increase their operation time away from port, and—more disturbing still—enhance their capacity to operate in the Gulf of Mexico. This capacity would bring additional American territory within range of Soviet submarine-launched missiles.[146]

Kissinger concludes that the American arsenal alone could not preserve international equilibrium. Worse yet, doing nothing or deferring action would send the wrong message: the Soviets might be emboldened to make even more provocative moves elsewhere. The situation cried out for the intervention of a physician/statesman at the right moment to titrate the balance of power. Only such a man could find the right words to prevent the crisis from becoming a disaster. Pleading with Nixon, Kissinger urged that he and Dobrynin should use the secret channel to resolve the situation. Nixon denied the request and prepared for his vacation. Kissinger claims that a fortuitous event occurred a few days later: a DOD official inadvertently briefed the press on Soviet actions. (In *The Price of Power*, Seymour Hersh claims that Kissinger was ultimately responsible for this leak.[147]) In any case, Kissinger remarks that the press responded predictably with alarmist headlines: the Soviets were establishing a nuclear submarine base in Cuba.[148]

He persuaded Nixon that due to this leak, an exceedingly dangerous public confrontation was imminent. Accordingly, he must be permitted to settle matters quickly and quietly through the secret channel. Nixon reluctantly agreed to allow

Kissinger to meet briefly with Dobrynin. But he insisted that Kissinger must accompany him to Europe, lest Kissinger promote the confrontation as a crisis. (It is tempting to suggest that Nixon also wanted to be present to take credit for settling the episode.)

Dr. Kissinger took charge. As usual, the premier specialist ignored the advice of associates. He defined the provocation as a crisis because—according to his metaphorical narrative—Soviet actions were akin to those of nineteenth-century imperial states that upset the delicate constitution of the international body politic. Much to his credit, unlike the ideologues in the Kennedy administration who demonized the Soviets, Kissinger likened the Soviets to the benign, legitimate states that participated in the Congress of Vienna. (In Kissinger's view, malign, illicit states—such as Nazi Germany—had to be excised forcibly from the body politic. He argued, of course, that benign states became malignant unless their growth was checked by judiciously balancing antagonistic forces.) Precisely for this reason, the Soviets had to be cut down to size: a Soviet nuclear base ninety miles from American shores would bestow unprecedented strategic advantage, undermine American credibility, and encourage Soviet adventurism.

Kissinger's account of his Cienfuegos press conference presents awesome interpretive difficulties. He is obviously proud of what he portrays as cleverly contrived dissembling and duplicity. But it is difficult not to suspect that Kissinger's accounts of himself are less than candid—even depictions of his wile and cunning. In any case, I see no prima facie reason to hold that Kissinger is absolutely candid with his readers or with himself. Putting these understandable suspicions aside, Kissinger presents a bravura account of masterful, diplomatic dissembling, a gloss on a virtuoso performance—whether true or not—that would have bedazzled Hermes. We read that Kissinger conjured up a carefully crafted mixture of ambiguity, half-truth, and guile designed to quell public alarm while bestowing diplomatic leverage with Dobrynin.

During the press conference, he eagerly awaited questions that would serve as a pretext for his bravura performance. With carefully chosen words he minimized domestic apprehension while giving the Soviets a graceful way to withdraw. Predictably, he was asked whether the president was going abroad at a bad time: Shouldn't Nixon remain in Washington to resolve the confrontation involving the Soviet submarine base? Unlike Kennedy, who dramatically escalated a comparable confrontation by going public and issuing an ultimatum, Kissinger decided not to promote the confrontation as a crisis—at least in public. After reiterating the informal understanding that resolved the 1962 episode, he asserted the opposite of what he believed (or so he claims): "We are not . . . in a position to say exactly what they [Soviet actions in Cuba] mean. . . . [And] nothing very rapid and dramatic is likely to occur."[149] Ironically, as we shall see shortly, even those who were justly suspicious of Kissinger got the right message precisely because they were suspicious! In any case, as Kissinger would shortly discover, the construction of the Soviet base stopped just after the press conference.

In order not to alarm Dobrynin unduly (and, perhaps, to maintain the element of surprise), Kissinger used the proposed summit conference as a pretext for meeting with the Soviet ambassador shortly after the press conference. He explained to Dobrynin that his pronouncements at the press conference "had been carefully chosen to suggest that the United States had not yet made up its mind about the precise nature of Soviet activities in Cienfuegos."[150] Kissinger stressed that this misleading public representation of the situation was designed expressly to give the Soviets a face-saving opportunity to withdraw from Cuba without a public spectacle. However, in reality, the American leaders viewed the situation with the "utmost gravity": the base simply could not remain. The United States would take any steps necessary to force a Soviet withdrawal. However, if the Soviets withdrew immediately, their provocative activities would simply be dismissed as a "training exercise." According to Kissinger, Dobrynin comported himself like a professional representative of a legitimate state. While he was not enthusiastic about Kissinger's message, he "coolly said that he would report to Moscow and be in touch."[151]

Nixon vacationed as planned, and Kissinger joined him at the president's insistence. No one remained inside the Beltway to promote a crisis atmosphere. Nevertheless, Kissinger had good cause for apprehension: "The fact remained that less than forty-eight hours after the end of the Syrian invasion of Jordan, we were close to another confrontation, this time with a superpower."[152]

The Curse of Hermes worked in Kissinger's favor, at least for a time. The first wave of suspicion undermined Kissinger's efforts to conceal Soviet actions, or so it seemed. However, the Nixon/Kissinger reputation for duplicity saved the day. Kissinger intimates that he prevailed because the second wave of suspicion was suspicious of the first! According to Kissinger, the first wave was generated by the always suspicious liberal press. The *Washington Post* proclaimed: "U.S. Warns Reds on Cuba Sub Base." And influential columnists warned that Kissinger was trying to cover up a grave threat to American security. Naturally, Kissinger was apprehensive about such publicity fomenting a public confrontation. The second wave generated a convoluted, Byzantine suspicion that worked to Kissinger's advantage. As he suggests, such heightened suspicion was prevalent because, "this was the era of Vietnam." Kissinger's convoluted, deceitful plot worked. As he intended, the truly suspicious critics of the Nixon administration reasoned that Kissinger used reverse psychology at his press conference: playing upon his dissembling reputation, Kissinger claims he hoped that the public would conclude that he was not truthful—he was concealing a momentous crisis. However, Nixon administration critics such as senators Frank Church and William Fulbright fell for the trap—they would not be taken in, or so they thought. They convinced themselves that they saw through Kissinger, and concluded that the Soviet submarine base was a fiction contrived for domestic politics. As Kissinger quips, "Fulbright voiced his skepticism on 'Issues and Answers,' helpfully just as the Nixon party departed from Washington." The senator expressed this second-wave suspicion when he complained that "nearly every year just before we have an appropriations bill in the Senate, we get these stories."[153]

Nixon and Kissinger returned in early October. Kissinger met with Dobrynin, and learned—with some satisfaction—that the Soviets agreed to abide by the informal understanding: no submarines with operational ballistic nuclear missiles would be based in Cuba. Due to Dobrynin's dissembling qualification, Kissinger was put to the test again. Through supple maneuvering, he got the Soviets to agree not to construct offensive naval bases in Cuba. This verbal agreement failed to resolve the situation. Kissinger's diplomatic acumen would be tested continually over the next six months. On a monthly basis the Soviets removed offending ships and supplies only to redeploy them a few weeks later. With a notable absence of frustration, Kissinger explains that the Soviets were seeking loopholes in what became the formal understanding regarding American and Soviet policy toward Cuba. [154] He remarks that he patiently reiterated his position to Dobrynin. His patience paid off. The Soviets stopped testing Kissinger's resolve in May 1971. He concludes, "Rather than a dramatic confrontation on the order of 1962, we considered that quiet diplomacy was best suited to giving the USSR an opportunity to withdraw without humiliation."[155]

Kissinger turned in a virtuoso performance; Hermes himself would not have been more impressive. His resolve was tested continually, yet he prevailed. Using the prescribed mixture of charm, deception and dissembling, he chose the right words: Dobrynin got the message: the status quo forged in October 1962 was reestablished in May 1971. Nixon's impression managers permitted Admiral Thomas Moorer (chairman of the Joint Chiefs) to tell the Economic Club of Detroit that the Soviet Union did not have a submarine base in Cuba.

There is, of course, no end to interpretation. This account of the forgotten Cienfuegos crisis is based upon interviews and available data. However, due to the obscurity of the episode, interpretive commentary is minimal. And, most significantly, it appears that much remains to be discovered. As Haldeman discloses, "Most of the material relating to this incident [Cienfuegos] was deleted from my diary by the government for national security reasons."[156]

Sic Transit Gloria

I'm the only secretary of state who has lost two countries in three weeks.
—Kissinger's lamentation following Communist
victories in Vietnam and Cambodia[157]

Successes such as Cienfuegos, along with editorial cartoons and op-ed pieces, reinforced Kissinger's belief in magic. The quintessential realist came to believe that he had found the magic formula, the right words and gestures, to bend realpolitik to his will. However, within a few years, it appeared to most observers that the magic was gone. Kissinger was constantly put to the test by foreign and domestic crises. He survived the demise of the Nixon administration, only to endure a series of foreign policy calamities while Ford's secretary

of state. As fate would have it, he served another president who preferred vacations to foreign policy; as he discloses:

> The North Vietnamese and their Viet Cong allies were bearing down on Saigon.
> With the Mideast peace process in tatters, relations with the Soviets at a four-year
> low, [and] Cambodia collapsing . . . Ford left Washington for a golfing vacation
> in Palm Springs.[158]

This time, however, Kissinger's considerable efforts were to no avail. Congress refused to allocate funds to pursue the war; indeed, disregarding Kissinger's counsel, Ford publicly declared the war at an end. No resolution of the
Arab/Israeli conflict was in sight, and detente unraveled. It was as if Hermes
exacted revenge for Kissinger's presumption: he became overly-confident due to
his early success; and as his charm faded, his image of a trickster emerged.

Like many academics, Kissinger presupposed that the real world had the
decency—if not the good sense—to conform to his congenial assumptions. In his
earlier academic writing he realized that international relations amounted to
choosing the right metaphor. Not only did his admirable initial successes rein-
force his metaphors; he seemed to forget that international relations theory is
constructed with contested metaphors rather than the uncontested theories of
textbook science. Implementing "triangular diplomacy" (balancing relations between the United States, China, and the Soviet Union); the breakthrough on the
SALT negotiations; and, of course, Cienfuegos seemed to convince Kissinger of
two things: the health and survival of the international body politic required the
continual balancing of antagonistic forces; and he—*the* Doctor of Diplomacy—
was the man to do it.

Unlike his predecessor, Dean Acheson, Kissinger did not consider the possibility that successful crisis management sometimes merely results from "plain
dumb luck." Perhaps Kissinger's initial successes occurred because he was in the
right place at the right time. This possibility does not discredit his successful
management of the Cienfuegos incident, but it does suggest that Kissinger drew
unwarranted generalizations from incidents such as Cienfuegos. Because, at the
time, the Soviets were realists does not imply that all adversaries are realists
motivated by cost/benefit/risk analysis. Time and again, Kissinger would learn
that the real world did not conform to his cherished presuppositions. He discovered that America's Vietnamese adversaries willingly endured hideous
costs—as did the Americans themselves. And, in trying to end the Vietnam War
through his usual Byzantine shuttle diplomacy, he learned more than he cared to
about the role of domestic politics in the formulation and execution of foreign
policy.[159] Likewise, at a later date, Kissinger came to realize that concerns he
routinely dismissed—ideology and domestic politics—unraveled détente. He
laments, "Conservatives who hated communists, and liberals who hated Nixon
came together in a rare convergence, like an eclipse of the sun."[160]

Unlike Hermes, Kissinger's supply of charm was finite. Friend and foe alike
saw through Kissinger. Given his association with the Nixon administration, and
his well-deserved reputation for duplicity, his dissembling began to fail. During a

round of Middle East shuttle diplomacy—which involved convoluted dissembling beyond that of any Byzantine court or academic department—Kissinger's credibility was bluntly questioned. Responding to yet another of Kissinger's dubious claims, his former friend Yitzhak Rabin expressed himself with admirable clarity: "I don't believe you."[161]

REMEMBERING AND FORGETTING

> In autumn of 1970 Moscow chose to test whether . . . [détente] reflected indecision, domestic weakness due to Vietnam, or the strategy of a serious government. Having been given the answer, Moscow permitted Cienfuegos to recede once more into well-deserved obscurity.
>
> —Henry Kissinger[162]

The year 1995 commemorated the surrender of Germany and Japan, and the advent of nuclear weaponry. However, the twenty-fifth anniversary of peaceful resolution of a potential Götterdämmerung—the 1970 Cienfuegos Bay crisis—merited no attention whatsoever. Initially, the popular press headlined the event, and prominent journalists such as Hersh scrutinized Nixon's and Kissinger's responses. Today, however, the episode has faded into oblivion.

However, we can't get the Cuban missile crisis out of our minds—it is unforgettable. There is every reason to anticipate a fiftieth anniversary commemoration of the "missiles of October" in 2012. (We will probably be part of the action in a televised, holographic celebration of Kennedy's joust on the abyss; indeed, due to technological advances, we may experience Khrushchev's apprehension—the smell of burning will be in the air.)

The Cienfuegos episode receded into obscurity with astonishing rapidity—Kissinger's wish was granted. Not only is it unknown in popular culture, but it seldom merits more than an annotation in the international relations literature. His indifference to the episode is puzzling. Cienfuegos was surely a quintessential Kissinger crisis. While Kissinger's management of his other crises remains the subject of heated controversy, there is virtual consensus in the scant literature on Cienfuegos: his resolution of the Cienfuegos challenge reflects admirable patience and adroit diplomacy. Perhaps further explication of the medical crisis narrative can dissolve some of the puzzlement.

Even the most exalted physician/statesman is but a passing celebrity, not an unforgettable hero. Heroes are legendary miracle workers who defy the Fates by venturing beyond known boundaries. Heroes do the unexpected; celebrities do not. Unlike heroes, they attain passing fame for their accomplishments within established venues. Larger-than-life heroes perform in our fantasy world. A physician/statesman, however, barters with reality; the tradeoffs are seldom heroic. I am not the first to recognize that it is difficult to live without heroes. Millions are captivated by James Bond; realistic accounts of the life saving techniques of a gifted surgeon are, to say the least, less popular.

The Cienfuegos episode, a successful instance of nuclear age crisis management, is forgotten because heroic dramas are far more captivating than routine medical procedures—*Agamemnon* is a classic, *General Hospital* is not. Skilled specialists are not immortalized for saving a patient undergoing a potentially fatal, but routine, medical crisis. Likewise, heroic posturing is immortalized, while routine titration of the balance of power merits nary a mention.

More surprising still, Nixon represents the Cienfuegos incident as a vindication of his mature statesmanship. Contrasting himself with Kennedy, Nixon claims that, unlike the reckless youth who risked everything in 1962, he averted a potential conflagration through his wise leadership:

> Through strong but quiet diplomacy we had averted what would have been known as the Cuban Nuclear Submarine Crisis of 1970 and which, like its predecessor, might have taken us to the brink of nuclear confrontation with the Soviet Union.[163]

Yet, despite this encomium to himself, and despite the fact that Nixon authored voluminous accounts of his career and his reflections on international politics, he devotes but four pages to this episode in his Memoir, *RN*. As in his previous works, such as *Leaders*, Nixon uses *In the Arena* as a pretext to narrate and picture the triumphant occasions in his life. Through these photographs we witness an ebullient Nixon celebrating his vindication in the Hiss case. We look in upon an unusually happy and content Nixon with Checkers (and a less illustrious dog named Vicky) seated beside him. And, to be sure, we are favored with yet another print of the classic Nixon photo opportunity: an animated vice president jabbing Khrushchev in the ribs. And, needless to say, these episodes are once again rehearsed in prose. The Cienfuegos incident, however, merits but two sentences.

Michael Korda, an editor of a work by Julie Nixon Eisenhower, recounts a dinner party with the Nixons. His experience reveals what Nixon regards as his heroic moments, and what he ignores. After dinner the former president toured his home with Korda and three Chinese diplomats. He insisted on giving the Chinese visitors a memento—a quintessential expression of the American spirit. He explained that his guests would receive a book, "one of the most important books of the twentieth century"; a book with a universal message. The book was not a celebration of Nixon diplomacy, and there was no mention of resolving the Cienfuegos incident quietly and peaceably—As Korda explains, Nixon commemorated what he regarded as a truly momentous event:

> We stood around Nixon, spellbound by his emotion, for he was speaking . . . from the heart, and his eyes, normally piercing, were humid. . . . Nixon bent down and opened the bottom drawer of his big desk, and withdrew a copy of Whittaker Chambers' "Witness." I was fascinated to see the drawer was full of hardcover copies of Chambers' book.[164]

For Korda it was not merely ironic that Nixon expanded upon his triumph over communist subversion before three Chinese communist bureaucrats; it was surrealistic:

I left feeling like Dorothy leaving Oz. As I drove home, around me in the night was suburban New Jersey, and behind me was a kind of magic world—as remote . . . as Oz—where the past was still alive . . . where Whittaker Chambers was still an American hero.[165]

As we have seen, the president is the interpreter in chief. Like the public at large, most analysts echo Nixon's interpretation: Cienfuegos is not worth remembering. For Nixon, it is not worth remembering because it did not affect him personally. Had Brezhnev jabbed Nixon with his finger while the whole world watched, and threatened to deploy nuclear submarines in Cuba, the shelves would groan with accounts of the Cuban nuclear submarine crisis—if any authors and readers survived the confrontation. Like the public at large, it appears that many analysts find fearful jousts on the abyss more intriguing than the subtleties of quiet diplomacy.

Finally, our collective memory of Nixon the man must be considered. A Yiddish proverb comes to mind: "All brides are beautiful; all the dead are holy." Nixon was neither. Given his ethos and his disgrace, any temptation to praise him—if only for declining to attend what could have been the gravest crisis of the nuclear age—is easy to resist. But, like Oliver Stone, after learning more about Nixon's tormented life, I experience a newfound compassion for the thirty-seventh president. I hope Nixon was sincere when he concluded in one of his last works:

But win or lose, I feel fortunate to have come to that time in life when I can finally enjoy what my Quaker grandmother would have called 'peace at the center.'[166]

NOTES

1. Richard Nixon, *RN: The Memoirs of Richard Nixon* (New York: Grosset & Dunlap, 1978), 485.

2. Steven Ambrose, *Nixon,* vol. 2 (New York: Simon and Schuster, 1989), 69.

3. Ibid., 95.

4. Ibid., 49.

5. Ibid., 9–20.

6. Ibid., 380.

7. Quoted by Robert D. Schulzinger in his *Henry Kissinger: Doctor of Diplomacy* (New York: Columbia University Press, 1989), 32.

8. Marvin Kalb offers a detailed and perceptive account of Nixon's post-Watergate impression management in his *The Nixon Memo* (Chicago: University of Chicago Press, 1994).

9. Secret communiqué from Nixon to Haldeman, March 13, 1972; quoted in *From The President: Richard Nixon's Secret Files,* Bruce Oudes, ed., (New York: Harper & Row, 1989), 384–387.

10. Nixon, 486.

11. See Fen Hampson's account in "The Divided Decision-Maker: American Domestic Politics and the Cuban Crises," in *The Domestic Sources of American Foreign Policy,* Charles Kegley and Eugene Wittkopf, eds. (New York: St. Martin's Press, 1988).

12. Henry Kissinger, *The White House Years* (Boston: Little, Brown, 1979), 633–644.

13. Richard Nixon, *In the Arena* (New York: Simon and Schuster, 1990), 196.

14. Kissinger, 635.

15. Ambrose, 33–34.

16. "Buchanan's Letter to Nixon, September 17, 1971," quoted in *From the President*, Bruce Oudes, ed. (New York: Harper & Row, 1989), 317–318.

17. Kissinger, 633–644.

18. Ibid., 639.

19. Ambrose, 382.

20. Quoted by Christopher Matthews in "Great Debate" in the *San Francisco Examiner Magazine*, April 28, 1996, 12.

21. See, for example Schulzinger; and Walter Isaacson, *Kissinger* (New York: Simon and Schuster, 1992).

22. Nixon, *RN*, 489.

23. Arthur Miller, "Introduction to Collected Plays" in *Willy Loman*, Harold Bloom, ed. (New York and Philadelphia: Chelsea House, 1991), 39.

24. Richard Nixon, *Six Crises* (New York: Simon and Schuster, 1990), 254.

25. Quoted by Christopher Matthews in his *Kennedy & Nixon* (New York: Simon and Schuster, 1996), 124.

26. Quoted by Matthews in "Great Debate," 14.

27. Ambrose, 462.

28. Garry Wills, *Nixon Agonistes* (Boston: Houghton Mifflin, 1969), 406.

29. Gerald S. Strober and Deborah Hart Strober, *Nixon: An Oral History of His Presidency* (New York: HarperCollins, 1994), 34.

30. Wills, 406.

31. Miller, 99.

32. Tom Wicker, *One of Us: Richard Nixon and the American Dream* (New York: Random House, 1992), 6.

33. Quoted by James David Barber, *The Presidential Character*, 2nd ed. (Englewood Cliffs: Prentice-Hall, 1977), 400.

34. William Popkin, "Arthur Miller: The Strange Encounter" in *Willy Loman*, Harold Bloom, ed. (New York: Chelsea House, 1991), 12.

35. In addition to the sources cited above, see Fawn Brodie, *Richard Nixon: The Shaping of His Character* (Cambridge: Harvard University Press, 1983); John Dean, *Blind Ambition* (New York: Simon and Schuster, 1976); H. R. Haldeman, *The Haldeman Diaries* (New York: Putnam, 1994); Jonathan Schell, *The Time of Illusion* (New York: Vintage Books, 1976); and Theodore White, *The Making of the President, 1968* (New York: Atheneum, 1969).

36. Quoted by Matthews in *Kennedy & Nixon*, 137.

37. Strober and Strober, 39.

38. Ibid., 38.

39. Quoted by Wicker, 9.

40. Ibid., 31.

41. Strober and Strober, 43.

42. Ibid., 50.

43. Ambrose, "Introduction" in H. R. Haldeman, *The Haldeman Diaries* (New York: Putnam, 1994), 6.

44. Ambrose, *Nixon*, 197.

45. See Arthur Larson's account in his *Eisenhower: The President Nobody Knew* (New York: Charles Scribner's Sons, 1968), 9.

46. See Steven Ambrose's "Afterword," in H. R. Haldeman, *The Haldeman Diaries* (New York: Putnam, 1994), 677–682.

47. Quoted by Wicker, 653.

48. Barber, 387.

49. Quoted by Ambrose, *Nixon*, 96.

50. Ibid., 472.

51. Anatoly Dobrynin, *In Confidence* (New York: Times Books, 1995), 197.

52. Quoted in *Willy Loman*, Harold Bloom, ed. (New York: Chelsea House, 1991), 8.

53. Miller, 2.

54. Haldeman, 116.

55. Quoted in *From the President*, Bruce Oudes, ed. (New York: Harper & Row, 1989), 579.

56. Haldeman, 132.

57. Ambrose, "Introduction," 2.

58. Miller, 33–34.

59. Barber, 347.

60. Richard Nixon, *Six Crises* (New York: Simon and Schuster, 1976), xx.

61. See Richard Nixon, *Leaders* (New York: Warner Books, Inc., 1982).

62. These representative excerpts are taken from ibid., 332–345.

63. Barber, 395.

64. Nixon, *Leaders*, 170.

65. Ibid., 335.

66. H.R. Haldeman, with Joseph DiMona, *The Ends of Power* (New York: Times Books, 1978), 219.

67. Quoted by Wicker, 209.

68. Barber, 386–387.

69. Ibid., 362.

70. Isaacson, 146.

71. Arthur Miller, *Death of a Salesman* (New York: Viking Press, 1949), 36.

72. Quoted by Kalb, 14.

73. Wills, 2.

74. Nixon, *Six Crises*, xvii.

75. Joan Hoff-Wilson, "Richard M. Nixon: The Corporate President" in *Leadership in the Modern Presidency,* Fred I. Greenstein, ed. (Cambridge: Harvard University Press, 1988).

76. He indicts these "un-American ideologies" in *Six Crises*, 67.

77. Ibid., 51, 58.

78. Wicker, 57.

79. Ibid.

80. Nixon, *Six Crises*, 18.

81. Ibid., 6.

82. Ibid., 28.

83. Quoted by Wicker, 64.

84. Ibid., 64–68.

85. Nixon, *Six Crises*, 54.

86. Ibid., 55.

87. Ibid., 69–70.

88. Quoted by Wicker, 107.

89. See Larson, 8–10.

90. Barber, 369.

91. Nixon discusses this phase of the crisis in *Six Crises*, 80–82.

92. Ibid., 83.

93. Jeremy Hawthorn, "Sales And Solidarity," in *Willy Loman*, Harold Bloom, ed. (New York: Chelsea House, 1991), 90.

94. Nixon, *Six Crises*, 86.

95. Ibid., 84.

96. Wicker, 89.

97. Nixon, *Six Crises*, 100. According to Wicker, Nixon actually said, "There comes a time in matters like these when you have to shit or get off the pot."

98. Ibid., 102.

99. Ibid., 110–111.

100. Ibid., 112.

101. Ibid., 115.

102. Ibid., 123.

103. Christopher Matthews, "Dogs in the News," in *San Francisco Examiner and Chronicle*, May 4, 1997, B–4.

104. Nixon, *Leaders*, 174.

105. Nixon, *Six Crises*, 245.

106. Ibid., 246.

107. Haldeman, *Diaries*, 25.

108. Quoted by Nixon, *Six Crises*, 253.

109. Ibid., 254.

110. Ibid., 255.

111. Ibid., 256–257.

112. Ibid., 258.

113. Seymour Hersh, *The Price of Power* (New York: Summit Books, 1983), 447.

114. Hoff-Wilson, 168.

115. Barber, 441.

116. See Matthews, *Kennedy & Nixon*, 36.

117. Quoted by Barber, 478.

118. Ibid., 462.

119. Raymond Williams, "Modern Tragic Literature From Hero to Victim," *Modern Tragedy* (Stanford: Stanford University Press, 1966) 103–104.

120. Wicker, 687.

121. Plato, "Statesman," in *The Collected Dialogues of Plato*, Edith Hamilton and Huntington Cairns, eds., (New York: Pantheon Books, 1961), 1062.

122. Kissinger, 55.

123. Isaacson, 296.

124. Ibid., 100.

125. Ibid., 61.

126. Bruce Mazlish, *Kissinger: The European Mind in American Foreign Policy* (New York: Basic Books, 1976), 218–222.

127. Isaacson, 146.

128. Quoted by Kalb, 16–17.

129. Nixon, *Leaders*, 324.

130. Quoted by Isaacson, 94.

131. Seymour Hersh, "Kissinger and Nixon in the White House," *Atlantic Monthly* 249, (May 1982): 50.

132. Quoted by Isaacson, 140.

133. Mazlish, 285.

134. Kissinger, 65.

135. Kissinger's arrogance spawned a host of anecdotes. According to Isaacson, when Henry's brother Walter was asked why he lost his German accent but Henry didn't, he quipped, "Henry listens to no one!" Mazlish repeats a joke that was popular during the Kissinger era: Superman seeks psychiatric help because he thinks he's Kissinger!

136. Mazlish, 96.

137. Henry Kissinger, *Diplomacy* (New York: Simon & Schuster, 1994), 811.

138. Ibid., Chapter 9.

139. Ibid., 42.

140. Ibid., 301.

141. Kissinger, *White House Years*, 639.

142. Ibid., 638.

143. Ibid., 642–643.

144. Ibid., 643.

145. Ibid., 644.

146. Ibid., 640.

147. See Hersh, *The Price of Power*, Chapter 20.

148. Kissinger, *White House Years*, 645.

149. Ibid., 646.

150. Ibid., 647.

151. Ibid.

152. Ibid.

153. Ibid., 648.

154. Ibid., 651.

155. Ibid.

156. Haldeman, *The Haldeman Diaries*, 197.

157. Quoted by Isaacson, 647.

158. Ibid., 640.

159. See Isaacson's discussion, Chapter 28.

160. Ibid., 607.

161. Ibid., 632.

162. Kissinger, *White House Years*, 652.

163. Nixon, *RN*, 197.

164. Michael Korda, "Nixon, Mine Host," *The New Yorker*, May 9, 1994, 80.

165. Ibid., 80.

166. Nixon, *In the Arena*, 369.

CHAPTER 5

THE PAST AS PROLOGUE

I faced 12 international crises during the first two years of my tenure [as chairman of the Joint Chiefs], and the only thing I am sure of is there is a 13th out there.

—Colin Powell[1]

Despite the unforeseen end of the Cold War, the world remains a realm of interminable suspense. Recent events in the Caribbean, Africa, and the Middle East attest to the unpredictable, if not ineffable, dimension of international politics. One prediction, however, inspires confidence: the past is prologue—crises will remain a prominent and dangerous feature of international relations. Indeed, it is a veritable truism that, like the poor, crises will always be with us.

This chapter subjects this truism to closer scrutiny. I argue that, in the overdeveloped world, more American-style crises are on the horizon, but not for the reasons widely supposed. I explore this possibility that more crises are ahead because the institutionalized practice of reading crisis narratives into captivating texts and performances can produce extraordinary personal and political dividends. And, as the explication of the Cuban crises suggests, the nature of these future crises will depend, in large measure, on the genre of the crisis narratives invoked and improvised to interpret and resolve these situations.

Like their predecessors, it is unlikely that future leaders will take responsibility for their crises. They will rely upon two unthought, unquestioned tactics to deny their complicity in crisis promotion: blaming adversaries, and likening crises to predestined natural disaster beyond their control. Blaming others is not without precedence: Nixon blamed communist sympathizers and the liberal press for his personal embarrassments; Kennedy blamed Khrushchev for the joust on the abyss; and Kissinger blamed Brezhnev for risking the health of détente.

Putting blame aside, crises seem inevitable because they are likened to certain arresting metaphors: just as San Francisco is destined to suffer "The Big

One" (a catastrophic earthquake), so those inside the Beltway are fated to endure earthshaking crises. No wonder Powell is fatalistic: the thirteenth crisis will occur regardless of his intentions and efforts; one can only hope that it will not be the unlucky one that precipitates a catastrophic war.

Former CIA Director James Woolsey invokes more virile metaphors. He anticipates more crises because of the intractable danger of international life: "It's a jungle out there." True, the "Soviet dragon" has been slain, but "We live now in a jungle filled with a bewildering variety of poisonous snakes, and in many ways the dragon was easier to keep track of."[2] In the world according to Woolsey and his associates, crises are inevitable because—to press the metaphor— vipers like Saddam Hussein await in ambush.

The frequent, if not promiscuous, invocation of "crisis" is nothing new. Crises, and rumors of crises, abound in each generation. As political analyst Charles Hermann observes, crises were the idée fixe of the 1960s:

> References to crises pervade observations on the contemporary world. On the first two pages of a Sunday edition of the New York Times, six of the thirteen news stories mention crises . . . [and] Rusk told a Senate subcommittee that the world experienced forty-seven international political crises in . . . the years between January 1961 and the middle of 1966.[3]

Indeed, even before the Republic existed, the first European settlers imported their Puritanism and their affinity for crises. To be sure, as political theorist Sacvan Bercovitch explains, traditional European jeremiads used fear to gain acceptance of the established order. But "The American jeremiad went much further. It made anxiety its end as well as its means. Crisis was the social norm it sought to inculcate."[4] Evidently, "crisis"—the jeremiad of American civic religion— quickly attained canonical status. Quoting Bercovitch, communication theorist Denise Botsdorff writes:

> Puritan political sermons made use of crisis talk . . . to provide the community with a sense of purpose and direction. According to [Sacvan] Bercovitch, Puritan leaders exploited crisis for their own ends; they "fastened upon it, gloried in it, even invented it if necessary."[5]

Crises are variations on an ancient theme. After examining the origin of the concept from ancient Greece through modern times, historian Randolph Starn suggests that virtually every epoch suffers from a collective narcissism, a compulsion to represent itself as an age of crisis—a critical juncture demanding momentous choices that determine the fate of civilization, if not of the cosmos itself.[6] Our age is no different:

> That this is an "age of crisis" seems the least controversial of statements. Old enemies . . . Right and Left, swear by it; all the evidence is said to prove it. It is hardly surprising that crises have become a favorite theme of historians. . . .[7]

There is much talk of crises, especially in high places. The alarm, and breathless excitement, reverberate within the halls of power and resound through the popular media and international relations literature. Pundits and theorists of every stripe agree: crises are inevitable. Rhetorical critic Dan Hahn argues that *"all non-ceremonial national presidential speeches are crisis speeches."*[8] Hahn may not be exaggerating; however, he misses a crucial point: crises also play a vital ceremonial function. These social dramas *are* ceremonies that punctuate the monotony of everyday experience. More significantly, they are rites of atonement and redemption: elite rites of passage—epiphanies that supposedly reveal a leader's character, if not the character of the nation as a whole. By experiencing and commemorating a crisis, the abstract state becomes incarnate in the lives of the polity. In the American civic religion crises are condensation symbols that simultaneously absolve a leader and a nation of past indiscretions, and consecrate new nationalistic myths.

Like their predecessors, recent presidents welcomed crises. It is no secret that Ford, Carter, Reagan and Bush promoted these episodes. Indeed, in his closing statement during the October 15, 1992, Presidential Debate in Atlanta, Bush urged the public to consider which candidate would be more trustworthy and reliable the next time an inevitable crisis occurred. (It appeared that he was trying to reap dividends from what many regarded as his triumphant resolution of the Persian Gulf crisis.) Clinton has already had crises in Iraq, Somalia, Haiti, and Bosnia; and as I write, he warns that weapons development must continue because of the inevitability of crises. Despite the radical unpredictability of international affairs, there is little doubt that Clinton's successors will also promote crises that define their presidency.

The invocation of "crisis" to account for a diverse array of texts and performances is virtually second nature. This conceptual habit—or addiction—is not without justification. Like the political actors they study, many analysts presuppose that crisis discourse is the métier of international relations because there are innumerable crises "out there" waiting to happen. In other words, discourse mirrors reality. I wrote this book because I suspect the obverse: crises will occur precisely because crisis discourse has become the lingua franca inside the Beltway—reality mirrors discourse. It seems likely that American political actors will continue to speak English and to represent a broad variety of events as critical junctures that demand risk and sacrifice, in a word, crises.

The tyranny of crisis discourse over officialdom's conceptual universe is revealed by a simple fact: once an actor construes a situation as a crisis, he/she will not recant. I can think of no instance when an actor confessed that rather than promoting an incident as a crisis, he or she could have ignored the situation, construed it as a problem to be resolved in due course, or lamented the episode as hopeless tragedy. Why is it that elites never allow that they were wrong in promoting a crisis? As philosopher Greg Tropea remarks: "If you expect a crisis, mirabile dictu, sooner or later you will get one."[9] As we have seen, however, actors seldom get the one they want.

Situating crises in their historical and cultural contexts is an effective anti-dote to the prevailing naturalized notion of "crisis": it should erase any doubt that a crisis is a concept, not a thing. Unlike an earthquake, which occurs apart from human volition, and with predictable consequences (regardless of culture and language), a crisis is a social practice. As such, its significance depends upon the linguistic and social practices of a particular community of discourse. And, like a crisis itself, crisis interpretation bears the indelible mark of time and place—how could it be otherwise?

Looking at the historical context, I have already suggested that a crisis spark-ed by an unmistakable threat to the early Republic—such as the British setting the White House afire—is qualitatively different from reading a crisis narrative into cryptic communiqués and reconnaissance data. Looking at contemporary crises, historian Michael Hunt argues that American-style crisis interpretation labors under parochial and ethnocentric presuppositions. He urges colleagues to eschew congenial, one-dimensional, academic models of "crisis" that celebrate American exceptionalism and rationality in favor of international sensibilities attentive to the marginalized narratives of other cultures in these confrontations. In other words, the time has come to entertain diverse perspectives, multifaceted approaches that recognize that not all crises have an American accent. Amer-icans tend to reconstruct their actions as "bottom line" exercises in pragmatic rationality, but, as Hunt suggests, a broader perspective may be revealing and unsettling:

> Viewed in international terms, "crisis management" ceases to be a simple exer-cise in cool ends-means analysis . . . and becomes instead a kind of psycho-logical Saint Vitus' dance that two rivals induce in each other and that ends only after exhaustion sets in.[10]

American analysts, for example, conveniently assume that crises can be rep-resented with considerable precision. These episodes supposedly begin and end at discernible times. (The Cuban missile crisis, as we've seen, is neatly encap-sulated in a thirteen-day social drama.) This retrospective scripting of crises is convenient, but misleading. Notions of "crisis" originate in particular cultures—how could it be otherwise? Indeed, such notions reveal more about a culture and its leaders than about international relations. As we have seen, like American ceremonial architecture, American style crises are rooted in ancient Greek ex-perience. Accordingly, the Cuban crises explicated in this inquiry were depicted as variations on an ancient, but all-too-familiar themes.

To make a philosophic distinction, there are crises, and there are crises: the world is not limited to (let alone bound by) American cultural conceptions. My graduate students at the United Nations University in Austria explicated diverse cultural appropriations—and non appropriations—of "crisis" in their research. It appears that in certain traditional cultures, there is no notion of "crisis" what-soever. Ojakol explains that traditional histories written by Ugandans have no term for "crisis." However, recently introduced British and American texts use the term unsparingly. And Penjor claims that in Bhutan—the "Land of the Peaceful Dragon"—native narratives eschew confrontational terms such as "crisis." But, due to recent strife between Nepalese immigrants and native Bhutanese, the term has entered discourse.[11]

And ironically, it seems that in nations enduring unmistakable threats to national survival, leaders are reluctant to use the term "crisis" lest the population become overly alarmed and demoralized. The term is usually used in retrospect for self-promotion if fortunate leaders somehow survive and resolve the threat. However, in nations free of unmistakable threats, "crisis" is invoked promiscuously to excite and distract an apathetic population. Botsdorff aptly quotes Mencken: "The whole aim of practical politics is to keep the populace alarmed (and hence clamorous to be led to safety) by an endless series of hobgoblins, most of them imaginary."[12]

Finally, Peña reminded me that Cubans refer to the events of the fall of 1962 as the "October Crisis." (This designation seems to suggest that, from a Cuban perspective, the missiles should not have provoked a crisis.) She added that Cuban officials do not refer to their current economic woes as a crisis, lest the population become agitated. "Crisis" is generally invoked retrospectively to refer to strife between Cuba and imperial powers such as the United States.

However, as if to corroborate Turner's account of the universality of certain essential crisis features, the students concluded that political crises have essential, defining elements. Despite their significant cultural variations, crises are informed by common themes:

1. Metaphorical narratives in which a daunting present is likened to a crisis of the remembered past; the remembered heroics of crises of yesteryear provide the favored metaphors. (For example, triumphant struggles against would-be European colonizers are a favored metaphor in Ethiopia.)

2. Liminal phases are common because the venerable ancient metaphors often fail and no new ones are on the near horizon to take their place. (Ugandans, for example, liken latter-day crises to the daunting phases of tribal initiation rites.)

In any case, when Powell and the others claim there are more crises "out there" waiting to happen, they are not thinking of the unmistakable threats precipitated by occurrences such as a civil war in Ethiopia or immigration problems in the "Land of the Peaceful Dragon." The crises they have in mind have a distinctly American accent: typically American interpretations of symbolic action. More specifically, they seem to anticipate the ersatz and the genuine crises endemic to American political culture.

Accordingly, this chapter concludes by examining the personal and political dividends paid by the ersatz and the genuine crises that typify American political culture. More crises are "out there" because these social dramas will continue to pay handsome dividends. Ersatz crises will occur when actors deem it expedient to deliberately fabricate and publicly promote crises with great alarm and fanfare even though they believe no crisis exists. The political motives for such episodes are transparent to most analysts, at least in retrospect. Two illustrative cases, the Grenada crisis and the Cuban Brigade crisis, are discussed.

Genuine crises will occur when actors truly believe a crisis move is justified because they confront an acute threat that demands urgent, perilous decisions. As
we have seen, such episodes may be public or private affairs. In the present
American context, such episodes are not precipitated by unmistakable threats to
national survival or even to obvious, tangible values. The dividends of promoting such episodes are more symbolic and personal than strategic and tangible.
Nevertheless, genuine crises are more dangerous than the ersatz variety. Unaware of their complicity in crisis construction and promotion, those who manage genuine crises have convinced themselves that events somehow demand an
immediate return to the status quo ante despite the risk of catastrophic conflict.

Due to institutional inertia more ersatz and genuine crises can be unanticipated. Since crisis discourse has long been the lingua franca inside the Beltway,
anticipating future crises in American culture is no more remarkable than anticipating more freeways and shopping centers—it's simply the unthought, unquestioned way things are done. I see nothing corrupt, let alone conspiratorial, in all
this. Just as shamans preconsciously read tribal myths into their experience, and
scholastics read medieval morality plays into their texts, so today's political
actors read their morality plays—crisis narratives—into their texts. The remain-
der of this chapter examines the handsome personal and political dividends that
perpetuate these episodes. Due to these dividends, it is unlikely that any twelve-
step program will cure political actors of their addiction to "crisis."

THE DIVIDENDS OF ERSATZ CRISES

> The trivialization of crisis, while it testifies to a pervasive sense of danger—to a
> perception that nothing, not even the simplest domestic detail, can be taken for
> granted—also serves as . . . [an elite] survival strategy in its own right.
> —Christopher Lasch[13]

Tracing "crisis" to its ancient Greek origins, Botsdorff aptly stresses the
double meaning of the concept. It can refer to the critical moment of decision in
the life of an issue *or* an auspicious time for an advantageous decision.[14] Ersatz
crises are of the latter variety. Perhaps psychiatrist Jerold Post gained rare insight into the opportunistic nature of such crises when a senior government official confided that a crisis is "An optimal opportunity for a bureaucratic power
player to gain senior level visibility and maximize his organizational position."[15]

I suspect that actors rationalize such opportunism as a necessary evil practiced to attain higher ends—self-deception is not unknown in high places. In any
case, as the Grenada incident illustrates, actors will likely continue to devise very
good reasons for ersatz crises for public consumption. However, the real reasons
such crises occur are considerably different: these episodes bestow a wealth of
personal and political dividends—if properly managed. (Of course, what actually
occurs during the episode and its aftermath is incidental: crisis management has
become impression management.) However, as the Cuban Brigade episode demonstrates, ersatz crisis promotion can fail to achieve its objectives or can make
matters worse.

Grenada

In October, 1983, Americans found themselves in the midst of two crises. . . . In Beirut . . . the United States suffered both humiliation and a great loss of life with a suicide terrorist attack on U.S. marines. A second crisis, one that quickly eclipsed events in Beirut, was Operation Urgent Fury, the U.S. invasion of Grenada.

—Denise Botsdorff[16]

The Reagan administration had a penchant for promoting such distracting, ersatz crises.[17] In his cameo role as president, the "Great Communicator" attempted to alarm the public about a possible Sandinista invasion: South Texas, we were warned, was but a two-day drive from Nicaragua. (He was less communicative about the Iran/Contra affair and a savings and loan scandal that would have embarrassed Boss Tweed.)[18] However, perhaps the Grenada episode offers the best illustration.

In October 1983 a coup occurred on the small Caribbean island of Grenada. (Until then, Grenada's main export had been nutmeg, not crises.) General Hudson Austin overthrew the regime of Prime Minister Maurice Bishop. In his public pronouncements President Ronald Reagan interpreted the event as a crisis for two reasons:

1. The new regime was even more sympathetic to communist causes than the old regime. The Austin regime, Reagan insisted, would tyrannize the local population while exporting terrorism. The construction of an airfield, with the assistance of Cuban comrades, was cited as proof.

2. American medical students on the island were in jeopardy.

Almost immediately, the president decided to resolve the crisis with weapons rather than words. The press was prevented from covering the American invasion: the Reagan administration, not the journalists, would manage impressions. According to official reality, the invasion was a "rescue mission" that unselfishly and courageously deposed communist despotism and brought the students home. Reagan framed the incident as a Manichaean drama, a decisive, unprecedented victory against the Evil Empire. According to Reagan, it was: "the first time in history that a communist regime . . . was replaced by democracy."[19] His popularity soared.

Like most analysts, Botsdorff does not take Reagan's account at face value. Unlike the president, who urged that the crisis was a selfless struggle against communist tyranny, she argues that the crisis was about the president's personal and political vulnerabilities; it was a pretext for distracting attention from the fiasco in Beirut while reasserting triumphant leadership. She suggests that while Grenada had been a minor chronic problem, the fiasco in Lebanon gave Reagan incentive to promote the coup as a major, acute crisis.

Reframing the incident, Botsdorff recalls that Reagan placed American marines in harm's way in Beirut in 1982 as part of a multinational force to restore order and to facilitate the evacuation of Palestinians. His decision was criticized in Congress and questioned by various military officials, who argued that Reagan's actions were a perilous, symbolic gesture, rather than a carefully planned, achievable military mission. The legality of Reagan's unilateral actions also was questioned. American intervention ended in October 1983, when a suicide bombing killed more than 200 marines in their barracks at the Beirut airport. The Grenada invasion occurred two days later. As Botsdorff concludes, "Reagan was able to mask his Mideast foreign policy failure and to bask, instead, in the glory of an obvious success."[20]

She does not revel in the glory. That Grenada posed a threat to the continental United States—or even to some crucial American interest—defies credulity. The triumph of history's greatest military colossus against a remote isle is no cause for celebration. She aptly quotes Larry Speakes, Reagan's deputy press secretary, who opined that the invasion "was the equivalent of the Washington Redskins scheduling my old high school team, the Merigold Wildcats."[21] It also appears that the students were free to leave after the coup, and that they were not in jeopardy until the invasion occurred. Finally, scores of innocent Grenadans were killed, including most of the inmates of a mental asylum. And, of course, American personnel died in a cause that had no connection with the defense of the continental United States.

Naturally, Reagan emphasized the positive—there was no mourning in America. He played to cherished myths—the collective wishful thinking—of the civic religion. As communication theorist W. Lance Bennet explains, such political myths "are like the lenses in a pair of glasses in the sense that they are not the things people see when they look at the world, but they are the things they see with. Myths are truths about society taken for granted."[22]

Representations of crises such as Grenada can be honed into truly remarkable conceptual lenses. Grenada became a "condensation symbol." Such symbols play a vital ritual role in ceremonial democracy by simultaneously absolving leaders of their sins while consecrating their destiny, if not the fate of the American people. Reagan, of course, was absolved of the Beirut disaster, and anointed a wise and courageous leader. Such ersatz crises:

1. *Focus attention on the president by portraying the commander in chief as an indispensable, if not heroic, leader.* Reagan was transformed from an avuncular, aging actor into a resolute, larger-than-life leader in times of trouble.

2. *Distract public attention from embarrassing or intractable problems.* The seemingly refractory Vietnam Syndrome was overcome, and, amid the celebration, the debacle in Beirut was forgiven and forgotten.

3. *Vindicate official policies and pronouncements.* Reagan had long warned of the communist menace. The coup in Grenada was represented as part and parcel of Soviet/Cuban plans to brutally dominate the Western Hemisphere. In his nationwide address the president explained that Grenada had ceased to be a salubrious tropical isle. It was a "Soviet-Cuban colony, being readied as a major military bastion to export communism and undermine democracy. We got there just in time."[23] Such rhetoric validates cherished civic myths, such as the fable of American exceptionalism. America—unlike other nations—does not intervene abroad for self-serving ends. Legendary America is altruistic, and can be faulted only for being "too good"—naive about the cunning and treachery of lesser

nations. The "Redeemer Nation" selflessly sacrifices its blood and treasure to promote freedom and prosperity. Reagan's gloss on Grenada expressed this Manifest Destiny: "In foreign policy, we've let the world know once again that America stands for the political, religious, and economic freedom of mankind."[24]

4. *Demonizes adversaries, foreign and domestic.* Rather than acknowledging his role in constructing and promoting the crisis, Reagan blamed the confrontation upon perfidious adversaries. Surplus meaning was also attached to the event. Grenada was not represented as an insignificant incident played out against an inconsequential palace coup. The president attached world-historical significance to the event: it became a Manichaean struggle between the forces of light and the powers of darkness. Analyzing presidential rhetoric, Bottsdorff notes that the president represented the crisis as a momentous struggle against communist world domination. Indeed, communists—not Islamic fundamentalists—were blamed for the deaths of the marines in Lebanon. Likewise, the coup in Grenada was not merely the palace politics of an insignificant nation, it was a sinister machination of the international communist conspiracy.[25] Given what Robert Jay Lifton calls the "Cold War cosmology," questioning or criticizing the invasion of Grenada seemed unpatriotic, even traitorous. As Botsdorff observed, opponents "had to make the unenviable choice either to remain silent about their qualms or to voice their concerns and thereby commit blasphemy."[26]

5. *Promotes willingness to sacrifice.* During times of crisis—ersatz or otherwise—it seems selfish and unpatriotic to be preoccupied with immediate personal concerns such as health care, economic security, and other issues that profoundly affect our lives. One must be willing and eager to sacrifice security and comfort—perhaps even the lives of sons and daughters—to abstractions. Crises, then, ready the public for the ultimate sacrifice—war.

Botsdorff aptly concludes:

Through the successful promotion and management of a crisis in Grenada, Reagan unified a nation divided by events in Beirut, and his approval rating soared to its highest level in two years. An ABC-*Washington Post* survey found that 71 percent of American citizens supported . . . intervention in Grenada.[27]

Crisis promotion, of course, does not always pay handsome dividends.

The Cuban Brigade Crisis

Fighting a National Conservative Political Action Committee campaign in Idaho which branded him "soft" on . . . the Soviet Union, [Senator Frank] Church was worried that a news leak [about the brigade] would make his earlier denial of Soviet forces look either gullible or irresponsible. An anti-Church commercial had shown Church and Fidel Castro smoking cigars together on Church's recent trip to Havana. . . . Church decided the news [of the brigade] had to come from him. He was fighting for his political life in the face of a growing wave of conservatism.

—Fen Osler Hampson[28]

In the summer of 1979, as President Jimmy Carter and his party prepared for the election, a new, sophisticated satellite photographed a brigade of approximately 5,000 Soviet troops in Cuba. The brigade's significance was contested. The National Security Agency (NSA) suspected that the brigade was deployed to engage in combat or to protect nuclear weapons installations. However, the CIA and the Department of State did not share this assessment. In any case, due to its size and the fact that it lacked air and amphibious support, no one concluded that the brigade constituted an invasion force preparing to attack the United States.[29] Indeed, no one in the Carter administration construed the brigade as a strategic threat. However, Carter and his associates were not indifferent to the political implications of appearances and symbols.

Predictably, the ascendant conservative movement attempted to use the NSA report to its advantage. For example, conservatives on the Foreign Relations Committee argued that the newfound brigade indicated that the Soviets could not be trusted, and therefore the recently negotiated SALT II Treaty should not be ratified. Senator Frank Church (Chairman of the Foreign Relations Committee) was attacked for his alleged naiveté regarding Soviet ambitions and capability. In response, he initially reiterated the Carter administration's claim that no Soviet brigade existed in Cuba. (Ironically, Church had also denied Republican claims in August 1962 regarding the deployment of Soviet missiles in Cuba.)

When it appeared that the intelligence reports would be leaked to the press, Church obtained permission from Secretary of State Cyrus Vance to preempt the conservatives and the press by publicly denouncing the existence of the brigade. The senator, the secretary, and the president concurred that this move would be politically expedient. Carter used grave and dramatic oratory to describe the threat posed by the brigade and by Soviet actions in general. Despite their initial enthusiasm for SALT II, Carter and his associates succumbed to political exigencies and insisted that the treaty could not be ratified while the brigade remained in Cuba.

Outraged and incredulous, Dobrynin—still Soviet ambassador after all these years—reminded Ambassador Ralph Earle (the principal SALT II negotiator at the time) that, as part of the understanding forged by Kennedy and ratified by Nixon, the United States had agreed to allow Soviet troops in Cuba. Indeed, Dobrynin reminded Earle that, in accord with the understanding, Soviet troops had been in Cuba for years, advising various military and civilian projects. Moreover, he urged that it was inconceivable that 5,000 troops without air or sea support posed a threat to the United States.[30] Further intelligence analysis corroborated Dobrynin's claims. Nevertheless, the majority of the Foreign Relations Committee argued that the Soviets could not be trusted, and they rejected SALT II. The treaty was never ratified.[31] Despite their efforts to promote an ersatz crisis, Carter, Church, and other liberal Democrats lost the election, American foreign policy was subject to derision, and U.S./Soviet relations reached new lows. As Hampson explains, "The Treaty was withdrawn with enormous cost to the Carter Presidency and to détente itself."[32]

GENUINE CRISES

> Many historians have a rather vague and certainly varied sense of what "crisis" really means, for on examination, the impact of the word dissolves in ambiguity.
> —Randolph Starn[33]

Actors, of course, may sincerely believe that they confront a crisis, and they may promote the crisis for their highest ideals. However, virtue has its rewards. If their impression management is successful, they and their anointed successors will reap the dividends listed above, along with extraordinary bonuses. As we have seen, Kennedy believed that he confronted genuine crises. Given his ethos and adroit impression management, he enjoyed considerable dividends, even from debacles such as the Bay of Pigs. (Apparently, due to his willingness to take military action—using a CIA-controlled Cuban exile brigade—against Cuba, his popularity in the polls surged; and sympathetic analysts deem the debacle part of JFK's learning experience.) And due to his public performance in the Cuban missile crisis, he enjoyed all the dividends listed above and more: he was immortalized as a profile in courage. The crisis became a venerated metaphor with a halo effect: his successors evoked the hallowed memory of the crisis to justify themselves and their crises.

Nixon, of course, did not fare as well. Despite his aspirations, he is not lionized for the successful resolution of his personal embarrassments. No one lauds him for what he did not do (or for doing the right thing for the wrong reasons) in response to the Cienfuegos base. And it is no secret that Watergate—his defining life-crisis—ended in disaster. Unlike Kennedy, Nixon's doctor of diplomacy, Kissinger, is remembered as a celebrity with passing fame, not as an enduring hero. Indeed, even international relations specialists seldom recall his successful, secret resolution of the Cienfuegos incident.

However, the lure of public acclaim was not the only reason for vintage Kennedy, Nixon, and Kissinger crises. A brief summary of the findings of this study reveals that, in addition to the public dividends listed above, private dividends may accrue from genuine crises. These episodes accomplish the following:

1. *Enable an actor to escape the daunting ambiguity endemic to international life.* Prevailing approaches seem to suggest that by anticipating crises, actors embrace the vagaries of international relations. I conclude that a crisis is not a robust recognition of the vagaries of international life. On the contrary, it is a retreat from such vicissitudes A crisis, in effect, is self-confessional; these episodes reveal that actors prefer certainty to uncertainty. Since they are thrown into a world of dangerous uncertainty, actors are possessed by an even more disturbing quest for certainty. Since certitude eludes them in the external world, they manufacture it in the conceptual realm—a dimension seemingly within their control. By defining a cryptic text or symbolic performance as a crisis, an actor unwittingly imposes a facile, resonant narrative upon the event, and scripts his/her response. By embracing crisis narratives, actors, in effect, convince themselves that they are not enduring a disaster that they are powerless to remedy, nor are they confronting a chronic problem they can live with, to be ameliorated

patiently and quietly in due course. Rather, they are confronting an acute crisis that must be resolved with the right words or weapons.

To reiterate, these crisis narratives are not merely cognitive maps, as is widely supposed. They are teleological and normative: in addition to representing what is happening, crisis narratives disclose why it is happening and what is expected of the actor. They do so by imposing a metaphor that exaggerates similarities between past and present while concealing differences. They minimize puzzlement by imposing a storyline that scripts the episode; and they ultimately dissolve ambiguity by eliminating competing narratives from discourse.

Actors, of course, are not content with conceptual clarity. It does not suffice to define a situation as a crisis rather than a tragedy or a problem. A crisis is also a form of self-expression.

2. *Satiate the desire for drama.* It is not without reason that every epoch represents itself as an "age of crisis," a critical juncture demanding momentous choices that determine the fate of civilization, if not of the cosmos itself. As Edelman explains, this representation is widespread in this age of popular media: "All times are 'the times that try men's souls.' The age one lives in is always in crisis, and especially so since newspaper reading became common."[34]

Leaders are not accustomed to envisioning themselves as lackluster caretakers making routine decisions, and coping with chronic, possibly intractable, problems as best they can. Like their ancestors, today's leaders seem possessed by a desire to dramatize the personal significance they impose upon unforeseen events. Nixon extols the quasi-religious peak experiences sparked by genuine crises:

> A man who has never lost himself in a cause bigger than himself has missed one of life's mountaintop experiences. Only in losing himself does he find himself. Crises can be agony. But it is the exquisite agony which a man might not want to experience again—yet he would not for the world have missed.[35]

3. *Engage in deep acting.* Nixon suggests that the agony and the ecstasy of crises reveal the authentic self. Thrown into a crisis, an actor must choose, and such fateful decisions reveal what an actor is made of. Prevailing accounts of crises seem to endorse this facile existentialism when they suppose that there is an authentic self manifested during a crisis. While it is beyond the scope of this study to consider the extensive literature on selfhood—including the postmodern suggestion that the very notion of authentic selfhood is mythic—I have argued that transparent authenticity is not the hallmark of crises or of crisis managers. Crises, as Lebow suggests, often involve self-deception.

The Curse of Hermes transforms actors into impostors. As we have seen, crises involve bluffing and posturing, what Jervis aptly calls "threatening on the cheap." Impression management is about dissembling rather than revealing one's sensibilities to adversaries, foreign and domestic. A crisis offers a pretext for enacting one's dreams and concealing one's vulnerabilities. As my explication of Kennedy and his crises suggests, he was captivated by heroic dreams and bedeviled by pragmatic sensibilities. As biographer Christopher Matthews notes:

"One campaign worker, stopping by Kennedy's home one evening, caught his candidate listening to the booming voice of Winston Churchill on his record player. The pupil was studying the master."[36]

Kennedy's grandiose reverie was more dangerous than Nixon's modest dream of merely being well-liked and respected in the here and now. The Cuban missile crisis provided a pretext to act out his fantasies in public while facing reality in camera. Kennedy's performance convinced the public and many of his associates, but we will probably never know whether he convinced himself.

And turning to the thirty-seventh president, could it be that Nixon had no authentic self to reveal? Perhaps Nixon, as I've suggested, was nothing but personae improvised for every occasion. If men like Kennedy and Nixon constantly sell themselves, perhaps little remains of an authentic self. As Wills and other Nixon biographers suspect, despite his astonishing resurrection from political death, and despite his impressive accomplishments, Nixon remained profoundly insecure. Could it be that he was haunted by the possibility that, he too, was an impostor not worthy of the presidency? As Wills concludes, "Nixon's triumphs were always his greatest tragedies."[37]

4. *Script a rite of passage.* Today, crises are not about national rights; they are (as I have urged) about elite rites of passage. These social dramas—when successfully staged and concluded—mark the transition from opportunistic politician to forthright statesman. Cast in this perspective, crises are about mastery, mastering one's preconceived destiny. As Post explains:

> Some individuals may even seek out and create crises as a way of feeling a sense of mastery, of giving a channel to their own aggressive and combative instincts. . . . [For] Nixon, involvement in a crisis imbued him with a sense of power.[38]

After the Cuban missile crisis, Kennedy was no longer a "reckless youth," the playboy son of Joe Kennedy—the appeaser who "carried Chamberlain's umbrella." He became a martyred statesman, a profile in courage who "had the guts to stand up to Khrushchev." Likewise, at least during the early halcyon days of his shuttle diplomacy, Kissinger was transformed from an obscure academic into a world-class celebrity, the celebrated "doctor of diplomacy." Nixon—ever struggling for recognition and respect from the privileged classes he at once envied and despised—sought adulation for his management of the personal embarrassments recounted in *Six Crises*. He had little success. The Alger Hiss case was treated with derision and soon forgotten; and the Checker's speech and Kitchen Debate are the stuff of parody, not legend. Watergate, his defining life crisis, is no cause for celebration. And those who would promote Nixon as a respected elder statesman cannot invoke the glamorous images of Camelot—to say nothing of the Kennedy resources—to attain their end.

Perhaps those who have reaped handsome dividends from successfully completing their elite rites of passage prior to their presidency can resist the temptation to transform the cryptic texts and symbolic performances of international life into dangerous bravura crises. The Eisenhower presidency comes to mind.

By all accounts the general completed his rite of passage with World War II. As Matthews writes:

> Gen. Dwight D. Eisenhower, Supreme commander of Allied Forces in Europe, accepted the Nazi surrender documents . . . on May 7, 1945. Days later, he was driven through the canyons of Wall Street, ticker tape flying down from the highest windows as the general stood . . . both hands held high with the V sign, a gesture he and the world learned from . . . Churchill.[39]

To be sure, his presidency should not be romanticized. Nevertheless, unlike his successor he tended to construe challenges as problems he could live with, rather than acute crises. For example, unlike Lyndon Johnson, he resisted considerable pressure to commit massive forces to the civil war in Vietnam. And, unlike George Bush, he avoided a crisis mentality—let alone a war—in response to the messianic ambitions of an Arab leader, Gamal Abdel Nasser.

It is prudent for actors and analysts to anticipate the radical unpredictability endemic to international life. While some regarded former CIA Director Robert Gates' intelligence assessments with suspicion, few would dispute his confirmation hearing testimony that: "the very idea of change, the idea that, for years to come, change and uncertainty will dominate international life, and that the unthinkable, and the not-even-thought-about will be common place."[40]

It appears that political actors will heed Nixon's advice for interpreting this daunting uncertainty. In one of his last pieces he admonished: "Because we are the last remaining superpower, no crisis is irrelevant to our interests."[41] However, contrary to received wisdom, these symbolic challenges need not be interpreted as crises demanding urgent, perilous choices. More crises are ahead because Nixon's exhortation will be heeded while Eisenhower's wise counsel in his Farewell Address will continue to be disregarded:

> To meet . . . [international challenges] successfully there is called for not so much the emotional and transitory sacrifices of crisis but rather those which enable us to carry forward . . . the burdens of a prolonged and complex struggle.[42]

NOTES

1. Quoted in the *San Francisco Chronicle*, October 14, 1991, 10.
2. Quoted by John Prados in "Woolsey And The CIA," in *Bulletin of the Atomic Scientists*, Vol. 49, no. 6 (July/August 1993): 6.
3. Charles Hermann, *International Crises* (New York: The Free Press, 1972), 3.
4. Sacvan Bercovitch, *The American Jeremiad* (Madison: University of Wisconsin Press, 1978), 23.
5. Denise Botsdorff, *The Presidents and the Rhetoric of Foreign Crisis* (Columbia: University of South Carolina Press, 1994), 204.
6. Randolph Starn, "Historians and Crisis" *Past and Present*, 52 (Fall 1971): 4–12.
7. Ibid., 3.
8. Botsdorff, 24.
9. Greg Tropea, "Crisis and Divination," [unpublished MS.].

10. Michael H. Hunt, *Crises in U.S. Foreign Policy* (New Haven: Yale University Press, 1996), 424.

11. It is not possible to pursue a fascinating and sorely needed inquiry in this volume: a cross-cultural comparison of "crisis." However, the student research projects present intriguing possibilities. The following cross-cultural commentary on "crisis" is indebted to the research and insights of Altaye Alaro of Ethiopia; Moses Ojakol of Uganda; Suzette Peña of Cuba; and Deki Penjor of Bhutan.

12. Quoted by Botsdorff, 237.

13. Christopher Lasch, *The Minimal Self* (New York: W.W. Norton, 1984), 62.

14. Botsdorff, 207.

15. Quoted by Jerold M. Post in his "The Impact of Crisis-Induced Stress on Policy Makers," in *Avoiding War: Problems of Crisis Management*, Alexander L. George, ed. (Boulder: Westview Press, 1991), 481.

16. Botsdorff, 175. This account of public crisis promotion and its dividends is indebted to her perceptive analysis of the diverse rhetorical techniques used to promote crises.

17. Ibid., 175–204.

18. While I cannot resist the temptation to criticize the excesses and improprieties of the Reagan administration, it is not my intention to reduce Reagan to a caricature. It appears that during his second term, his personal contact with Gorbachev enabled him to abandon abstract, symbolic representations of the Soviet Communist threat. At the Reykjavik meetings he astonished friend and foe alike by advocating nuclear disarmament by the year 2000. Indeed, more attuned to relating to the immediate and personal than the abstract and symbolic, he presided over unprecedented arrangements to dismantle strategic nuclear weapons in Europe. Nevertheless, his first term provides abundant illustrations of ersatz crisis promotion.

19. Quoted by Botsdorff, 196.

20. Ibid., 182.

21. Ibid., 175.

22. Ibid., 177.

23. Ibid., 197.

24. Ibid., 191.

25. Ibid., 184.

26. Ibid., 200.

27. Ibid., 202. Kennedy also attained a 71 percent approval rating in the Gallup Poll after his ill-fated Bay of Pigs invasion.

28. Fen Osler Hampson, "The Divided Decision-Maker: American Domestic Politics and the Cuban Crises," in *The Domestic Sources of Foreign Policy*, Charles W. Kegley, Jr. and Eugene R. Wittkopf, eds., (New York: St. Martin's Press, 1988), 244–245.

29. See ibid., 242–246; see also Gloria Duffy's "Crisis Mangling" in *Avoiding War*, Alexander George, ed. (Boulder: Westview Press, 1991).

30. Interview with Ralph Earle; Chico, Calif.; November 16, 1990.

31. The treaty was never ratified. Nevertheless, the Reagan administration abided by its provisions with minor exceptions. Of course critics of the administration charged that its enthusiasm for the Strategic Defense Initiative violated the provisions of SALT I—a treaty formally endorsed by the United States.

32. Hampson, 243.

33. Starn, 3.

34. Murray Edelman, *The Symbolic Uses Of Politics* (Urbana: University of Illinois Press, 1985), 13.

35. Richard Nixon, *Six Crises* (New York: Simon & Schuster, 1976), xx.

36. Christopher Matthews, *Kennedy & Nixon* (New York: Simon and Schuster, 1996), 138.

37. Garry Wills, *Nixon Agonistes* (Boston: Houghton Mifflin, 1969), 12.

38. Post, 485.

39. Matthews, 33.

40. Robert Gates' testimony before the Senate Intelligence Committee, quoted in *San Francisco Chronicle*, November 4, 1991, 10.

41. Quoted by John C. Hawley in "Bosnia—Human Nature at Its Worst," *San Francisco Chronicle*, Book Review, February 25, 1996, 3.

42. Dwight Eisenhower, "Farewell to the Nation," *U.S. Department of State Bulletin*, (February. 6, 1961): 44.

SELECTED BIBLIOGRAPHY

Abrahams, Roger D. "Ordinary and Extraordinary Experience." In *Anthropology of Experience*. University of Illinois Press, 1986.

Allison, Graham. *The Essence of Decision: Explaining the Cuban Missile Crisis.* Boston: Little Brown, 1971.

Allyn, Bruce J., James G. Blight and David A. Welch. "Essence of Revision." *International Security*, 14, no. 2 (Winter 1989/1990).

Ambrose, Steven E. *Nixon*, Vol. 2. New York: Simon and Schuster, 1989.

Arendt, Hannah. *The Human Condition.* Chicago: University of Chicago Press, 1958.

Ball, George. "JFK's Big Moment." *New York Review,* February 13, 1992.

Barber, James David. *The Presidential Character*, 2nd ed. Englewood Cliffs: Prentice-Hall, 1977.

Bauman, Zygmunt. *Hermeneutics as Social Science.* New York: Columbia University Press, 1978.

Berlin, Isaiah. "On Political Judgment." *New York Review,* October 3, 1996.

Bernstein, Barton J. "The Week We Almost Went to War." *Bulletin of the Atomic Scientists*, February 1986.

Beschloss, Michael. *The Crisis Years.* New York: HarperCollins, 1991.

Betts, Richard. *Nuclear Blackmail and Nuclear Balance.* Washington: Brookings Institution, 1987.

Bliecher, Joseph. "On Hermeneutics." *The Blackwell Dictionary of Twentieth Century Thought.* London: Blackwell, 1989.

Blight, James G. *The Shattered Crystal Ball: Fear and Learning in the Cuban Missile Crisis.* Lanham: Rowman & Littlefield, 1992.

Blight, James G., and David A. Welch, eds. *On The Brink: Americans and Soviets Reexamine the Cuban Missile Crisis.* New York: Hill and Wang, 1989.

Bloom, Harold, ed. *Willy Loman.* New York: Chelsea House, 1991.

Bottsdorff, Denise. *Presidents and the Rhetoric of Foreign Crises.* Columbia: University of South Carolina Press, 1994.

Brodie, Fawn. *Richard Nixon: The Shaping of His Character.* Cambridge: Harvard University Press, 1983.

Bruner, Edward M. "Ethnography as Narrative." In Victor W. Turner and Edward M. Bruner eds., *The Anthropology of Experience.* Urbana: University of Illinois Press, 1986.

Bulfinch, Thomas. *The Golden Age of Myth and Legend.* Hertfordshire: Wordsworth Editions, 1993.

Bundy, McGeorge. *Danger and Survival.* New York: Random House, 1988.

Burke, Kenneth. *Permanence and Change*. Rev. ed., Los Altos: Hermes Publications, 1954.

Carroll, Tim. "The Cuban Missile Crisis: Representations and Misrepresentations." Presented to the American Popular Culture Conference, Las Vegas, March 26, 1996.

Cassirer, Ernst. *An Essay of Man*. Garden City: Doubleday Anchor, 1956.

Chang, Laurence, and Peter Kornbluh. *The Cuban Missile Crisis, 1962*. New York: New Press, 1991.

Chomsky, Noam. "Interventionism & Nuclear War." In Michael Albert and David Delllinger, eds., *Beyond Survival*. Boston: South End Press, 1983.

Clinch, Nancy. *The Kennedy Neurosis*. New York: Grosset & Dunlap, 1973.

Cockburn, Alexander. "No Smoking Gun." *The Nation*. December 23, 1996.

Dean, John. *Blind Ambition*. New York: Simon and Schuster, 1976.

Divine, Robert, ed. *The Cuban Missile Crisis*. Chicago: Quadrangle Books, 1971.

Dobrynin, Anatoly. *In Confidence*. New York: Times Books, 1995.

Duffy, Gloria. "Crisis Prevention in Cuba." In Alexander George, ed., *Managing U.S.– Soviet Rivalry*. Boulder: Westview Press, 1979.

Durrenmatt, Friedrich. *The Physicists*. New York: Grove Press, 1984.

Edelman, Murray. *The Symbolic Uses of Politics*. Urbana: University of Illinois Press, 1981.

_____. *Constructing the Political Spectacle*. Chicago: University of Chicago Press, 1992.

Fentress, James, and Chris Wickham, Chris. *Social Memory*. Oxford: Blackwell, 1992.

Fisher, Walter. *Human Communication as Narration: Toward a Philosophy of Reason, Value, and Action*. South Carolina University Press, 1987.

Foucault, Michel. "The Order of Discourse." In Michael Shapiro, ed., *Language and Politics*. New York: New York University Press, 1989.

Frye, Northrop. *The Great Code: The Bible and Literature*. Toronto: Academic Press, 1981.

Gadamer, Hans-George. "Rhetoric, Hermeneutics, and the Critique of Ideology: Metacritical Comments on Truth and Method." In Kurt Mueller-Vollmer, ed., *The Hermeneutics Reader*. New York: The Continuum, 1989.

Garthoff, Raymond L. "Handling the Cienfuegos Crisis." *International Security* 8, no. 1 (1983).

_____. *Reflections on the Cuban Missile Crisis*. Washington: Brookings Institution, 1987.

Geertz, Clifford. *The Interpretation of Cultures*. New York: Basic Books, 1973.

_____. *Local Knowledge*. New York: Basic Books, 1983.

_____. "Epilogue." *Anthropology of Experience*. Urbana: University of Illinois Press, 1986.

George, Alexander. "A Provisional Theory of Crisis Management." In Alexander George, ed., *Avoiding War: Problems of Crisis Management*. Boulder: Westview Press, 1991.

George, Jim. *Discourses of Global Politics: A Critical (Re)Introduction to International Relations*. Boulder: Lynne Rienner, 1994.

Glynn, Patrick. *Closing Pandora's Box*. New York: Basic Books, 1992.

Goffman, Erving. *The Presentation of Self in Everyday Life*. Garden City: Doubleday, 1959.

Habermas, Jürgen. *Legitimation Crisis*. Boston: Beacon Press, 1975.

_____. "On Hermeneutics' Claim to Universality." In Kurt Mueller-Vollmer, ed., *The Hermeneutics Reader*. New York: Continuum, 1989.

_____. "What Does a Crisis Mean Today? Legitimation Problems in Late Capitalism." In Steven Seidman, ed., *Jürgen Habermas on Society and Politics*. Boston: Beacon Press, 1989.

Haldeman, H. R.; with Joseph DiMona. *The Ends of Power*. New York: Times Books, 1978.

_____. *The Haldeman Diaries*. New York: Putnam, 1994.

Hampson, Fen Osler. "The Divided Decision-Maker: American Domestic Politics and the Cuban Crises." In Charles Kegley and James Wittkopf, eds., *The Domestic Sources of American Foreign Policy*. New York: St. Martin's Press, 1988.

Hermann, Charles. *International Crises*. New York: The Free Press, 1973.

Hersh, Seymour. "Kissinger and Nixon in the White House." *Atlantic Monthly*, May 1982.

_____. *The Price of Power*. New York: Summit Books, 1983.

Hiley, David, et al. eds., *The Interpretive Turn*. Ithaca: Cornell University Press, 1991.

Hirschbein, Ron. *Newest Weapons/Oldest Psychology: The Dialectics of American Nuclear Strategy*. New York: Peter Lang, 1991.

_____. "A Suspicious Look At Nuclear Deterrence." In William Gay and T.A. Alekseeva, eds., *On The Eve of the 21st Century*. Lanham: Rowman & Littlefield, 1994.

_____. "Support Our Tropes: A Critique of Persian Gulf Discourse." In Lawrence F. Bove and Laura Duhan Kaplan, eds., *In the Eye of the Storm*. Amsterdam: Rodopi, 1995.

Hoff-Wilson, Joan. "Richard M. Nixon: The Corporate President." In Fred I. Greenstein, ed., *Leadership in the Modern Presidency*. Cambridge: Harvard University Press, 1988.

Holsti, Ole. *Crisis Escalation War*. Montreal: McGill-Queen's University Press, 1972.

_____. "Crisis Decision-Making." In Philip Tetlock, Jo Husbands, et al. *Behavior, Society and Nuclear War,* Vol. 1. Oxford, New York: Oxford University Press, 1989.

Hunt, Michael H. *Crises in U.S. Foreign Policy*. New Haven: Yale University Press, 1996.

Isaacson, Walter. *Kissinger*. New York: Simon and Schuster, 1992.

Jervis, Robert. *The Logic of Images in International Relations*. Princeton: Princeton University Press, 1970.

_____. *Perception and Misperception in International Politics*. Princeton: Princeton University Press, 1976.

Kaplan, Fred. *The Wizards of Armageddon*. New York: Simon and Schuster, 1983.

Kennedy, John F. *Why England Slept*. New York: Wilfred Funk, 1940.

_____. *Profiles in Courage*. New York: Harper & Brothers, 1956.

Kennedy, Robert F. *Thirteen Days: A Memoir on the Cuban Missile Crisis*. New York: W.W. Norton, 1969.

Keohane, Robert O. *International Institutions and State Power*. Boulder: Westview Press, 1991.

Khrushchev, Nikita. *Khrushchev Remembers*. Boston: Little Brown, 1970.

Kissinger, Henry. *The White House Years*. Boston: Little Brown, 1979.

_____. *Diplomacy*. New York: Simon and Schuster, 1994.

Korda, Michael. "Nixon, Mine Host." *New Yorker*, May 9, 1994.

Kuhn, Thomas. *The Structure of Scientific Revolutions*, 2nd ed. Chicago: University of Chicago Press, 1970.

_____. "The Natural and Human Sciences." In David R. Hiley, James F. Bohman, and Richard Shusterman, eds., *The Interpretive Turn*. Ithaca: Cornell University Press, 1991.

Kundera, Milan. *The Book of Laughter and Forgetting*. New York: Penguin, 1987.

Larson, Arthur. *Eisenhower: The President Nobody Knew*. New York: Charles Scribner's Sons, 1968.

Lebow, Richard Ned. *Between Peace and War: The Nature of International Crises.* Baltimore: Johns Hopkins University Press, 1981.

_____. "Domestic Politics and the Cuban Missile Crisis: The Traditional and Revisionist Interpretations Reevaluated." *Diplomatic History,* Fall 1990.

Lebow, Richard Ned, and Janice Gross Stein. *We All Lost the Cold War.* Princeton: Princeton University Press, 1994.

Machiavelli, Nicolo. *The Prince.* Ware: Wordsworth Editions, Ltd., 1993.

Madison, G. B. *The Hermeneutics of Postmodernity.* Bloomington: Indiana University Press, 1990.

Mandelbaum, Michael. *The Nuclear Question.* New York: Cambridge University Press, 1979.

Matthews, Christopher. *Kennedy & Nixon.* New York: Simon and Schuster, 1996.

Mazlish, Bruce. *Kissinger: The European Mind in American Foreign Policy.* New York: Basic Books, 1976.

McNamara, Robert S. "The Military Role of Nuclear Weapons." *Foreign Affairs,* 62, no. 4, (Fall 1983).

_____. *In Retrospect.* New York: Times Books, 1995.

Miller, Arthur. *Death of a Salesman.* New York: Viking Press, 1949.

_____. "Introduction to Collected Plays." In Harold Bloom, ed., *Willy Loman.* New York: Chelsea House, 1991.

Morgenthau, Hans J. *Politics Among Nations: The Struggle for Power and Peace.* 3rd ed. New York: Alfred Knopf, 1960.

Mueller-Vollmer, Kurt, ed. *The Hermeneutics Reader.* New York: Continuum, 1989.

Nathan, James A. *The Cuban Missile Crisis Revisited.* New York: St. Martin's Press, 1992.

Niebuhr, Reinhold. *Moral Man and Immoral Society.* New York: Scribners, 1933.

Neustadt, Richard. *Presidential Power.* New York: John Wiley, 1980.

Neustadt, Richard, and Ernest May. *Thinking in Time.* New York: Free Press, 1986.

Nixon, Richard M. *In the Arena* New York: Simon and Schuster, 1990.

_____. *Leaders.* New York: Warner Books, 1982.

_____. *RN: The Memoirs of Richard Nixon.* New York: Grosset & Dunlap, 1978.

_____. *Six Crises.* New York: Simon and Schuster, 1976.

Ormiston, Gail, and Alan D. Schrift, *The Hermeneutic Tradition.* Albany: State University of New York Press, 1990.

Oudes, Bruce, ed. *From the President.* New York: Harper & Row, 1989.

Oye, K. A. *Cooperation Under Anarchy.* Princeton: Princeton University Press, 1986.

Polanyi, Michael. *Personal Knowledge.* London: Routledge, 1958.

Poster, Mark. *The Mode of Information.* Chicago: University of Chicago Press, 1990.

Prus, Robert. *Symbolic Interaction and Ethnographic Research.* Albany: State University of New York Press, 1996.

Reeves, Richard. *President Kennedy: Profiles of Power.* New York: Simon and Schuster, 1993.

Rhodes, Richard. "The General and World War III." *The New Yorker,* June 19, 1995.

Rosen, Stanley. *Hermeneutics as Politics.* Oxford: Oxford University Press, 1987.

Rosenau, Pauline. *Postmodernism and the Social Sciences.* Princeton: Princeton University Press, 1992.

Samuels, David. "The Call of Stories." *Lingua Franca,* May/June 1995.

Schlesinger, Arthur M., Jr. *A Thousand Days: JFK in the White House.* Boston: Houghton Mifflin, 1965.

_____. *Robert Kennedy and His Times.* Boston: Houghton Mifflin Company, 1978.

Schulzinger, Robert D. *Henry Kissinger: Doctor of Diplomacy.* New York: Columbia University Press, 1989.

Shapiro, Michael J. *Reading the Postmodern Polity.* Minneapolis: University of Minnesota Press, 1992.

Shusterman, Richard. "Beneath Interpretation." In David R. Hiley, James F. Bohman, and Richard Shusterman, eds., *The Interpretive Turn.* Ithaca: Cornell University Press, 1991.

Singer, David J. "The Behavioral Science Approach to International Politics: Payoffs and Prospects." In James N. Rosenau, ed., *International Politics and Foreign Policy.* New York: Free Press, 1969.

Sorensen, Theodore. *Kennedy.* New York: Harper & Row, 1965.

_____. *The Kennedy Legacy.* New York: Macmillan Company, 1969.

_____. "Kennedy Vindicated." In *The Cuban Missile Crisis.* Robert Divine, ed., Chicago: Quadrangle Books, 1971.

Starn, Randolph. "Historians and Crisis." *Past and Present,* 52 (Fall 1971).

Strober, Gerald S. and Deborah H. Strober. *"Let Us Begin Anew": An Oral History of the Kennedy Presidency.* New York: HarperCollins, 1993.

_____. *Nixon: An Oral History of His Presidency.* New York: HarperCollins, 1994.

Thompson, Robert Smith. *The Missiles of October.* New York: Simon and Schuster, 1992.

Trachtenberg, Marc. "The Influence of Nuclear Weapons in the Cuban Missile Crisis." In Sean Lynn-Jones, Steven Miller and Stephen Van Evera, eds., *Nuclear Diplomacy and Crisis Management.* Cambridge: MIT Press, 1990.

Tuchman, Barbara. *The March of Folly.* New York: Alfred Knopf, 1984.

Turner, Victor. *The Ritual Process.* Chicago: Aldine Company, 1969.

_____. "Dewey, Dilthey, and Drama." *Anthropology of Experience.* University of Illinois Press, 1986.

_____. "Social Dramas and Stories about Them." In *Critical Inquiry* 7, (1980).

_____. *Dramas, Fields and Metaphors.* Ithaca: Cornell University Press, 1974.

Underhill, Evelyn. *Mysticism.* New York: Meridian Books, 1955.

Van Gennep, Arnold. *The Rites of Passage.* Chicago: University of Chicago Press, 1960.

Weinberg, Steven. "Sokal's Hoax." *The New York Review.* August 8, 1996.

White, Theodore. *The Making of the President, 1968.* New York: Atheneum, 1969.

Wicker, Tom. *One of Us: Richard Nixon and the American Dream.* New York: Random House, 1992.

Wills, Garry. *Nixon Agonistes.* Boston: Houghton Mifflin, 1969.

_____. *The Kennedy Imprisonment.* Boston: Little Brown, 1981.

Wolfers, Arnold. "'National Security' as an Ambiguous Symbol," In John Vasquez, ed., *Classics of International Relations.* 3rd ed. Upper Saddle River, NJ: Prentice Hall, 1996.

INDEX

experience, 82–83

Vienna Conference, 70, 115–116
Vietnam, 11, 29, 88–89, 164, 180, 202;
    and Cuban missile crisis syndrome,
    135, 139–141; and Kissinger's dip-
    lomacy, 186

Warner, Lloyd: eschatological refer-
    ence, 87
Watergate, 29, 48, 82, 90, 98, 150, 155,
    158, 160, 162, 165, 205, 207; and
    liminality, 160, 169, 174; tapes, 177
Weinberg, Steven, 79
Why England Slept, 15, 28, 90, 106,
    contesting narratives, 108–109, 111,
    122. *See also* Kennedy, John F.
Wickham, Chris, 23–24, 46. *See also*
    Fentress
Wills, Garry, 25, 113, 157, 165, 207
Wittgenstein, Ludwig, 49
Wolfers, Arnold, 54
Woolsey, James, 196
WSAG (Washington Strategic Action
Group), 181

About the Author

RON HIRSCHBEIN is Professor of Philosophy and Coordinator of War and Peace Studies at California State University, Chico. He has served as a visiting research philosopher at the University of California, San Diego, and as a visiting professor in Peace & Conflict Studies at the University of California, Berkeley. Hirschbein has published extensively on crisis management and nuclear strategy.